Environmental Justice in India

T0313240

Modern environmental regulation and its complex intersection with international law has led many jurisdictions to develop environmental courts or tribunals. Strikingly, the list of jurisdictions that have chosen to do this include numerous developing countries, including Bangladesh, Kenya and Malawi. Indeed, it seems that developing nations have taken the task of capacity-building in environmental law more seriously than many developed nations.

Environmental Justice in India explores the genesis, operation and effectiveness of the Indian National Green Tribunal (NGT). The book has four key objectives. First, to examine the importance of access to justice in environmental matters promoting sustainability and good governance Second, to provide an analytical and critical account of the judicial structures that offer access to environmental justice in India. Third, to analyse the establishment, working practice and effectiveness of the NGT in advancing a distinctively Indian green jurisprudence. Finally, to present and review the success and external challenges faced and overcome by the NGT resulting in growing usage and public respect for the NGT's commitment to environmental protection and the welfare of the most affected people.

Providing an informative analysis of a growing judicial development in India, this book will be of great interest to students and scholars of environmental justice, environmental law, development studies and sustainable development.

Gitanjali Nain Gill is a Reader in Law at Northumbria Law School, UK.

Gitanjali Nain Gill brings us a stunning volume on green jurisprudence in India. Painstakingly providing a 'holistic' theory of adjudication and social movement for environmental justice, she documents regulatory failures as well as cultures foregrounding international state obligations and constitutional mandates. All those anxious about the future of human rights in the Anthropocene era will cherish this volume.

Upendra Baxi, *Emeritus Professor of Law, University of Warwick, UK and Delhi, India*

Gitanjali Nain Gill's analysis of the National Green Tribunal provides an indispensable guide to a question faced by most jurisdictions in the World: whether the environment might be better protected under the particular jurisdiction of an environmental tribunal. Founded on interviews with Tribunal members, this rich analysis proceeds to offer a unique insight into wider and weightier issues concerning the place of environmental justice in the face of competing pressures of development and the sustainability of natural resources and at the interface between law and science.

Robert Lee, *Professor, Birmingham Law School, UK*

Routledge Explorations in Environmental Studies

Environmental Justice in India
The National Green Tribunal

Gitanjali Nain Gill

Routledge
Taylor & Francis Group
LONDON AND NEW YORK

earthscan
from Routledge

First published 2017
by Routledge
2 Park Square, Milton Park, Abingdon, Oxon OX14 4RN

and by Routledge
711 Third Avenue, New York, NY 10017

First issued in paperback 2018

Routledge is an imprint of the Taylor & Francis Group, an informa business

British Library Cataloguing-in-Publication Data
A catalogue record for this book is available from the British Library

Library of Congress Cataloging in Publication Data
Names: Gill, Gitanjali Nain, author.
Title: Environmental justice in India : the National Green Tribunal / Gitanjali Nain Gill.
Description: New York, NY : Routledge, 2016.
Identifiers: LCCN 2016025442 | ISBN 9781138921108 (hb) | ISBN 9781315686592 (ebook)
Subjects: LCSH: Environmental justice–India. | India. National Green Tribunal. | Environmental law–India.
Classification: LCC KNS1507 .G55 2016 | DDC 344.5404/6–dc23
LC record available at https://lccn.loc.gov/2016025442

ISBN 13: 978-1-138-62580-8 (pbk)
ISBN 13: 978-1-138-92110-8 (hbk)

Typeset in Goudy
by Wearset Ltd, Boldon, Tyne and Wear

Dedicated to my loving parents, Narinder Singh and Sawinder Kaur Nain

Contents

Illustrations

Figures

Table

Table of cases

All judgments cited are National Green Tribunal judgments unless otherwise stated.

Foreword

Dr Gitanjali Nain Gill, Reader in Law at Northumbria University, Newcastle, UK, makes an extremely important contribution to the international literature on environmental justice and specialised environmental courts and tribunals (ECTs) with the publication of this book. *Environmental Justice in India: The National Green Tribunal* provides an in-depth analysis of the development and significance of this new environmental tribunal in India – meticulously field researched by this distinguished scholar and written to be of use to environmental scholars, judges, officials and the interested public everywhere. It is the first book of its kind to provide such comprehensive analysis of a single emerging ECT in a major developing country, going far beyond the existing literature on longer-standing ECTs, such as those in Australia, New Zealand, Scandinavia and the USA.

This book is especially important given the ongoing proliferation of ECTs – one of the most dramatic developments in environmental law in the twenty-first century. In the 1970s, only a handful of these ECTs existed. In 2009, when our University of Denver ECT Study published its pioneering report, *Greening Justice: Creating and Improving Environmental Courts and Tribunals*, we documented some 300+. Now, just seven years later, over 1200 ECTs exist at the national or regional level in 44 very diverse nations – in rich developed countries and the poorest developing ones, large nations and small, democratic and non-democratic regimes, on every inhabited continent, in every major type of legal system, and at all government levels. And ECTs are dramatically changing the way environmental disputes are resolved.

Nothing illustrates this adjudication revolution as well as this impressive new book by Dr Gill. While our University of Denver studies (to which Dr Gill has been an expert contributor) focus on comparative ECT systems analysis, in this book she uses her detailed knowledge of one of the world's newest and most progressive ECTs to show how such specialised bodies can broaden access to environmental justice, increase environmental protection, engage scientists and other non-law technical experts as essential decision-makers, and advance the environmental rule of law.

The National Green Tribunal (NGT) makes a very exciting case study. Established just six years ago, its authorising legislation gives it broad trial and appellate jurisdiction over virtually all environmental and natural resources laws and cases, review only by the Supreme Court, flexibility in its procedures, strict standards for judicial appointments, recognition of 'the right to a healthy environment', some of the broadest rules on the planet for public participation and access to justice, a mandate to apply international treaties and principles, and sets up five branches in New Delhi, Bhopal, Pune, Kolkata and Chennai covering the country. Dr Gill's analysis shows how the NGT has successfully expanded its openness, procedural flexibility, transparency and progressive judgments, with detailed analysis of numerous cases.

India's NGT is noteworthy for a number of remarkable features. Its decision-makers include both judicial and expert members, reflecting the multidisciplinary scientific nature of environmental cases. Its judicial members must be former judges or justices of the Supreme Court or High Courts, and the technical experts must be persons from the life sciences, physical sciences, engineering or technology with 15 years' experience including five years of environmental practice. Dr Gill has done extensive fieldwork, having been given unique access to interview numerous NGT judges, expert members, staff and lawyers. Her work demonstrates the innovative role of scientific experts as judges in their ability to shape and legitimise NGT decisions.

In terms of outreach and public participation, the judges and expert members often go to the site of the dispute and make inspections, analyses and recommendations. Rather than decide cases simply on legal precedent, the NGT can organise fact-finding commissions and participation groups of other experts, political leaders, advocacy groups and aggrieved parties to help hammer out workable solutions.

Standing (*locus standi*) to file or participate in an NGT case does not require aggrieved persons to show any personal interest or injury, only that protection of the environment is in their interest.

The NGT has taken upon itself *suo motu* powers to 'on its own motion' take jurisdiction over adverse environmental events, even just from reading newspaper reports and without plaintiffs or defendants.

It has encouraged public interest litigation (PIL), as has the Indian Supreme Court, with the result that nearly half of all its cases are filed by non-governmental organisations (NGOs), social activists and citizen advocates.

The NGT is not a passive decisional body. It uses a wide variety of proactive information-gathering techniques, including adversarial, inquisitorial, investigative and collaborative procedures in reaching its decisions. It provides a welcoming atmosphere for parties seeking to advance environmental interests, while simultaneously discouraging litigation by those using the judicial process for delay or other improper motives.

The organisation of this book is admirable in the way it springboards off this one ECT to reach larger issues of environmental adjudication of benefit to both specialised and general jurisdiction courts everywhere. Voluminous NGT cases are described and analysed giving the work serious scholarly and practical depth. One wishes there were more follow-up on how the tribunal's decisions in these cases are being implemented or carried out in the real world, but that would be another book.

Chapter 1, 'Environmental justice: a global perspective', sets the backdrop, explaining the need for environmental justice, a fair adjudication process, public access to justice and why ECTs can be superior to the general court system.

Chapter 2, 'Genesis and establishment of the National Green Tribunal', traces the history, growth and benefits of PIL in India, and how it led to the creation of the NGT.

Chapter 3, 'The National Green Tribunal Act 2010: interpretation and application', presents an insightful analysis of the NGT's authorising act and how those broad statutory powers are being progressively interpreted by the tribunal through its cases. Not all is smooth sailing with the implementation of NGT decisions, Dr Gill notes, for example with the tribunal's sweeping orders about various cities' air pollution or municipal solid waste problems.

Chapter 4, 'National Green Tribunal: normative principles', is a review of the international treaties and principles that are made part of the NGT's jurisprudence by its enabling act – particularly the precautionary, polluter-pays and sustainable development principles. Balancing environmental protection with economic development is a supremely challenging task, and criticisms of NGT decisions from both ends of the spectrum are discussed.

Chapter 5, 'National Green Tribunal: science and law', the results of Dr Gill's unique interview fieldwork, is a stand-out chapter. Her interviews elicit an amazing perspective on scientific knowledge utilisation by the NGT and the innovative role of its scientific decision-makers in their ability to guide and legitimise NGT decisions and policy and to assist government officials in implementing both.

Chapter 6, 'National Green Tribunal: judgments and analysis', presents the author's fascinating analysis of the over-1000 NGT cases from the beginning (2011) through 30 September 2015. It charts the caseload growth, dispute subjects, and types of plaintiffs and defendants. The findings reveal a pattern of a repeat group of public interest plaintiffs bringing regular actions against powerful national, state and local government regulatory authorities for non-compliance with laws and administrative misconduct – with plaintiffs winning a majority of the time.

The concluding Chapter 7, 'The National Green Tribunal's journey: challenges and success', highlights problems the NGT faces, while finding it 'is changing the environmental jurisprudential landscape in India'. Not without difficulties, it has 'developed wide-ranging environmental policies and exposed serious administrative weaknesses', such that 'its public credibility is widespread and the results of its decisions continue to reach even further across India'.

This book provides readers a unique understanding of the NGT, but, more, it lays a foundation for practical use by all policy-makers and scholars interested in environmental law, environmental compliance, access to justice, scientific decision-making, and provides a solid basis for the author's and others' future research. We hope Dr Gill will continue her research and publications on the

NGT, perhaps by documenting the implementation and longer-range impacts of their ground-breaking decisions. Analysis of the social, economic and environmental effectiveness of decisions by ECTs is sorely lacking, in spite of the growing popularity of ECTs as an institutional tool to enhance sustainable development and protect the environment for future generations. Documenting ECT effectiveness and the political and public acceptance of its decisions over time would be another ground-breaking study.

We wish Dr Gill continued great success in her endeavours.

George (Rock) Pring, Professor of Law Emeritus,
University of Denver Sturm College of Law
Catherine (Kitty) Pring, Principal, Global Environmental Outcomes LLC
Co-Directors, University of Denver Environmental Courts and Tribunals Study

Acknowledgements

This book bears the name of the sole author: Dr Gitanjali Nain Gill. In reality it would not have been written without the support and involvement of many other contributors. Consequently, I name a few and acknowledge many more people.

I am grateful to the Chairperson and bench members of the National Green Tribunal (NGT) (present and former) whom I interviewed and who made me feel welcome, were generous with their time, and open with their recorded comments: Chairperson, the Honourable Mr Justice Swatanter Kumar, who authorised these interviews; Honourable Judicial Members Mr M Chockalingam, Mr V R Kinganonkar, Mr P Jyothimani, Mr Dalip Singh and Mr U D Salvi; Honourable Expert Members Professor R Nagendran, Dr Devendra K Agarwal, Gopal K Pandey, Professor (Dr) P C Mishra, Mr P S Rao, Mr Ramesh C Trivedi, Dr Ajay A Deshpande and Mr Ranjan Chatterjee. I am particularly thankful to the Chairperson and the bench members for their hospitality and frankness. Their inside stories provide substance and meaning to the text. Their words thread throughout the book particularly in Chapter 5. I also thank the former Registrar General of the Principal Bench in Delhi and my friend, Sanjay Kumar, who was helpful in arranging my visits and interviews in Pune, Bhopal, Chennai and Kolkata. The lawyers, non-governmental organisation (NGO) members and litigants whom I talked with provided an external, objective account of the work of the NGT and it was invariably positive.

This research owes much to my rakhi brother, Judge Vinay Gupta, who opened heavy doors for me to conduct my fieldwork.

I thank Professor Philip Thomas, of Cardiff University Law School, for being a constant mentor, supporter and critic of this book.

I also wish to acknowledge and thank John Clayton of Northumbria University, Newcastle, who guided me through the mysteries of Statistical Package for the Social Sciences (SPSS) analysis. Thanks to Marie Selwood, my copy-editor, who kept telling me that I would meet the publisher's deadline. Fortunately for me, she proved to be correct. Samarth Luthra proved a valuable research assistant in Delhi.

I have published several articles and chapters which after revision appear in various chapters of this book. I acknowledge the support of the publishers of the academic papers: 'Environmental justice in India: the National Green Tribunal and Expert Members' (2016) 5(1) *Transnational Environmental Law Journal* 175–205 (CUP); 'Human rights and environment protection in India: a judicial journey from public interest litigation to the National Green Tribunal' (2015) in A Grear and E Grant (eds), *Thought, Law, Rights and Action in an Age of Environmental Crisis*, (Edward Elgar) 123–154; 'The National Green Tribunal of India: a sustainable future through the principles of international environmental law' (2014) 16(3) *Environmental Law Review* 183–202; 'Environmental protection and development interests: a case study of the river Yamuna and the Commonwealth Games, Delhi 2010' (2014) 6(1/2) *International Journal of Law in Built Environment* Special Issue on Environmental Law 69–90; 'A green tribunal for India' (2010) 22(3) *Journal of Environmental Law* 461–474; and 'Human rights and the environment in India: access through public interest litigation' (2012)14(3) *Environmental Law Review* 200–218.

Finally, I thank Ishvinder, Amrinder and the rest of my family and everyone who believed in me.

Dr Gitanjali Nain Gill
Newcastle-upon-Tyne
31 May 2016

Abbreviations

AA	Achanakmar-Amarkantak
ADB	Asian Development Bank
ADR	alternative dispute resolution
AJNE	Asian Judges Network on Environment
AOL	Art of Living
ASEAN	Association of Southeast Asian Nations
BARC	Bhabha Atomic Research Centre
BR	Biosphere Reserve
CAG	Comptroller and Auditor General
CEIA	Cumulative Environmental Impact Assessment
CETP	common effluent treatment plant
CIDCO	City and Industrial Development Corporation
CPC	Civil Procedure Code
CRZ	Coastal Regulation Zone
CWGV	Commonwealth games village
DRDO	Defence Research and Development Organisation
EAC	Expert Appraisal Committee
EC	environmental clearance
ECT	environmental courts and tribunals
EIA	environmental impact assessment
ELC	Environment and Land Court
ELMA	Environmental Law (Management) Act
EMCA	Environmental Management and Coordination Act
ET	environmental tribunal
FFC	fact-finding committee
GDP	gross domestic product
HLC	High Level Committee
IEA	independent regulatory agencies
IGI	Indira Gandhi International
IISc	Indian Institute of Science
ISIC	Indian Spinal Injuries Centre
ISRO	Indian Space Research Organisation
JFM	joint forest management

JNPT	Jawaharlal Nehru Port Trust
MCZMA	Maharashtra Coastal Zone Management Authority
MEC	Malaysian Environment Court
MLJCA	Ministry of Law, Justice and Company Affairs
MMRDA	Mumbai Metropolitan Region Development Authority
MoEF	Ministry of Environment and Forests
MoEFCC	Ministry of Environment, Forest and Climate Change
MSW	municipal solid waste
NCT	National Capital Territory
NDZ	No Development Zone
NEAA	National Environment Appellate Authority
NEMA	National Environment Management Authority
NET	National Environment Tribunal
NGO	Non-governmental organisation
NGT	National Green Tribunal
NHAI	National Highway Authority of India
NSW	New South Wales
ONGC	Oil and Natural Gas Corporation
PEPA	Pakistan Environmental Protection Act
PIL	public interest litigation
PNJ	principles of natural justice
SAARC	South Asian Association for Regional Cooperation
SDG	Sustainable Development Goals
SEAC	State Expert Appraisal Committee
SEIAA	State Level Environment Impact Assessment Authority
SEMA	State Environment Management Authority
STP	sewage treatment plants
UCIL	Union Carbide Indian Ltd
UN	United Nations
UNEP	United Nations Environment Programme
VIDC	Vidharba Irrigation Development Company
WGEEP	Western Ghats Ecology Expert Panel
WHO	World Health Organization

Introduction

Every traveller should have a map identifying the best route to their destination and indicating appropriate stopping places. Readers are entitled to similar support, rather than simply opening the pages of a research monograph with little knowledge of its content beyond the expectation that it's an informative, worthwhile read. Consequently, this brief introduction describes my research journey and offers a short environmental account for the traveller who has yet to visit India or knows insufficient about it to appreciate the contents of this book. Thereafter, there follows an account of the fieldwork and case analysis methodology and I conclude with a precis of the seven chapters.

My involvement in environmental law was triggered by family reasons. I lived and taught in Delhi and at the time of the birth of my son, Tejeshwar, I became acutely aware and concerned about Delhi's environment, particularly its air quality.[1] My concerns over my child's health and that of hundreds of thousands of children in the capital city promoted my long-term personal and academic involvement in India's environmental challenges.

The human and geographical scale of India is gigantic, as are its ongoing internal issues that include population growth,[2] poverty,[3] inflation[4] and corruption.[5] Modern India has embarked on an economic pathway to promote itself as a development juggernaut. Successive governments have focused on achieving high growth of its gross domestic product (GDP) believing it will also help the reduction of poverty and secure social and economic equality. Growth gurus argue the importance of maximising the efficient exploitation of the country's resources in order to achieve economic development. The latest economic strategy has assumed heightened significance under the leadership of India's current Prime Minister, Narendra Modi. He is known for his ability to drive change and his commitment to accelerate growth in Asia's third largest economy. Modi, known as a pro-business, market-oriented reformer, aims to boost India's growth to 8 to 10 per cent per annum.[6] Resurgence in manufacturing, (including cars and car parts, pharmaceuticals, textiles and other goods); fast-tracking major infrastructure projects in power, roads, ports and rail; improving the business environment; and encouraging foreign direct investment are some of the government's key projects. Prime Minister Modi, at the 2015 United Nations (UN) Sustainable Development Summit,[7] stated that the development process must be inclusive and sustainable resulting in benefits to all stakeholders:

> Addressing the needs of 1.3 billion poor people in the world is not merely a question of their survival and dignity or our moral responsibility. It is a vital necessity for ensuring a peaceful, sustainable and just world. Our attack on poverty today includes expanded conventional schemes of development, but we have also launched a new era of inclusion and empowerment, turning distant dreams into immediate possibilities ... We are focusing on the basics: housing, power, water and sanitation for all – important not just for welfare, but also human dignity ... We are making our farms more productive and better connected to markets; and, farmers less vulnerable to the whims of nature ... Nations have a national responsibility for sustainable development ... There is no cause greater than shaping a world, in which every life that enters it can look to a future of security, opportunity and dignity; and, where we leave our environment in better shape for the next generation ... May all be happy, may all be healthy, may all see welfare ...[8]

Notwithstanding these ambitious goals, the social reality within India remains disturbing. A 2015 UN report states that, in India, nearly 300 million people live in extreme poverty and face deprivation in terms of access to basic services including health, education, water, sanitation and electricity (UN Food and Agriculture Organization 2015: 46).[9] The UN annual hunger report, 'The State of Food Security in the World 2015',[10] notes that India is home to 194 million hungry persons: a figure that surpasses China. The federal and state governments' policies and legislation to acquire for a pittance fertile land for speculative investment, for mines and factories, for highways and expressways and the resulting urban sprawl have trapped desperate farmers in crippling debt and resulted in numerous suicides.[11] These land-grabbing actions have detrimentally affected the livelihood of farmers and indigenous people. Sixty-five per cent of India's population remains agrarian. According to Vandana Shiva, a leading activist:

> ...while land has been taken from farmers at Rupees 300 ($6) per square metre by the government – using the Land Acquisition Act – it is sold by developers at Rupees 600,000 ($13,450) per square metre – a 200,000 percent increase in price – and hence profits. This land grab and the profits contribute to poverty, dispossession and conflict.[12]

The target of high GDP within this development agenda indicates worrying trends in the context of its social and environmental impact. The convergence of the right to environment and the right to development has created a national paradox. For example, the right to a healthy environment is affected by industrialisation, modernisation and the impact of consumerism that has resulted in increased air and water pollution. According to the 2016 WHO Urban Ambient

Air Pollution database,[13] India has 16 of the world's 30 most-polluted cities. Six Indian cities – Gwalior, Allahabad, Patna, Raipur, Ludhiana and Delhi – rank among the most polluted in the world. The levels of ultra-fine particles of less than 2.5 microns (PM2.5s) – which can cause fatal damage to heart and lungs – are highest in India. In relation to water, Delhi has undrinkable water. India has the highest number of people without safe water. Nearly 76 million people have no access to a safe water supply. Approximately 140,000 Indian children die annually from diarrhoea (WaterAid 2016: 9). Sadly, air and water quality are merely illustrative of the many challenges that people live with on a daily basis.

The right to development is commonly perceived as being a reflection of powerful commercial vested interests rather than supporting equitable social welfare. Economic globalisation has created opportunities for investment which has resulted in the displacement of local people and damage to the local ecosystem. Across India, approximately 40 per cent of those displaced by dams, power plants and mines are poor tribal people although they make up only 8 per cent of the country's population (Ministry of Tribal Affairs 2014: 49–50). Investment by foreign companies and industry, enthusiastically supported by government, into sectors including energy and mining has on occasions resulted in unsustainable development. Such 'development' leaves the poor and marginalised to suffer and die. The construction of an integrated steel plant in the state of Odisha (popularly known as the POSCO project) and mining extraction by Vedanta Resources in the Niyamgiri Hills illustrate this point.[14]

In March 2016, the Minister of Environment and Forests, Prakash Javadekar stated his ministry granted environmental clearance (EC) to 943 projects in 21 months[15] for 'ease of doing business' and to create a conducive environment for investors. However, evidence suggests that regulatory environmental laws and procedures were ignored or short-circuited in the race for economic returns.[16] Errors include failure to provide mandatory documentation, inadequate stakeholder participation, and deliberate concealment or submission of false or misleading information for the EC process. A study by the Centre for Science and Environment, a Delhi-based research and advocacy organisation, stated, between June 2014 and April 2015, 103 mining projects and 54 infrastructure projects were granted ECs. The coal-mining sector was a special beneficiary as projects were allowed in critically polluted areas via a diluted public hearing requirement.[17] The data showed that 'projects were being cleared and processes were made so convoluted that they stopped working to protect the environment'.[18] These developmental and infrastructure projects result in the displacement of the marginalised, the poor and in particular the tribal population. The 'backwash effects' (Mohanty 2011: 67) of displacement, deforestation, loss of agricultural land and environmental degradation led to further exclusion of the tribal poor from mainstream society rather than aspirational integration. The primary thrust of state agencies to pursue an economic development model accommodates corporate interest and manipulates and subverts laws and safeguards that protect the rights of the tribal poor and marginalised. The controversial draft legislative proposal of reducing tribal rights over forest land in favour of industries without securing the prior consent of Gram Sabha or village councils is an example of non-recognition of the forest rights of tribal communities (Sethi 2016).

The Modi promise of '*achhe din*'[19] (good times including good governance, transparency, development and jobs) remains unfulfilled. Previous governmental focus was myopic and economically blinkered. The challenge of the current government is whether or not to perpetuate historic injustices, inequities and discrimination against the weaker sections of society, particularly the tribal. Are the poor to be left experiencing impoverishment, displacement, dispossession and unaccountable environmental degradation?

Resuscitating India's economy is necessary, but not to the detriment of the environment. Striking a balance between human needs, economic growth and the environment is required to create an 'inclusive development' that provides facilities and opportunities for the welfare of people in order that they may live with dignity and equal status. In this context, the vital role of the judiciary and, in particular, that of the National Green Tribunal (NGT) is to act as the primary guardian of the environment for the benefit of present and future generations. The historic importance of the Supreme Court of India, its creation of the procedural tool of public interest litigation (PIL), which provides access to justice for poor people, and its willingness to speak out for the 'underdog' in environmental cases are a matter of public record.

Today, it is the turn of the NGT to assume the principal position of adjudicating environmental issues and build upon the environmental jurisprudence of the Supreme Court. The tension between economic development and protection of the environment is reflected in the relationship between the working practices of federal and state agencies and the corporate sector and the institutional growth and functionality of the NGT. The tribunal's procedures and case law indicate a willingness to support sustainable development subject to the strict application of the NGT Act 2010, the constitutional mandate and relevant environmental regulations. The NGT is proving to be stubbornly determined and successful in enforcing the environmental regulations laid down by the state and its agencies to protect the environment and promote the welfare of the public. Its case law demonstrates its ability and willingness to require transparency and accountability that ultimately constitute the building blocks of good governance and environmental democracy.

Methodology

In 2014, I began a research project that resulted in the publication of this book. Nevertheless, my environmental research journey continues. The financial support of the British Academy through its research grant programme made my frequent visits to India both longer and more productive than anticipated and I undertook several trips between 2014 and 2015. This allowed me to spend extended time in Delhi, Pune, Bhopal, Chennai and Kolkata: the cities where NGT are sited. NGT bench members and registrars were both open and generous with their time, experiences and thoughts. Their support made my fieldwork productive and enjoyable. The interviews were semi-structured, open-ended, recorded and transcribed. Some were one-to-one and others involved two bench members. On subsequent visits the interviews followed a similar pattern and allowed me to trace the 'growth' of the regional benches, thereby providing a pattern of the national development of the NGT. For many reasons institutions change over time and such is the dynamic of law that it has supported the growth of the NGT's competence and impact.

Additionally, I interviewed lawyers who appeared in front of the NGT, NGO representatives and people who saw the NGT as the problem-solving, relief-giving forum they sought. The NGT's outreach has become extensive as people increasingly recognise it as an institution willing to act both to preserve the environment and also make decisions that recognise and support the public interest. In all I undertook 110 interviews. There is no substitute for 'being there' and I spent time in tribunals, sitting and observing cases as they were presented, debated and decided. For example, I was in the Chennai tribunal in July 2014 when Amrit Mahal Kaval case was heard.[20] Because of my university teaching commitments I was obliged to travel to India during the hot season when temperatures rise to 40-plus centigrade. Travelling throughout India and undertaking research in those temperatures was challenging and made me grateful for air-conditioning in the tribunals! I also read, analysed and categorised 1130 NGT reported judgments, excluding daily orders, published on the NGT's website between July 2011 and September 2015 and coded them for SPSS analysis. The results are presented in Chapter 6. Indian English has its own grammar and punctuation conventions. All extracts from interviews and cases are faithful to the original. To a limited extent the book draws upon some of my previous published work on the NGT.

Structure of the book

This book is divided into seven chapters. The first introduces the reader to the growing awareness and acceptance that the environment is the responsibility of everyone, be they individuals, organisations, sovereign states, regions or international partners. It examines the role and functions of an informed and progressive judiciary actively exercising the environmental rule of law. Finally, it identifies and describes several types of environmental courts and tribunals (ECTs), both in the developed and developing world.

The second chapter traces the history of need, growth and activities associated with PIL. Judicial activism is demonstrated by illustrative PIL cases. In particular, PIL and environmental protection are examined and the substantive and procedural uses of PIL are traced. The debate about the need for a specialised environmental tribunal (ET) is documented by reviewing supportive *dicta* in Supreme Court judgments and recommendations of the Law Reform Commission of India. The Parliamentary passage of the NGT Act is also documented and, finally, the earliest days of the establishment of the NGT benches are discussed.

Chapter 3 examines sections of the NGT Act 2010 and how these statutory powers continue to be liberally interpreted by the NGT. In particular, the bench composition, jurisdiction and procedure of the NGT are examined. They demonstrate how the Tribunal's successful expansion of its procedural ambit and progressive judgments have moved its decisional impact beyond the court room door and has resulted in wider social and economic consequences.

The fourth chapter identifies international treaties and obligations that have been accepted by India and are embedded in the NGT Act. Established global principles that underpin environmental jurisprudence include the precautionary principle, the polluter-pays principle and sustainable development. Examples of the application of these principles by the NGT in deciding cases are provided throughout the chapter.

The fifth chapter notes that there are limited empirical studies on scientific knowledge utilisation at the institutional level. Hass' theory of 'knowledge utilisation' (2007, 2014) and that of Schrefler's work (2010, 2014) and her three categories of symbolic, instrumental and strategic scientific knowledge are explored and tested in the light of the judgments of the NGT. The role of science and scientific experts is examined. The interview fieldwork undertaken in India, particularly at the bench level, demonstrates the innovative role of scientific experts as NGT bench members and their ability to both shape and influence NGT decisions. The judgments demonstrate that decisions are capable of going beyond the courtroom by offering scientifically-based policy changes affecting or introducing both national and regional regulation.

Chapter 6 interogates NGT case data examined during the research. Some 1130 NGT cases were coded and analysed statistically. There has been a rapid growth, year on year, in cases heard by the NGT. It demonstrates increasing public awareness and the readiness to approach the NGT as a new and appropriate forum offering environmental justice. Appreciation of the importance of being an 'aggrieved person', reflecting the expansive interpretation of 'standing', has been taken up by NGOs, social activists and public-spirited persons, evidenced by the fact that almost half of all cases were brought by them. Conversely, regulatory failure by national, state and public bodies and also industry is illustrated by the number of cases brought against them.

The final chapter examines both the challenges faced by and the overall success of the NGT. Its initial difficult start was a consequence of the lack of effective support and commitment at national and state levels. Only after the Supreme Court's intervention was the necessary support forthcoming from ministries obligated by statute to ensure the effective establishment of the NGT benches throughout India. The NGT's life history, difficulties and activities are placed and reviewed within the theoretical framework developed by Suddaby and Viale (2011) thereby providing a holistic account and understanding of the NGT.

The seven chapters chart and analyse the growth of the NGT, a powerful, specialised judicial entity staffed by technical experts and lawyers that functions not only as an adjudicatory body but also moves its focus beyond traditional, individualised legal issues and associated common law remedies. Additionally, its ability to engage, produce and enforce scientifically supported policy has taken its remit beyond the courtroom and into the wider community. The outcome is that the NGT has changed and continues to change the landscape of India's environmental jurisprudence.

Notes

1 I address the question of air pollution in Delhi and India generally in Chapter 3.
2 The current population of India is 1.32 billion and is estimated to rise to 1.53 billion by 2030. See www.indiaonlinepages.com/population/india-current-population.html.
3 India now has 172 million people below the poverty line (although the World Bank has revised the line upwards from $1.25 (Rupees 81) to $1.90 (Rupees 123.5) per day) http://economictimes.indiatimes.com/news/economy/indicators/indias-poverty-rate-lowest-among-nations-with-poor-population-world-bank/articleshow/49225412. cms; according to India's 2015 Socio-economic and Caste Census Report, out of 300 million households surveyed, 73 per cent lived in rural areas. Of these less than 5 per cent paid income tax, 75 per cent earned less than Rupees 5000 ($78) each month, less than 10 per cent had salaried jobs and 35.7 per cent were illiterate http://edition.cnn.com/2015/08/02/asia/india-poor-census-secc/.
4 The rate of inflation (March 2016) in India is 5.51 per cent www.inflation.eu/inflation-rates/india/inflation-india.aspx.
5 India is ranked 76th among 176 nations in the global corruption index released by Transparency International www.transparency.org/cpi2015.
6 'India's Modi signals country won't join FX devaluation race to boost trade' Reuters Business, 12 March 2016 www.reuters.com/article/india-economy-modi-idUSL4N16K063; 'India's Modi says his government will push for economic development', *Wall Street Journal*, 11 June 2014; www.wsj.com/articles/indias-modi-says-his-government-will-push-for-economic-development-1402505104.
7 UN General Assembly Sustainable Development Summit, 25 September 2015, New York: www.un.org/press/en/2015/ga11688.doc.htm; also see Prime Minister Modi's inaugural address, 2016 International Conference on Rule of Law for Supporting the 2030 Development Agenda/Sustainable Development Goals (4 March 2016, New Delhi) www.narendramodi.in/pm-modi-at-the-international-conference-on-rule-of-law-for-supporting-the-2030-development-agenda-427789.
8 See n 6.
9 UN Economic and Social Commission for Asia and the Pacific, 'India and the MDGs: towards a sustainable future for all' UN India Report, 5 February 2015 www.unescap.org/resources/india-and-mdgs-towards-sustainable-future-all.
10 www.fao.org/hunger/en/.
11 'There is no reason why India should face hunger and farmers should commit suicide' EcoWatch, 14 August 2015 http://ecowatch.com/2015/08/14/vandana-shiva-india/; see also 'Indian land bill: "We're losing not just land, but a whole generation of farmers"', *Guardian*, 12 May 2015 www.theguardian.com/global-development-professionals-network/2015/may/12/agriculture-in-india-collapse-farmer-debt-land-acquisition-bill.
12 'The great land grab: India's war on farmers' Aljazeera (Opinion Environment) 7 www.aljazeera.com/indepth/opinion/2011/06/20116711756667987.html.
13 www.who.int/phe/health_topics/outdoorair/databases/cities/en/.
14 An independent report, published by a human rights NGO in 2013 on the POSCO project tells the story of a human rights crisis induced by mega-development projects that would lead to the forced migration of many thousands of poor people (International

Human Rights Clinic, ESCR-Net: 2013); Vedanta Resources is a London-based company. Its slogan is 'Creating happiness', exercised through its social responsibility programmes. It received the Golden Peacock Award for environmental management. Nevertheless, in India it has been repeatedly found to violate laws on environment protection and human rights. See 'Vedanta Resources lawsuit (re Dongria Kondh in Orissa)' (2014) Business and Human Rights Resource Centre and the extensive resources linked to the report   http://business-humanrights.org/en/vedanta-resources-lawsuit-re-dongria-kondh-in-orissa.

15 'Green nod for 943 projects in 21 months' *Indian Express*, 31 March 2016 http://indian-express.com/article/india/india-news-india/prakash-javedekar-environment-projects/.

16 See e.g. Scheduled Tribes and Other Traditional Forest Dwellers (Recognition of Forest Rights) Act 2006; Scheduled Tribes and Other Traditional Forest Dwellers (Recognition of Forest Rights) Rules 2007 and 2012; Panchayats Extension to Schedule Areas 6 1996. Often there is failure to implement the letter of the law thereby making it of symbolic value.

17 'NDA's environmental clearance record not significantly different from UPAs' Centre for Science and Environment, 26 May 2016 www.cseindia.org/content/nda%E2%80%99s-environmental-clearance-record-not-significantly-different-upa%E2%80%99s-says-analysis-cse.

18 Ibid.; also see South Asia Network on Dams, Rivers and People, 'Rampant environmental violation of Maharashtra water resource department' 21 June 2014, http://sandrp.wordpress.com/2014/06/20/press-release21–06–14-rampant-environmental-violations-of-maharashtra-water-resource-department/.

19 '*Achhe din*' was the Hindi slogan of the ruling Bharatiya Janata Party for the 2014 Indian general election.

20 *Leo Saldhana v Union of India* (Judgment 27 August 2014). See Chapter 4.

References

Haas, P M (2007) 'Epistemic communities' in D Bodansky, J Brunee and E Hey (eds), *Oxford Handbook of International Environmental Law* (OUP) 791–806.

Haas, P M (2014) 'Ideas, experts and governance' in M Ambrus, K Arts, E Hey and H Raulus (eds) *The Role of 'Experts' in International and European Decision-Making Processes: Advisors, Decision Makers or Irrelevant Actors?* (CUP) 19–43.

International Human Rights Clinic, ESCR-Net (2013) *The Price of Steel: Human Rights and Forced Evictions in the POSCO-India Project* (NYU School of Law).

Ministry of Tribal Affairs (May 2014) *Report of the High-Level Committee on Socio-Economic, Health and Educational Status of the Tribals of India* (Ministry of Tribal Affairs).

Mohanty, R (2011) 'Impact of development project on the displaced tribals: a case study of a development project in eastern India' September–October *Orissa Review* 67–73.

Schrefler, L (2010) 'The usage of scientific knowledge by independent regulatory agencies' 23(2) *Governance* 309–330.

Schrefler, L (2014) 'Reflections on the different roles of expertise in regulatory policy making' in M Ambrus, K Arts, E Hey and H Raulus (eds) *The Role of 'Experts' in International and European Decision-Making Processes: Advisors, Decision Makers or Irrelevant Actors?* (CUP) 63–81.

Sethi, N (2016) 'Opposition criticises government's move to dilute Forest Rights Act' Business Standard (e-paper), 5 May www.business-standard.com/article/economy-policy/opposition-criticises-government-s-move-to-dilute-forest-rights-act-1160505 00042_1.html.

Suddaby, R and Viale, T (2011) 'Professionals and field-level change: institutional work and the professional project' 59(4) *Current Sociology* 423–442.

UN Food and Agriculture Organization (2015) *The State of Food Insecurity in the World: Meeting the 2015 International Hunger Targets: Taking Stock of Uneven Progress* (FAO UN).

WaterAid (2016) *Water: at What Cost? The State of the World's Water 2016* www.wateraid.org/news/news/water-at-what-cost-our-latest-report-reveals-the-state-of-the-worlds-water.

1 Environmental justice

A global perspective

The globalisation of environmental concerns and the internationalisation of environmental law have promoted the development of environmental justice discourse. This discourse discerns, analyses and calls for the distribution of environmental benefits and burdens (Walzer 1983: 6; Brighouse 2004: 2), the recognition of oppressed individuals and communities in political and cultural realms (Taylor 1986; Young 1990: 22; Honneth 1992) and procedural dimensions focusing on participatory mechanisms (Schlosberg 2007: 25–29; Holifield *et al.* 2011: 10). The discourse initially concentrated on the disproportionate effects of environmental degradation on people and places and on distributional inequity. The term 'environmental justice' originated in events in Warren County, North Carolina, in 1982 (Agyeman 2005: 14). Toxic waste was dumped within and resisted by a marginalised community. The result was 'people went to jail trying to stop a toxic waste landfill' (Geiser and Waneck 1994: 52; Agyeman 2005: 14). Because of its similar timeline, this dispute is commonly associated with the Love Canal residential and community development on toxic land in New York State (Dobson 1998: 18). These appalling incidents demonstrated a connection between poor or low-income neighbourhoods and the poisoned environment where they were located. Szasz observed: 'toxic victims are, typically, poor or working people of modest means. Their environmental problems are inseparable from their economic condition. People are more likely to live near polluted industrial sites if they live in financially strapped communities' (1994: 151). Similarly, Pulido argued: 'it is … the poor and marginalized who often bear the brunt of pollution and resource degradation – whether a toxic dump, a lack of arable land, or global climate change – simply because they are more vulnerable and lack alternatives' (Pulido 1996: xv–xvi).

The anti-toxic movement joined with the movement against environmental racism in American urban centres. Benjamin Chavis, coined the term 'environmental racism' stating:

> environmental racism is racial discrimination in environmental policy making and enforcement of regulations and laws, the deliberate targeting of communities of colour for toxic waste facilities, the official sanctioning of the presence of life threatening poisons and pollutants in communities of

colour, and the history of excluding people of colour from leadership of the environmental movement.

(Chavis 1993: 3)

Studies revealed environmental racism prevailed in 'certain communities, predominantly communities of colour' which were at 'disproportionate risk for commercial toxic waste' (United Church of Christ 1987; Bullard 1990; Adeola 1994: Agyeman 2005: 15). The 'Cancer Alley' region of Louisiana was one where 'a billion pound of toxic chemicals was emitted in the alley' (Shrader-Frechette 2002: 9).[1] Other examples include nuclear testing at Maralinga, early uranium mining in Australia (Jessup 2012: 50) and salt water infiltration into Dutch fields from potassium mines in Alsace, France (Kiss and Shelton 2003: 105). These environmental struggles, expressed within a framework of social justice and civil rights, helped create a pathway towards environmental justice, thereby, influencing public policy.

Over time, environmental justice discourse has been re-contextualised within numerous jurisdictions to include issues of fairness, equity, standing, rights of disadvantaged populations in developing countries and meaningful participation in the decision-making process to promote environmental governance and ecological conservation (Shrader-Frechette 2002: 8–12; Holifield *et al.* 2011: 6). The Bhopal gas tragedy, for example, illustrates how people in developing countries face worse environmental threats than those in the developed world.[2] Another illustration is the dumping of electronic waste (e-waste) in developing countries by the industrialised world. According to a 2015 UN report up to 90 per cent of the world's e-waste, worth nearly $19 billion (£12 billion), is illegally traded or dumped annually (UN 2015: 6–8). The key destinations for large-scale shipments of hazardous waste, such as electrical and electronic equipment, include Africa and Asia (ibid.).[3] The key driver for illegal waste shipments is the profit generated from payments for safe disposal of waste that in reality is either dumped or unsafely recycled (ibid.: 8).

Amid a constantly changing political climate and environmental priorities, defining environmental justice is challenging and debatable. There is growing recognition among scholars that the focus should not be confined to the distribution of environmental hazards and amenities, and resource conservation within bounded localities. The environmental paradigm needs to include the 'ways in which place-specific policies and practices can have consequences that cross national boundaries, affect multiple scales, and extend across global networks' (Holifield *et al.* 2011: 5).[4] Hence, environmental justice, with its shifting meaning, is an important entry point for enquiry. Schlosberg's work argues that environmental justice movements are 'often broad, plural and inclusive; likewise their definitions and discourses of justice range from those based on individual distributive complaints to those based on the survival of community functioning' (Schlosberg 2007: 5). Building on philosophical theories (Young 1990; Fraser 2000),[5] Schlosberg offers a definition of environmental justice. It is comprised of four notions: fair distribution of environmental goods and harm;

gaining individual and community recognition thereby asserting self-respect and autonomy; the existence of deliberative and democratic participation; and the construction of capabilities among individuals, groups and non-human parts of nature (Schlosberg 2007).

Contextualising environmental justice discourse in the global south's developing countries, including India, means addressing the challenges of poverty in its many dimensions. Unfortunately, economically and politically disenfranchised communities are denied equal opportunities in the fair distribution of environmental resources and involvement in environmental decision-making. Striking a balance between human needs, economic growth and the environment is required to create an 'inclusive development' that improves people's well-being and capabilities for a fully functioning life. Environmental justice discourse is thus necessarily linked to a sustainable development model that promotes environmental sustainability and participatory mechanisms in the development process (Ako 2013: 3–5). This chapter focuses on a strong procedural dimension that requires fair, open, informed and inclusive state institutional processes. In this regard, access to justice through an accessible judicial structure as a means to redress environmental damage or harm and protect and enforce legitimate interests becomes important.

Access to justice and environmental rule of law

Access to justice is a pillar of democratic governance. It promotes just and equitable outcomes thereby supporting the rule of law. Courts allow people to hold government agencies, companies and individuals accountable for the violation of their fundamental rights as enshrined in the constitutional mandate. The UN Development Programme defines access to justice as 'the ability of people to seek and obtain a remedy through formal or informal institutions of justice, and in conformity with human rights standards' (Jayasundere 2012: 11).

Principle 10 of the Rio Declaration 1992 sets out access rights in environmental matters that encompass not only access to information and participation in decision-making processes but also cover effective access to judicial and administrative proceedings, including redress and remedy. Principle 10 has been recognised as a global framework incorporating elements for good environmental governance. It is characterised as promoting environmental democracy and facilitating the rule of law (UN Environment Programme (UNEP) 2015).[6] Failure to include access rights may result in governmental decision-making outcomes being 'environmentally damaging, developmentally unsustainable, and socially unjust' (David et al. 2012: 8). The Aarhus Convention[7] promotes Principle 10 and mandates binding environmental obligations that emphasise governmental accountability, transparency and responsiveness thereby bolstering access to justice and the rule of law.[8]

The rule of law is a dynamic and multifaceted concept intricately interlinked and interwoven with values including dignity, freedom, fairness, justice, democracy and/or human rights. The rule stands as a 'pre-eminent legitimating political idea in the world today but its precise meaning has, however, proved elusive' (Preston 2011: 2 and 17).[9] The rule of law is the cornerstone of good governance and essential to economic and social development. Its attributes – namely participation, openness, accountability, predictability and transparency – for an effective and fair functioning of independent institutions instil confidence in the populace that no one is above law (ibid.).[10] The concept is central to the functioning of states at national level and ensures that justice permeates all levels. The UN defines the rule of law as:

> a principle of governance in which all persons, institutions and entities, public and private, including the State itself, are accountable to laws that are publicly promulgated, equally enforced and independently adjudicated, and which are consistent with international human rights norms and standards. It requires, as well, measures to ensure adherence to the principles of supremacy of law, equality before the law, accountability to the law, fairness in the application of the law, separation of powers, participation in decision-making, legal certainty, avoidance of arbitrariness and procedural and legal transparency.[11]

In relation to environmental matters, the rule of law received fresh affirmation as a consequence of important outcomes of international processes and developments since Rio+20 UN Conference on Sustainable Development 2012. *The Future We Want* report (UN 2012) acknowledges that the rule of law is central for sustainable development, including sustained and inclusive economic growth, social development, environmental protection, and eradicating poverty and hunger. An improved institutional framework based on effective, transparent, accountable and democratic characteristics makes it a prerequisite for achieving a sustainable development agenda.[12]

UNEP's World Congress on Justice, Governance and Law for Environmental Sustainability[13] contributed to Rio+20 by declaring environmental sustainability can only be achieved in the context of fair, effective and transparent national governance arrangements and the rule of law predicated on:

a   fair, clear and implementable environmental laws;
b   public participation in decision-making and access to justice and information in accordance with Principle 10 including exploring the potential value of borrowing provisions from the Convention on Access to Information, Public Participation in Decision-making and Access to Justice in Environmental Matters (Aarhus Convention) in this regard;
c   accountability and integrity of institutions and decision-makers, including through the active engagement of environmental auditing and enforcement institutions;
d   clear and co-ordinated mandates and roles;
e   accessible, fair, impartial, timely and responsive dispute resolution mechanisms, including developing specialised expertise in environmental adjudication and innovative environmental procedures and remedies;

f   recognition of the relationship between human rights and the environment; and

g   specific criteria for the interpretation of environmental law.[14]

Thus, without adherence to the rule of law and an open, just and dependable legal order, outcomes related to environmental sustainability, including from Rio+20, would remain unimplemented. A strong legal framework for environmental protection, diligent enforcement and effective access to justice is fundamental in supporting the rule of law and environmental sustainability.

The etymological creation of the term 'environmental rule of law' by UNEP's Governing Council Decision 27/9 in February 2013 reinvigorated the integration of the rule of law in environmental matters to reduce the violation of environmental law and achieve sustainable development. Decision 27/9 was the first internationally negotiated document to request the Executive Director to 'lead the United Nations system and support national governments upon their request in the development and implementation of *environmental rule of law* [emphasis added] with attention at all levels to mutually supporting governance features...'[15] The Global Symposium on Environmental Rule of Law (23–27 June 2014, Nairobi) reiterated that the environmental rule of law is indispensable for sustainable development and environmental justice.[16] The bases for the environmental rule of law are adherence to environmental law, constitutional rights to a healthy environment and human rights. The enforcement and independent adjudication of environmental laws would ensure that environmental rule of law reduces corruption and guarantees accountability to and fairness in the application of the law, the separation of powers, participation in decision-making, respect for human rights and the delivery of environmental justice.

The post-2015 Sustainable Development Goals (SDG) agenda, particularly Goal 16, acknowledge that access to justice, the rule of law and effective, inclusive institutions are essential ingredients of sustainable development.[17] The rule of law is no longer an option but a prerequisite without which equitable economic growth, inclusive social development and environmental sustainability are unachievable. The 2030 Agenda[18] places justice and environmental rule of law at the heart of development. Within the justice element, access to fair justice systems and accountable institutions of democratic governance are integral to achieving sustainable development. Stronger specialised judiciaries and environmental laws, underpinned by the rule of law, can ensure good governance and achieve SDGs.

At regional levels, the contribution of environmental rule of law towards the realisation of sustainable development is increasingly emphasised. This involves developing a common understanding of the concept, identifying current trends and providing a knowledge base to support development and strengthening environmental laws, policies and institutions, as the foundation for sustainable development. The Putrajaya Statement of the First Asia and Pacific International Colloquium on Environmental Rule of Law[19] and the Nairobi Statement of the First Africa Colloquium on Environmental Rule of Law[20] reiterated environmental rule of law is essential for environmental justice and sustainable development. The Inter-American Congress on the Environmental Rule of Law, 30–31 March 2015 in Jamaica aimed to foster the 'environmental rule of law' in the Americas and contribute towards good environmental governance.[21] Thus the vital components of environmental rule of law include, inter alia, adequate and implementable laws, access to justice and information, public participation, accountability, transparency, liability for environmental damage, fair and just enforcement with timely, impartial and independent dispute resolution, and human rights.

These recent developments underscore the environmental rule of law's contribution to sustainable human development as a system of environmental governance and justice. It provides a predictable and steadfast foundation to seek redressal of grievances and enforcement of legal rights and obligations through a system of legal and social institutions. It rests upon a rights-based approach to guide decision-making in environmental matters that ultimately leads to better results by addressing the impact of environmental degradation in general and, in particular, affecting the world's poorest and most vulnerable. The role of the judiciary in championing the environmental rule of law that guarantees equitable access to justice and legal empowerment initiatives thus becomes important.

Judiciary: environmental compliance and enforcement

The role of the judiciary is critical. It plays a 'lead role in shaping the normative interpretation of the legal and regulatory framework'.[22] Justice Weeramantry in the commentary on the Bangalore Principles of Judicial Conduct observed that 'a judiciary of undisputed integrity is the bedrock institution essential for ensuring compliance' (UN 2007: 5).[23] There is growing support for judges to play a central role in defining how environmental sustainability and protection of human rights at all levels is achieved. Agenda 21 emphasises the need to provide an effective regulatory framework for improving the legal–institutional capacities of countries to cope with problems of national governance and effective law-making and law-applying in this field.[24] UNEP plays a pivotal function by highlighting the judiciary's role. For instance, the Johannesburg Principles on the Role of Law and Sustainable Development adopted at the Global Judges Symposium in Johannesburg 2002 stated:

> We emphasize that the fragile state of the global environment requires the Judiciary as the guardian of the Rule of Law, to boldly and fearlessly implement and enforce applicable international and national laws, which in the field of environment and sustainable development will assist in alleviating poverty and sustaining an enduring civilisation, and ensuring that the present generation will enjoy and improve the quality of life of all peoples, while also ensuring that the inherent rights and interests of succeeding generations are not compromised. We are strongly of the view that there is an

urgent need to strengthen the capacity of judges, prosecutors, legislators and all persons who play a critical role at national level in the process of implementation, development and enforcement of environmental law, including multilateral environmental agreements ... especially through the judicial process.[25]

Klaus Toepfer, UNEP Executive Director, in the 2005 UNEP Global Judges Programme stated:

It is essential to forge a global partnership among all relevant stakeholders for the protection of the environment based on the affirmation of the human values set out in the UN Millennium Declaration: freedom, equality, solidarity, tolerance, respect for nature and shared responsibility. The judiciary plays a key role in weaving these values into the fabric of our societies. The judiciary is also a crucial partner in promoting environmental governance, upholding the rule of law and in ensuring a fair balance between environmental, social and developmental consideration through its judgements and declarations.

(UNEP 2005: v; see also Kaniaru *et al*. 1998; Decleris 2011)[26]

Again, facilitating judicial leadership in environmental matters and specialised environmental adjudication was recognised and promoted in various international forums and associated documentation. They recognise that an independent judiciary and judicial process are vital for the implementation, development and enforcement of environmental law. The judiciary at national, regional and global levels are crucial partners for promoting compliance with, and the implementation and enforcement of, international and national environmental law.[27]

In Asia and the Pacific, the Asian Development Bank (ADB) is active in promoting green justice through knowledge-sharing and capacity-building. According to the 2015 ADB report, over the previous decade the region lost 18 million hectares of forest to deforestation and 10 million hectares to forest fires; in financial terms, each year about $4.5 trillion of forest cover due to the fires, poor forestry practices, and uncontrolled legal and illegal logging. Asia's mountains and upland ecosystems are threatened by increasing human population, haphazard infrastructure development and low investment in conservation. Freshwater environments are threatened by large dam projects that alter natural water flow. Coastal and marine ecosystems and marine biodiversity are in danger from overfishing and destructive fishing practices, valued between $10 billion and $23 billion annually (ADB 2015: 21). The ADB's long-term strategic framework, Strategy 2020, recognises the environment as a core operational area, and good governance and capacity development as drivers of change.

The ADB is committed to 'strengthen the ... legal, regulatory, and enforcement capacities of public institutions on environmental considerations' (Hovland 2011: iv). This includes publishing a compendium on Capacity Building for

Environmental Law in the Asian and Pacific Region, launching the Asian Environmental Compliance and Enforcement Network and organising symposiums and conferences. In 2010, the ADB organised the Asian Judges Symposium on Environmental Decision-Making, the Rule of Law and Environmental Justice emphasising:

> ...improving environmental and natural resource decision making and adjudication within regional judiciaries, without assuming that any particular form or structure is the best way to achieve effective environmental decision making and adjudication in different country contexts; highlighting environmental specialisation within general courts, as well as exploring work done by specialist environmental courts, boards, and tribunals. Importantly, without drivers for increasing the demand for effective environmental judicial decision-making from the judiciary, environmental judicial specialisations could go unused.
>
> (ADB 2012: 1)

Subsequently, in 2012 the ADB organised the South Asia Conference on Environmental Justice at Bhurban, Pakistan. The Bhurban Declaration 2012[28] promised:

- an educated judiciary and specialised courts;
- that countries would improve the development, implementation, enforcement of and compliance with environmental laws and an action plan to achieve this;
- to strengthen the existing specialised ETs, and train judges and lawyers on environmental law;
- and a vow to establish green benches in courts for dispensation of environmental justice and to make necessary amendments or adjustments to the legal and regulatory structures to foster environmental justice in South Asia.

Further, the ADB approved and supported technical assistance to establish the Asian Judges Network on Environment (AJNE) in 2010. The AJNE is an informal trans-governmental network committed to providing a dynamic forum for judicial capacity-building and multilateral exchanges on environmental adjudication.[29] In this network, the chief justices and judges of the Association of Southeast Asian Nations (ASEAN) and South Asian Association for Regional Cooperation (SAARC) regions have harnessed the collective judicial experience in environmental decision-making in Asia. The AJNE's contribution has been to encourage senior judiciary to realise that they share a professional mission of advancing environmental justice that extends beyond their national jurisdiction. The ASEAN judiciaries that include Brunei Darussalam, Cambodia, Indonesia, Lao People's Democratic Republic, Malaysia, Myanmar, the Philippines, Singapore, Thailand and Vietnam have held five chief justices' roundtable conferences. The fifth roundtable conference held in Cambodia from 4–5 December 2015 highlighted the powerful leadership role of the ASEAN judiciaries regarding environmentally sustainable development and domestic and regional action. The conference noted the progress made in creating national or regional environmental working groups for a mutual understanding of the issues, 'greening benches' and building capacity for environmental adjudication, including judicial training and certification programmes on the environment.[30] The judiciaries in the SAARC region include Afghanistan, Bangladesh, Bhutan, India, Maldives, Nepal, Pakistan and Sri Lanka. To date there have been four South Asia judicial roundtables on environmental justice, the latest being in November 2015 in Kathmandu, Nepal. The Kathmandu roundtable reaffirmed the commitment of the judiciaries to promote environmental protection in the region and the need for capacity development in environmental adjudication.[31]

Global and regional judicial networking and capacity-building aim to promote the sharing of legal information, harmonisation of the approach and non-formal peer-level supervision towards the implementation of global and regional environmental instruments. Anne-Marie Slaughter's exploratory essay (1994)[32] analyses the importance of 'transjudicial communication' of courts (national and supranational courts) talking to one another globally. The courts are bound to the

> …process of cross-fertilisation among legal systems for dissemination of ideas from one national legal system to another, from one regional legal system to another, or from the international legal system or a particular regional legal system to national legal systems. The purpose or effect of such cross-fertilisation may be to provide inspiration for the solution of a particular legal problem, such as the appropriate balance between individual freedom of expression and the needs of the community. Alternatively, and more broadly, cross-fertilisation may foster the development of fledgling national legal systems through the reception of entire bodies of foreign law.
>
> (Slaughter 1994: 117)

Slaughter's analysis complements judicial networking on environmental matters. Environmental problems are complex and increasingly transnational in nature. Transjudicial communication promotes better environmental decisions through regular and intensive communication of information thereby sharing developments and good practices on environmental adjudication in legal systems. Environmental judges play a unique and distinct leadership role in the environmental enforcement chain as members of a transnational community of law and mould normative interpretations of environmental law. The legal transplantation and adoption of legal doctrines from one nation state to another and/ or international laws to the receiving state have introduced innovative approaches to environmental governance. This is typically helpful for legal systems where environmental law is in an embryonic stage or is slow to respond to environmental crises. The legal transplant helps improve the content and design of national environmental laws of the borrowing nation. The adoption of the precautionary principle (Indonesia and Pakistan), polluter-pays principle (India and South Africa), intergenerational equity (Philippines) and public trust doctrine (Sri Lanka) are examples of such transplants. Slaughter rightly observes 'in a situation in which a number of states are contemplating acceptance of a particular international legal obligation, references to the activity of fellow courts in other states can act as both a security blanket and a stick' (ibid.: 116; see also Wiener 2000/2001; Kotzé 2012: 282).

Judicial globalisation fosters a pluralist and contextualised understanding of environmental law. The global environmental externalities and public goods make it imperative to draw on the laws of the shared ecological system, if not the same content, for environmental governance. By virtue of processes of transjudicial communication and legal transplant, the courts of many countries through their sound judgments and the example set by the judiciary itself have acted as 'protagonist judiciary ... or at least moving towards it' rather than 'spectator judiciary' (Benjamin 2012). In this regard, an environmentally trained and motivated judiciary increases opportunities for successful implementation of compliance and enforcement measures. ECTs are a way of concentrating expertise for fair and transparent balancing of competing interests between environment, development and human rights, efficient and effective conservation of natural resources, and promoting access rights (information, participation and access to justice) for just and equitable outcomes.

Environmental courts and tribunals: a specialised forum

A consequence of these international developments has led many jurisdictions to develop some form of specialised environmental court or tribunal, while embracing a flexible mechanism for dispute resolution. Dissatisfaction with the general court system is an establishment-driver of environmental courts in many countries, based on public perceptions of delay, lack of expertise, lack of independence and/or corruption. Judges in ordinary courts may lack sufficient experience of the practicalities of environmental law and may be uncomfortable dealing with expert testimony and the task of balancing anticipated environmental harm and economic benefits. Chief Justice Brian Preston of the State of New South Wales (NSW), Australia, Land and Environment Court, states:

> Increasingly, it is being recognised that a court with special expertise in environmental matters is best placed to play this role in the achievement of ecologically sustainable development ... Specialisation [is] not seen to be an end, but rather a means to an end. It [is] envisaged that a specialist court could more ably deliver consistency in decision-making, decrease delays (through its understanding of the characteristics of environmental disputes) and facilitate the development of environmental laws, policies and principles.
>
> (Preston 2012: 398 and 403)

The finely grained, comprehensive study of ECTs by George Pring and Catherine Pring in 2009 in *Greening Justice: Creating and Improving Environmental Courts and Tribunals* identified over 350 ECTs in 41 countries (Pring and Pring 2009).[33] In 2016, just seven years later, there were over 1200 ECTs operating in 44 countries, worldwide, in every major type of legal system (civil law, common law, mixed law, Asian law and Islamic law), at all government levels, from the richest to the poorest nations, with the majority created in the previous 10 years (Pring and Pring 2016 forthcoming).[34] Their updated 2016 study identifies five environmental court models and three ET models in operational ECTs. The environmental courts include:

1   operationally separate and fully independent environmental courts;[35]
2   decisionally independent environmental courts that are a part of court system but free to make their own rules, procedures and decisions;[36]
3   mix of law-trained and science-trained judges;[37]
4   generalist judges assigned environmental cases;[38]
5   generalist judges trained in environmental law.[39]

The ETs identified are:

1   operationally separate and fully independent ETs;[40]
2   decisionally independent ETs under the supervisory control of the government but not one whose decisions the ET reviews thereby retaining full independence over its decisions;[41]
3   captive ETs under the administrative, fiscal and policy control of an agency whose decisions they review.[42]

There is no optimal 'one-size-fits-all' model. Rather, it is driven by the cultural, and socio-economic conditions prevalent in each national jurisdiction (Pring and Pring 2016 and 2009: 3). There are 20 countries with pending or potential ECTs,[43] 15 with authorised but not established ECTs[44] and seven with discontinued ECTs.[45]

The exponential growth of ECTs has resulted in the concomitant advantages attached to the specialised forum (Pring and Pring 2009: 3; 2016). These include:

1   specialised expertise in complex legal, scientific and technical matters;
2   freeing the regular courts of significant and steadily increasing workload;
3   uniformity and consistency in decision-making processes;
4   greater dispatch in resolution of environmental controversies and more efficient adjudication;
5   more predictable environmental decision-making;
6   greater governmental accountability in environmental matters;
7   instilling public confidence and trust in the government and judicial system;

8　expanded notion of *locus standi* for effective public participation and vindication of rights;

9　reduced litigation costs;

10　adoption of flexible rules of procedure;

11　problem-solving approach that moves beyond traditional legal remedies to create innovative solutions resulting in promoting environmental sustainability including protection of human rights; and

12　demonstrating commitment to implement international obligations relating to access to justice, environmental rule of law and environmental sustainability.

Possible disadvantages include (Pring and Pring 2009: 17–18; 2016):

1　costs to establish and maintain a separate legal system;

2　jurisdictional location of the ECTs to assure convenient access to parties;

3　insufficient caseload;

4　generalist judges not sufficiently trained in environmental matters;

5　tendency of an activist judiciary usurping its power and adopting an unbalanced approach;

6　lack of expertise (judges and lawyers);

7　risk of creating an inferior court below the general courts with less power and status; and

8　scepticism about defining an environmental case and determining the appropriate forum.

Although potential difficulties exist, the advantages attributed to ECTs are dominant. The need to continuously adopt best practices and regularly monitor performance is necessary for a successful ECT. Chief Justice Preston, in an illuminating article, identifies 12 key characteristics for the successful operation of an ECT (Preston 2014). The identification of best practices helps not only those stakeholders and countries that are in the process of establishing ECTs but also those looking to improve the functioning and performance of their ECTs. These best practices are:

1　A superior status and authority ECT with comprehensive jurisdiction and public acknowledgment is considered a successful legitimate forum for environmental dispute resolution. The presence of expertise helps to develop environmental jurisprudence and maintain public confidence (NSW Australia; Sweden).

2　Independence and impartiality of ECT judges are essential components of good environmental justice and governance achieved through institutional safeguards in the form of selection of judges, long-term security tenure, substantive and procedural protection against their removal and sufficient remuneration (Brazil).

3　A comprehensive jurisdiction with respect to coverage of matters and disputes arising under all environmental laws and types of cases the ECT has authority to hear, such as merit review, judicial review, civil or criminal enforcement and others (NSW Australia; New Zealand).

4   In-house environmentally literate judges and other members of the ECT sensitive and responsive to environmental issues. Multidisciplinary environmental decision-making provides greater certainty and better quality decisions (Sweden; Environment, Resources and Development Court of South Australia).

5   Facilitation of alternative dispute resolution (ADR) without resorting to full-blown litigation. Conciliation, mediation and neutral evaluation are in-house ADR processes (NSW Australia; Planning and Environment Court, Queensland).

6   Access to external experts with excellent knowledge, experience, reputation and communication skills so as to be credible, reliable and persuasive on complex scientific and expert testimony areas (NSW Australia; Planning and Environment Court of Queensland).

7   Access to environmental justice by its substantive decisions and procedural requirements. The substantive decisions uphold the constitutional, statutory and human rights of access to justice. The procedural requirement relaxes the standing requirement and removes barriers to environmental public interest litigation (NSW Australia; Philippines).

8   Achieving just, quick and cheap dispute settlement through organised case-management policies and processes, use of technologies (e.g. teleconferencing, videoconferencing, court website and computer data management systems) (State Administrative Tribunal of Western Australia).

9   Innovative remedies, holistic solutions and responsiveness to environmental challenges are important characteristics of ECTs for environmental governance (NSW Australia).

10 Development of environmental jurisprudence on 'justice' (substantive, procedural, distributive and restorative) and cross-fertilisation of environmental law for a comparative approach are useful and valued contributions (NSW Australia).

11 Unifying ethos and mission to protect environment and promote sustainable development (Resource Management and Planning Appeals Tribunal, Tasmania).

12 ECTs may uphold, interpret and explicate environmental laws and values by developing environmental jurisprudence, formulating and applying non-binding principles to administrative decisions and developing innovative practices and procedures. Flexibility and innovativeness helps them adapt quickly and appropriately to inefficiencies in their own practices and procedures (NSW Australia).

For Chief Justice Preston, the court cannot rest on its laurels and should recognise the need for adaptive management. Quoting Gething, he observes: 'an excellent organization is one that is continually looking, learning, changing and improving towards the concept of excellence it has set for itself. Excellence is more of a journey than a static destination' (Preston 2014: 29).

A few cameo examples from developed and developing countries, with particular reference to the SAARC region, are discussed below to highlight the different ECT systems.

Developed countries

Australia (NSW)

The world's first specialist comprehensive Land and Environment Court of NSW, Australia, was established in 1980[46] with twin objectives – rationalisation (a 'one-stop-shop' for environmental, planning and land matters) and specialisation. The court consists of judges and commissioners with qualifications, knowledge and experience in environmental or town or country planning matters, environmental sciences, land valuation, architecture, engineering, surveying or building construction, resource management, urban design, heritage and land rights for Aborigines. It is a superior court of record having wide jurisdiction in relation to environmental, planning and land matters. Jurisdiction is exercised with reference to the subject matter of proceedings that involve impact on community interest or government policy. The court's jurisdiction includes merit review of governmental decisions, judicial review, civil enforcement, criminal enforcement (prosecutions), criminal appeals and sentences of the local court, and appeals against decisions of the commissioners of the court (Preston 2012: 403). Merit review is covered under three classes of court jurisdiction: Class 1 environmental, planning and protection appeals; Class 2 local government and miscellaneous appeals; and Class 3 land tenure, valuation, rating and compensation matters, plus Aboriginal land claims. The civil jurisdiction of the court extends to tree and mining disputes. Class 4 cases involve civil enforcement and judicial review of decisions under planning or environmental laws. The court's role in criminal enforcement is important. Class 5 involves summary criminal enforcement proceedings usually by governmental authorities against planning or environmental laws. Classes 6 and 7 cover criminal appeals against decisions of the NSW local court in proceedings for environmental offences related to conviction, sentence and dismissal of proceedings. The court's consistent and transparent decisions in sentencing for environmental offences have developed environmental crime jurisprudence and established the world's first sentencing database for environmental offences (Preston 2012: 406). Appeals can be made against its decisions depending upon type of proceedings, decision or order or whether the court was constituted by a judge or commissioner.

The court adopts innovative practices and procedures to facilitate access to justice including the development of PIL. Liberal interpretation of standing requirements, no summary dismissal proceedings on the ground of laches, representation in person or by agents (with the permission of the court) are other innovations. The concept of a multi-door courthouse is increasingly used. The court offers dispute resolution processes in-house and externally under one roof. This includes dealing with cases in an expeditious and timely manner, proportionate to their importance and complexity and cost-efficient to both private parties and public resource. Efficient case-management for just, quick and cheap settlement of disputes is fundamental. Last but not the least the court's approach of cross-fertilisation and legal transplant has led to the development of environmental jurisprudence on matters relating to justice. For instance, in *Telstra Corporation v Hornsby Shire Council* (2006) 146 LGERA 10, Chief Justice Preston in a remarkable judgment outlined six basic principles to explain the concept of ecologically sustainable development. In a matter relating to proposed mobile telecommunications antenna in the Sydney suburb of Cheltenham, and the local community's fear of harm from electromagnetic radiation, the judgment referred to judicial decisions from other foreign jurisdictions[47] and articulated principles for the application of ecologically sustainable development (ibid.: 35–37).[48] With its long-established history, the court has an outstanding international and national reputation. It is successful and acts as a role model for other ECTs.

Sweden

In Sweden, the Environmental Code is the most important piece of environmental legislation, promoting sustainable development and assuring a healthy and sound environment for present and future generations.[49] It encapsulates the underlying ethos and mission in the form of a statement that guides its operation and promotes responsibility for wise management of natural resources. The Code is comprehensive legislation giving environmental courts both civil and administrative jurisdiction and a range of enforcement powers. Since May 2011, Sweden has established five Land and Environment Courts (regional courts) that are part of the district courts in Nacka, Vänersborg, Växjö, Umeå and Östersund and one superior environmental court as the Svea Court of Appeal. The courts deal with many types of cases and matters including: permits for waterworks operations; environmentally harmful issues of health protection, environmental protection, sanitation, contaminated areas and toxic waste; damages and compensation issues with environmental ties; building, demolition and site improvement in accordance with planning and building laws; site leasehold rights cases; appeal of planning matters; cases pertaining to property registration, construction and utility easement; and expropriation cases.[50] Criminal cases are not within the jurisdiction of the courts.[51]

Judicial and technical experts sit as judges. Each regional environmental court has a panel consisting of one law-trained judge, one environmental adviser and two lay expert members.[52] The judge and the technical adviser are employed by the court and work full time as environmental judges. One of the expert members has experience of matters falling within the area of responsibility of the Swedish Environmental Protection Agency. The Land and Environment

Court of Appeal comprises three professional judges and one technical judge.[53] All members of the court have an equal vote. If in a case the outcome of the votes is equal, as a general rule the chairperson has the casting vote.[54] Inclusion of science–technical experts as decision-makers with judicially trained judges assures a comprehensive assessment. In the words of Ulf Bjällås, a former Presiding Judge of the Environmental Court of Appeal in Stockholm, 'technical expertise and trained judges make it easier to find the correct balance point' (2010: 183). Additionally, the environmental court may appoint one or more expert members to carry out special investigations or valuations for an assessment of a case and deliver their opinion.[55] On-site inspection is important in determining the real nature of problems and associated consequences. The above reflects instances of best practice to resolve environmental disputes by Swedish courts.

Ulf Bjällås states that Swedish environmental courts have 'high credibility and are fully accepted both by the Federation of the Swedish Industry and by NGOs focusing on environmental protection' (2010: 182). The adoption of an integrated and holistic approach to resolving disputes, effective management of environmental cases by adopting procedural flexibility, no filing fees, merit and judicial review by the courts and prioritising urgent cases for early disposal helps in maintaining credibility and inculcating public confidence (ibid.: 183).

UK

After over 20 years of debate[56] and political indolence, an ET was established in 2010. The approach to establishing the new tribunal '[was] typically British – cautious, pragmatic, learning from experience, yet containing elements of a radical vision' (Macrory 2010: 77).[57] The ET, being a part of the General Regulatory Chamber of the First-tier Tribunal, initially had limited jurisdiction and was confined to hearing appeals concerning civil sanctioning powers[58] of environmental regulators. However, other appeals have been added, notably, National Measurement Office appeals concerning civil sanctions under eco-design regulation[59] and appeals under Welsh plastic-bag regulations.[60] Criminal offences are outside its jurisdiction. The tribunal consists of judicial and non-legal members. In 2014 there were six judges each with at least seven years of professional standing together with 10 members with a wide range of expertise (Macrory 2014: 212). Procedures are governed by the Tribunal Procedure (First-tier Tribunal) (General Regulatory Chamber) Rules 2009 as amended.[61]

Developing countries

Malaysia

The Malaysian Environmental Court (MEC) was established on 3 September 2012[62] to ensure uniformity of decision-making and improvement of the administration of justice in environmental cases. The MEC is only functional at the level of the 42 Session and 53 Magistrate's Courts involving 38 Acts and Ordinances and 17 Regulations and Orders. It aims to provide expeditious disposal of cases within three to six months. According to Chief Justice Tun Arifin Zakaria, the MEC disposed of 96 per cent of cases from 2012–2015. Out of the 1140 cases registered at the Sessions Court, only 135 were still pending whereas, at the Magistrate's Court, the total number registered was 1017 and only 36 were pending.[63] An appeal lies to the High Court. The MEC does not have the jurisdiction to cover environmental civil cases.

However, there are challenges faced by the MEC. First, it only deals with criminal cases, the issue of *locus standi* becomes problematic. According to the federal constitution, the Attorney General can decide whether to institute criminal proceedings.[64] In *Ketua Pengarah Jabatan Alam Sekitar v Kajing Tubek* (1997) 3 MLJ 23, the Court of Appeal held the respondent lacked substantive *locus standi* as he was trying to impose a penal sanction on a Bakun dam developer. The power to prosecute lies with the Attorney General. In areas where there are no MECs established, the civil courts can exercise jurisdiction over environmental civil suits (Mulqueeny and Cordon 2014). The civil courts are, however, confronted with several problems in handling these environmental disputes. First, as the plaintiff needs to show real injury 'legal standing' becomes complex and limited resources of poor litigants make it difficult to access environmental justice (ibid.). Second, there is no established uniform standard of proof, particularly from environmental experts. In *Moslimin Bin Bijato v Public Prosecutor* (2011) MLJU 1061, as no evidence was adduced from the environmental expert to identify whether the carcass in question was that of a deer or not, the accused's appeal was allowed in the High Court. Third, lack of enforcement of implementing forest laws on the part of relevant agencies to prevent crimes against environment and wildlife is a huge challenge. Fourth, the judges are not adequately trained to handle complex environmental problems and, finally, the public needs to be more responsive and participative towards environmental issues and not merely spectators.

Kenya

On 30 August 2011, the Environment and Land Court Act provided for the jurisdiction, structure and operations of the Environment and Land Court (ELC). It is a specialised superior court with the same status as the High Court, comprised of the Presiding judge and such number of judges determined by judicial commission.[65] The ELC has original and appellate jurisdiction to hear and determine all disputes relating to environment and land,[66] including: environmental planning and protection; climate issues; land use planning; title, tenure, boundaries, rates, rents and valuations; mining, minerals and other natural resources; compulsory acquisition of land; land administration and management; public, private and community land and contracts; and choses in action or other instruments granting any enforceable interests in land.[67]

The ELC is guided by general principles of environmental management including sustainable development, public participation, cultural and social principles traditionally applied by any community in Kenya for the management of the environment or natural resources, international co-operation, intergenerational and intra-generational equity, and the polluter-pays and precautionary principles.[68] The ELC offers in-house ADR processes including conciliation, mediation and traditional dispute resolution mechanisms.[69] It has the power to grant any relief including interim or permanent preservation orders, covering injunctions, prerogative orders, award of damages, compensation, specific performance, restitution, declaration or costs.[70]

According to the Land Development and Governance Institute's report (2013), there was general optimism from the public on service delivery by the ELC. In areas where courts were established, they were publicly accessible although a section of the public was not actually aware of their existence. The report recommended that there was a need to increase the number of courts to cover all counties to reduce the cost of travelling. Capacity-building was necessary to increase public awareness of the jurisdiction and functions of the court and, where ADR mechanisms were established, they should be strengthened to reduce backlog (ibid.: 15).

Additionally, Kenya in 1999 established the National Environment Tribunal (NET) under section 125 and Part XII of the Environmental Management and Coordination Act (EMCA). Its principal function is to receive, hear and determine appeals arising from decisions of the National Environment Management Authority (NEMA) on issuance, denial or revocation of environmental impact assessment (EIA) licences, among other decisions, hear appeals on forestry matters and advise environmental authorities on questions of law when asked (Odote 2012: 142). Since 2005 the NET has decided 140 appeals. It consists of a chairperson and two advocates with judicial qualifications and three persons competent in the field of environmental management. It prescribes its own procedure (Pring and Pring 2016). Appeals from the NET are made to the ELC. However, there remains an overlap between the two and, in light of the establishment of the ELC, questions remain regarding the utility of having both a specialised court and a tribunal (ibid.).

South Asian Association for Regional Cooperation (SAARC) countries

SAARC is an organisation of eight countries with 1.7 billion people accounting for 21 per cent of the world population.[71] The region is facing a 'major challenge in achieving rapid economic growth to reduce poverty and attain other Millennium Development Goals in an era of accentuated risks posed by global climate change … and other environmental issues' (ADB 2014: 17). The judiciary helps shape the context and framework used for resolution of environmental disputes.

Afghanistan

Eighty per cent of the population is largely dependent upon the country's natural resource base for its economic well-being (UNEP 2007: 4). However, this resource base has been seriously degraded and damaged as a consequence of continuing political instability, civil unrest and weakly implemented environmental and resource management policies (ADB 2014: 10).[72] The Environment Management Act 2006 established the National Environment Protection Agency to protect the country's environmental integrity and promote sustainable use and management of natural resources and conservation and rehabilitation of its environment through the provision of effective environmental guidance and management services (Azimi 2007: 13). Afghanistan does not have an ECT for resolution of disputes.

Bangladesh

Bangladesh is a country fully aware of the implications of climate change. The Environment Court Act 2000 provided for the establishment of at least one environmental court in each of 64 districts and as many Environmental Appellate Courts as the government deemed fit. There are only two exclusive environmental courts functioning in the country, one in Dhaka and the other in Chittagong. The joint district judge acts as a judge of the environmental court in addition to being a civil judge.[73] The 2000 Act does not provide for technical experts acting as judges in the environmental court. An environmental court has the power and competence of a civil court when it decides a claim for compensation for causing harm to the environment or biodiversity and it functions as a criminal court when it performs as a trial court of an offence committed under the Environment Conservation Act 1995 or any other law relating to the environment.[74] No environmental court shall take cognisance of an offence or receive any suit for compensation except on the written report of an inspector or any other person authorised by the director general of the Department of Environment.[75] There is one Environmental Appellate Court, situated in Dhaka, to hear and dispose of appeals arising out of judgments and orders passed by the environmental court.[76]

There are major drawbacks in the Bangladesh system. The provisions of the 2000 Act are restrictive and fail to enhance access to environmental justice. Aggrieved persons must institute their case directly in the court without prior notice upon or report to the inspector of the Department of Environment (Preston 2014: 4). The consequence is an inactive court and a forum that lacks judicial and political independence. According to Chief Justice Md Muzammel Hossain:

> in 2013 there were 129 cases in the environmental court at Dhaka for trial and the Court disposed of 29 cases, as such, at the beginning of 2014, there were a backlog of 91 cases. In the environmental court in Chittagong, there

were 257 cases for trial in 2013 and the Court disposed of 23 cases in 2013 and there was a backlog of 234 cases at the beginning of 2014.[77]

Further, the lack of awareness about environmental laws and justice mechanisms among the legal fraternity including subordinate judges acts as a hindrance for accessing justice: 'In order to expedite the process of trial of environmental cases, it is necessary to establish more environmental courts, at least one exclusive environmental court in each of 17 old district Headquarters of the country.'[78]

Bhutan

Few environment-related cases have been brought before the courts. Bhutan plans to establish a green bench in its Supreme Court (ADB 2014: 11).[79]

Maldives

There is no specialised ECT in the Maldives. The constitutional provisions give importance to the preservation of the environment. These provisions highlight the obligation to respect the environment and the state's fundamental duty to protect and preserve the environment for the benefit of present and future generations and for fostering ecologically balanced sustainable development (ibid.).[80]

Nepal

The Supreme Court of Nepal is guided by its constitution to protect and improve the environment. There is no specialised ECT (ibid.).[81]

Pakistan

Pakistan Environmental Protection Act (PEPA) 1997 mandates the federal government to establish ETs as it considers necessary.[82] The ETs consist of a chairperson who is, or has been, or is qualified for appointment as, a judge of the High Court and two members to be appointed by the federal government of which at least one shall be a technical member with suitable professional qualifications and experience in the environmental field.[83] The tribunal has exclusive jurisdiction to try offences under it and to hear appeals against the orders of environmental protection agencies.[84] Appeals from the tribunal are forwarded to the Division Bench of the High Court.[85] The functioning of these tribunals has been ineffective due to 'interruptions in the continuous working of these tribunals leading to a backlog of cases, an increased workload, the absence of a specialised environmental forum, and burdening of the superior courts' (Ahsan and Khawaja: 2013: 13).[86]

The ineffectiveness of the environmental protection agencies has placed the burden on the Pakistan judiciary to enforce environmental rights and protect the environment. Consequently, the establishment of green benches (environmental courts) at all the High Courts and Supreme Court of Pakistan commenced from 2012. In 2016, there were 250 judges designated as 'green benches' in the High Court and district courts. The unwritten practice is to have one or two 'green benches' in the five High Courts and two green judges in each of the 133 districts courts (Pring and Pring 2016: Appendix A). The use of PIL in protecting and preserving the environment by the superior judiciary created inroads in developing an expansive environmental jurisprudence. The constitutionally protected right to life has been liberally interpreted to include the right to a clean environment.[87] The Pakistan judiciary creatively expanded the substance and scope of environmental justice to include matters such as: banning coal-mining activity polluting the water of a catchment area used by the residents of that area;[88] restraining industries from discharging untreated toxic effluents into drains and canals;[89] improving air quality to combat the menace of air pollution and noise caused by vehicles in Lahore[90] and restraining unauthorised and illegal groundwater extraction.[91]

Sri Lanka

Sri Lankan judiciary has developed judicial exegesis by defining social justice and human rights in the development process and in the context of environmental protection. The Supreme Court has played a pivotal role in expanding the scope of environmental justice by interpreting statutes in a liberal and eco-friendly manner. The active involvement of the Supreme Court in cases relating to illegal sand-mining,[92] air pollution[93] and noise pollution[94] illustrates the prevention, reduction and control of environmental pollution and the extinction and destruction of natural resources. The use of PIL and consequent expansion of the principle of *locus standi* have paved the way for the application of constitutional remedies on issues involving environment and development.[95] According to Justice S Marsoof: 'Sri Lanka does not have a permanent "green bench" but there is a specialised bench (of the Supreme Court) that receives environmental cases' (ADB 2014: 13).[96]

India

The subsequent chapters focus on environmental justice in India with particular reference to the NGT, a specialised forum for environmental justice.

Conclusion

'No man is an island', wrote John Donne.[97] Likewise, in terms of the environment, the days of the nation state functioning alone to protect the environment are past. The environment is here and everywhere, both in the present and in the future. The environment has taken on the widely accepted status of an international and global responsibility albeit with regional partners and individual states acting as local caretakers. This chapter has reviewed the international commitments that bind nation states alongside the recognition of the essential role of an enlightened judiciary in enforcing the environmental rule of law. Access to justice is a foundational pillar for environmental protection and appropriate court structures are required to provide such protection. The growth and varied operational strategies of ECTs have also been described. They take the reader into the following chapters which offer a detailed account of the creation, daily operation, powers, bench composition, procedure, caseload and functionality of the NGT of India.

Notes

1 Other instances include African-American communities with a lead smelter plant adjacent to their public housing; the native American Navajo tribe subjected to serious abuses from uranium mining in Churchrock, New Mexico.

2 This is a catastrophe without parallel in industrial history. At around midnight on 23 December 1984, there was a methyl-isocyanate gas and other toxins leak from the Union Carbide Indian Ltd (UCIL) pesticide plant in Bhopal, Madhya Pradesh. UCIL was the Indian subsidiary of US company Union Carbide Corporation, now a subsidiary of Dow Chemicals. Lax standards caused the tragedy which resulted in over 500,000 people being exposed to the deadly gas. The official death-count was 3787 but other agencies estimated 15,000. The horrific effects continue to this day. The plant continues to leak and pollute, affecting thousands who depend on the groundwater.

3 Ghana and Nigeria are among the largest recipients, although high volumes of e-waste are also transported to Cote d'Ivoire and Republic of Congo. In Asia, China, Hong Kong, Pakistan, India, Bangladesh and Vietnam bear the brunt of illegal e-waste shipments.

4 Holifield *et al.* (2011) provide instances, e.g. in Barcelona where policies to promote urban sustainability displace environmental problems to regional level and, in New York, community-based mobilisations against solid waste incineration helped rectify environmental health disparities at neighbourhood level but promoted regional injustices through export of waste to rural localities.

5 Reliance was also placed on the work of Nussbaum and Sen (1992).

6 See also the 12 Bali Guidelines 2010 that deal with access to justice in environmental matters, demonstrating the importance of the rights-based approach in implementing Principle 10 of the Rio Declaration: guideline 15 (access to review procedures relating to information requests); 16 (access to review procedures relating to public participation); 17 (access to review procedures relating to public or private actors); 18 (liberal standing provisions); 19 (effective procedures for timely review); 20 (access should be not prohibitively expensive and assistance should be available); 21 (prompt, adequate and effective remedies); 22 (timely and effective enforcement); 23 (information provided about access to justice procedures); 24 (decisions to be publicly available); 25 (promoting capacity-building programmes); and 26 (ADR).

7 Article 1 reads:

> each Party shall take the necessary legislative, regulatory and other measures, including measures to achieve compatibility between the provisions implementing the information, public participation and access-to-justice provisions in this Convention, as well as proper enforcement measures, to establish and maintain a clear, transparent and consistent framework to implement the provisions of this Convention.

8 Lord Carnwath, UK Supreme Court Justice, observed:

> No less important is Principle 10: the right to public participation. That has three 'pillars': the right of the public to relevant information held by public authorities, the right to participate in the decision-making process, and the right to effective access to judicial and administrative proceedings to enforce those rights. This simple, tripartite formula has proved pervasive and highly effective. It has been given more elaborate and binding form in Europe in the Aarhus Convention.
>
> (Carnwath 2015: 270–271)

9 For a detailed discussion on defining the concept of the rule of law, see Berg and Desai (2013): 5–8; Tamanaha (2004).

10 Preston stated:

> the idea of rule, of a government limited by law, involves two components. First, the government must abide by the currently valid law. The government may change the law, by Parliament enacting statutes or the executive exercising delegation to make subordinate rules, but until the law is changed, the law must be complied with. Second, even when the government wishes to change the law, it is not entirely free to change it in any way it desires because there are certain restraints on the law-making power. These restraints are to be found in constitutional, statutory and common law.
>
> (2011: 4)

11 UN GA Resolutions of the High-Level Meeting of the GA on the Rule of Law at National and International Level: Resolutions No 67/1, UN Doc A/Res/67/1, 24 September 2012 and No 67/97, UN Doc A/Res/67/97, 14 December 2012.

12 Preamble, point 10.

13 17–20 June 2012 Rio de Janeiro, www.unep.org/rio20/Portals/24180/Rio20_Declaration_on_Justice_Gov_n_Law_4_Env_Sustainability.pdf.

14 Part 2 Rio+20 Declaration on Justice, Governance and Law for Environmental Sustainability.

15 UNEP/GC.27/17, Decision 27/9, 26, para 5(a). www.unep.org/GC/GC27/Docs/Proceedings/K1350945.pdf.

16 www.unep.org/delc/worldcongress/.

17 www.un.org/sustainabledevelopment/peace-justice/.

18 UN, 'Transforming our world: the 2030 Agenda for sustainable development' https://sustainabledevelopment.un.org/post2015/transformingourworld.

19 Putrajaya, Malaysia, 12 December 2013 www.unep.org/delc/worldcongress/WorkshopsandEvents/ThePutrajayaStatement/tabid/132340/Default.aspx.

20 Nairobi, 14–16 October 2015. www.unep.org/delc/worldcongress/WorkshopsEvents/tabid/105856/Default.aspx.

21 www.oas.org/en/sedi/dsd/ELPG/aboutELPG/Events/IA_congress_2015.asp.

22 Keynote address, ADB Vice President B Davis, Fifth Asia–Pacific Judicial Reform Forum Meeting, 31 October–1 November 2013, Singapore.

23 The Bangalore Principles of Judicial Conduct 2007 highlight seven core values: independence, impartiality, integrity, propriety, equality, competence and diligence. www.unodc.org/documents/corruption/publications_unodc_commentary-e.pdf.

24 Chapter 8, Agenda 21, paras 8.13, 8.26 www.un.org/esa/sustdev/documents/agenda21/english/Agenda21.pdf. Article 23 World Charter for Nature 1982 provides: 'all persons, in accordance with their national legislation, shall have the opportunity to participate, individually or with others, in the formulation of decisions of direct concern to their environment, and shall have access to means of redress when their environment has suffered damage or degradation'. Additionally, the World Commission on Environment and Development Expert Group on Environmental Law Article 20 'Our common future', Annexe 1, adopted legal principles for environmental

protection and sustainable development ensuring 'due process and equal treatment in administrative and judicial proceedings to all persons who are or may be affected by trans-boundary interference with their use of a natural resource or the environment'.

25 www.unep.org/delc/judgesprogramme/GlobalJudgesSymposium/tabid/106158/Default. aspx. See also London Bridge Statement 2002 http://weavingaweb.org/pdfdocuments/ London%20Bridge%20Statement.pdf; Rome Symposium 2003 http://weavingaweb.org/ pdfdocuments/LN290304-Rome%20Statement%20FINAL.pdf; Stein 2006: 56; Justice Paul Stein, 'Why judges are essential to the rule of law and environmental protection'; https://portals.iucn.org/library/efiles/html/EPLP-060/section9.html; Justice Amedeo Postiglione, 'The role of the judiciary in the implementation and enforcement of environmental law' www.eufje.org/images/docConf/bud2014/presAP2%20bud2014.pdf.

26 See also UNEP Report (2004) UNEP/GC.23/INF/10: at 6, 14–15.

27 See nn 6, 14, 15, 19 above; First UN Environment Assembly Global Symposium on Environmental Rule of Law 2014; First African Colloquium on Environmental Rule of Law, Nairobi Statement 2015.

28 http://cmsdata.iucn.org/downloads/pk_bhurban_declaration_2012__20120410_.pdf.

29 www.asianjudges.org/about-ajne/.

30 www.asianjudges.org/fifth-asean-chief-justices-roundtable-on-environment/.

31 www.asianjudges.org/about-ajne/member-judiciaries/south-asia/.

32 Slaughter offers a typology of transjudicial communication: horizontal (courts of same status, national or supranational, across national or regional borders); vertical (between national and supranational courts); and mixed vertical–horizontal (a combination in several different ways – supranational tribunals serve as conduits for horizontal communication; and common legal principles in national legal orders are distilled and disseminated by a supranational tribunal).

33 www.law.du.edu/ect-study. The word 'court' indicates a body or individual in the judicial branch, and 'tribunal' reflects non-judicial dispute-resolution bodies in the administrative or executive branch of government.

34 For example, the countries include Antigua and Barbados, Australia, Bangladesh, Belgium, Bolivia, Brazil, Canada, Greece, Guatemala, Guyana, India, Ireland, Jamaica, Japan, Kenya, Malta, Malaysia, Mauritius, New Zealand, Nicaragua, Nigeria, Pakistan, Paraguay, Peru, Philippines, Samoa, South Korea, Spain, Sri Lanka, Sudan, Sweden, Thailand, Trinidad and Tobago, UK and USA.

35 New Zealand, Australia (NSW) and Brazil.

36 Australia (State of Queensland) and USA (State of Vermont).

37 Sweden.

38 Philippines and USA (state of Hawaii).

39 Indonesia. This is not an environmental court but is listed because Indonesia provides environmental training to select judges.

40 Kenya and Japan.

41 India, Canada (Province of Ontario) and USA (New York City, Environmental Control Board).

42 USA (Environmental Appeal Board).

43 Abu Dhabi, Argentina, Bahamas, Bhutan, Botswana, Ecuador, Honduras, Israel, Kenya, Kuwait, Lebanon, Malawi, Malaysia, Mexico, Nepal, Uganda, UK (Scotland), Vanuatu and Vietnam.

44 Bangladesh, Chile, El Salvador, Fiji, Gambia, Guyana, Lesotho, Liberia, Malawi, Mexico, Panama, Rwanda, Tanzania, Tonga and Zimbabwe.

45 Austria, Bahamas, China Jiangsu Province, Finland, Hungary, Netherlands and South Africa. According to Pring and Pring (2009), the reasons for the discontinued and authorised but not established ECTs include change in political leadership and commitment, insufficient caseload, inadequate funds, adverse special-interest pressure, judicial opposition or preferences and amalgamation of several environmental courts into one.

46   This part is derivative from the exhaustive works of Brian J Preston, Chief Justice NSW Australia; and the official website of the Land and Environment Court established by the Land and Environment Court Act 1979 (NSW Australia) www.lec. justice.nsw.gov.au/Pages/about/about.aspx#Classes_of_the_Court.

47   *Case C-236/01 Monsanto Agricoltura Italia v Presidenza del Consiglio dei Ministri* [2003] ECR I-8105; *Case C-241/01 National Farmers' Union v Secretary Central of the French Government* [2002] ECR I-9079; *Hungary v Slovakia, Re Gabcikovo-Nagymaros Project (Danube Dam case)* [1997] ICJ Rep 7; *Pfizer Animal Health SA v Council of the EU* [2002] ECR II–3305; *Mahon v Air New Zealand Ltd* [1984] 1 AC 808; *Vellore Citizens Welfare Forum v Union of India* AIR 1996 SC 2715 (India); *R v Secretary of State for Trade and Industry, ex parte Duddridge* [1995] Env LR 151; *Shehla Zia v WAPDA* (1994) PLD SC 693.

48   The principles include: (1) sustainable use; (2) integration (i.e. of economic and environmental considerations in the decision-making process); (3) the precautionary principle; (4) the principle of equity, including inter-generational; (5) the conservation of biological diversity; and (6) the internalisation of environmental costs – the need for full account to be taken of short-term and long-term costs of major projects.

49   Environmental Code, chapter 1, section 1.

50   www.domstol.se/funktioner/english/the-swedish-courts/district-court/land-and-environment-courts.

51   https://e-justice.europa.eu/content_access_to_justice_in_environmental_matters-300-se-maximizeMS-en.do?member=1#9.

52   Environmental Code, chapter 20, section 4.

53   Ibid.: section 11.

54   Ibid.: section 10.

55   Environmental Code, chapter 22, sections 12 and 13.

56   See, generally, Carnwath 1989; 1992; Woolf 1992; Grant 2000; Leggatt 2001; Royal Commission on Environmental Pollution 2002; Macrory and Woods 2003; Environmental Justice Project 2004; Macrory 2006; Sullivan Report 2008.

57   Macrory states:

> Paradoxically, the two main drivers for change providing the opportunity for establishing the environmental tribunal were not environmental factors. Rather, the new tribunal system was established as a result of a general recognition that the existing tribunal system could be run more efficiently and with greater flexibility. The new civil sanctions and rights of appeal to a tribunal are derived from a review of regulatory sanctions cutting across all areas of business regulation.

58   See Environment Civil Sanctions (England) Order 2010 and Environment Civil Sanctions (Wales) Order 2010.

59   Eco-design for Energy Using Products (Amendment) (Civil Sanctions) Regulations 2010.

60   Single Use Carrier Bags Charge (Wales) 2010 No 2880 (W 238).

61   SI 2009/1976 (L20) in force from 20 October 2014 www.gov.uk/government/uploads/ system/uploads/attachment_data/file/367600/tribunal-procedure-rules-general-regulatory-chamber.pdf.

62   Chief Registrar's Practice Direction No 3 2012; also see Keng 2015.

63   www.themalaysiantimes.com.my/96-pct-of-environmental-cases-disposed-cj/.

64   www.asianjudges.org/wp-content/uploads/2014/03/Embong_Biodiversity-Loss-and-Illegal-Wildlife-Trade-The-Role-of-the-Judiciary-Justice-Abdull-Hamid-Bin-Embong-Malaysia. pdf.

65   ELC Act, section 5.

66   Ibid.: section 13(1).

67   Ibid.: section 13 (2).

68   Ibid.: section 18.

69 Ibid.: section 20(1).
70 Ibid.: section 13(7).
71 www.saarc.com/the-south-asian-association-for-regional-corporation-saarc/.
72 Statement by Justice Abdul M Kamawi, Supreme Court of Afghanistan.
73 Environment Court Act 2000, section 4.
74 Ibid.: section 5.
75 Ibid.
76 Ibid.: section 12.
77 Presentation of Chief Justice of Bangladesh, Mr Justice Md Muzammel Hossain, on 'Developing a coherent and responsive environmental justice system; challenges and opportunities from the perspective of Bangladesh', in Global Symposium on Environmental Rule of Law, Nairobi, Kenya, 24 June 2014 www.unep.org/unea1/docs/erl/environmental-justice-system-muzammel-hossain.pdf.
78 Ibid.; also see www.bdlawdigest.org/reflections-on-environmental-adjudication-regime/.
79 Statement by Justice T Wangchuk, Supreme Court, Bhutan.
80 Statement by Justice A M Abdulla, Supreme Court, Maldives.
81 Statement by Justice O P Mishra, Supreme Court, Nepal.
82 PEPA, section 20(1).
83 Ibid.: section 20(2).
84 Ibid.: section 21.
85 Ibid.: section 23.
86 For a long time, the Khyber Pakhtunkhwa, Balochistan and Punjab Environmental Tribunal did not have a chairperson; the Sind Environmental Tribunal was without a chairperson and technical member; the tribunal in Islamabad was non-functional from March 2013, resuming work in November 2014.
87 *Shehla Zia* (n 47).
88 *General Secretary, West Pakistan Salt Mines Labour Union (CBA) Khewra, Jehlum v Director, Industries and Mineral Development, Punjab, Lahore* 1994 [SCMR] 2061.
89 *Rana Ishaque v Director General, EPA* (WP No 671 of 1995 before Lahore High Court).
90 *Syed Mansoor Ali Shah v Government of Punjab* (2007) CLD 533.
91 *Sindh Institute of Urology and Transplantation v Nestlé Milkpak* (2005) CLC 424.
92 *HeJiarachchige Don Chrishan Priyadarshana W ewardena v Geological Survey and Mines Bureau* SCFR No 81/2004.
93 *Geethani Wijesinghe v Patali Champika Ranawake, Minister of Environment and Natural Resources* SCFR No 87/2007.
94 *Al Haj MTM Ashik v RPS Bandula, OIC Weligama* (the Noise Pollution case) SCFR No 38/2005, decided 9 November 2007.
95 *Bulankulame v Secretary, Ministry of Industrial Development* (2000) 3 Sri LR 243; also see Guneratne (2015: 78).
96 Statement by Justice S Marsoof, Supreme Court, Sri Lanka.
97 Donne, 1572–1631, Meditation XVII, 1624.

References

ADB (2012) *Environmental Governance and the Courts in Asia* Law and Policy Reform Brief 1 (ADB).

ADB (2014) *Proceedings of the Third South Asian Roundtable on Environmental Justice for Sustainable Green Development* (ADB).

ADB (2015) *Proceedings: Fourth ASEAN Chief Justices' Roundtable on Environment: Role of the Judiciary in Environmental Protection* (ADB).

Adeola, F (1994) 'Environmental hazards, health and racial inequality in hazardous waste distribution' 26(1) *Environment and Behaviour* 99–126.

Agyeman, J (2005) *Sustainable Communities and the Challenge of Environmental Justice* (New York UP).

Ahsan, I and Khawaja, S A (2013) *Development of Environmental Laws and Jurisprudence in Pakistan* (ADB).

Ako, R T (2013) *Developing Countries: Perspectives from Africa and Asia–Pacific* (Routledge).

Azimi, A (2007) 'Environment Assessment for ADB's Program in Afghanistan' (ADB Country Partnership Strategy).

Benjamin, A H (2012) 'We, the judges, and the environment' 29(2) *Pace Environmental LR* 585.

Berg, L and Desai, D (2013) 'Overview on the Rule of Law and Sustainable Development for the Global Dialogue on Rule of Law and the Post-2015 Development Agenda' Background Paper.

Bjällås, U (2010) 'Experiences of Sweden's Environmental Courts' 3(1) *Journal of Court Innovation* 177.

Brighouse, H (2004) *Justice* (Polity Press).

Bullard, R (1990) 'Ecological inequalities and the New South: black communities under siege' 17(4) *Journal of Ethnic Studies* 101–115.

Carnwath, R (1989) *Enforcing Planning Control* (HMSO).

Carnwath, R (1992) 'Environmental enforcement: the need for a specialist court' September *Journal of Environmental Law* 799–808.

Carnwath, Lord (2015) 'Environmental law in a global society' 3 *Journal of Planning and Environment Law* 269–279.

Chavis, B (1993) 'Foreword' in R D Bullard, *Confronting Environmental Racisms* (South End Press).

David, B, Parmar, S, de Silva, L and Excell, C (2012) 'Moving from principles to rights: Rio 2012 and access to information, public participation, and justice' 12(3) *Sustainable Development Law and Policy* 8–14, 51.

Decleris, M, Honourable Vice President of the Hellenic Council of States (2011) 'Strengthening the judiciary for sustainable development' www.unep.org/delc/Portals/119/publications/Speeches/MICHAEL_DECLARIS.pdf.

Dobson, A (1998) *Justice and the Environment* (OUP).

Environmental Justice Project (2004) *Report by the Environmental Justice Project* (DEFRA) www.unece.org/fileadmin/DAM/env/pp/compliance/C2008-23/Amicusbrief/Annex-CEJP.pdf.

Fraser, N (2000) 'Rethinking recognition' 3 *New Left Review* 107–120.

Geiser, K and Waneck, G (1994) 'PCBs and Warren County' in R Bullard, *Unequal Protection* (Sierra Club).

Grant, M (2000) *Environmental Court Project: Final Report* (DETR).

Guneratne, C (2015) 'Using constitutional provisions to advance environmental justice: some reflections on Sri Lanka' 11(2) *Law, Environment and Development Journal* 72.

Holifield, R, Porter, M and Walker, G (2011) *Spaces of Environmental Justice* (John Wiley).

Honneth, A 'Integrity and disrespect: principles of morality based on the theory of recognition' (1992) 20(2) *Political Theory* 187–201.

Hovland, General Counsel J H (2011) 'Foreword', *Asian Judges Symposium on Environmental Decision Making* (ADB).

Jayasundere, R (2012) *Access to Justice Assessments in the Asia Pacific* (UNDP).

Jessup, B (2012) 'The journey of environmental justice through public and international law' in B Jessup and K Rubenstein, *Environmental Discourses in Public and International Law* (CUP).

Kaniaru, D, Kurukulasuriya, L and Okidi, C 'UNEP Judicial Symposium on the Role of the Judiciary in Promoting Sustainable Development', paper presented to Fifth International Conference on Environmental Compliance and Enforcement, Monterey, November 1998 (p. 22 conference proceedings).

Keng, R C W (2015) 'The Malaysian Environmental Court: the need to extend its reach to civil liability' July–December *PRAXIS* 36.

Kiss, A and Shelton, D (2003) *International Environmental Law* (UNEP).

Kotzé, L J (2012) *Global Environmental Governance* (Edward Elgar).

Land Development and Governance Institute (2013) *An Assessment of the Performance of the Environment and Land Court: 12th Scorecard Report* (Land Development and Governance Institute).

Leggatt, A (2001) *Report of the Review of the Tribunals*.

Macrory, R (2006) *Regulatory Justice* (Cabinet Office).

Macrory, R (2010) 'Environmental courts and tribunals in England and Wales: a tentative dawn' (2010) 3(1) *Journal of Court Innovation* 61–78.

Macrory, R (2014) *Regulation, Enforcement and Governance in Environmental Law* (Hart).

Macrory, R and Woods, M (2003) *Modernising Environmental Justice* (UCL).

Mulqueeny, K and Cordon, F J J (2014) 'Third ASEAN Chief Justices' roundtable on environment: ASEAN environmental challenges and legal responses', The Proceedings (ADB).

Nussbaum, M and Sen, A (1992) *The Quality of Life* (OUP).

Odote, C (2012), 'Country report: Kenya: the new Environmental and Land Court' 4(1) *IUCN Academy of Environmental Law e-Journal* 136–145.

Preston, B J (2011) 'The enduring importance of the rule of law in times of change' Environment and Planning Law Association (NSW) Annual Conference, 13 October, Sydney.

Preston, B J (2012) 'Benefits of Judicial specialisation in environmental law: the Land and Environment Court of New South Wales as a Case Study' 29(2) *Pace Environmental LR* 386.

Preston, B J (2014) 'Characteristics of successful environmental courts and tribunals' 26(3) *Journal of Environmental Law* 365–393.

Pring, G and Pring, C (2009) *Greening Justice* (Access Initiative, World Resources Institute).

Pring, G and Pring, C (2016 forthcoming) *The ABCs of the ECTs: A Guide for Policy-Makers for Designing and Operating a Specialised Environmental Court or Tribunal* (UNEP).

Pulido, L (1996) *Environmentalism and Economic Justice* (University of Arizona Press).

Royal Commission on Environmental Pollution (2002) *23rd Report: Environmental Planning* (HMSO).

Schlosberg, D (2007) *Defining Environmental Justice* (OUP).

Shrader-Frechette, K (2002) *Environmental Justice* (OUP).

Slaughter, A M (1994) 'Human Rights International Law Symposium: a typology of transjudicial communication' 29 *University of Richmond LR* 99–137.

Stein, Justice P (2006) 'Why judges are essential to the rule of law and environmental protection' in T Greiber (ed.), *Judges and the Rule of Law: Creating the Links: Environment, Human Rights and Poverty* IUCN Occasional Paper (Gland: IUCN).

Sullivan Report (2008) Ensuring Access to Environmental Justice in England and Wales (Royal Courts of Justice).

Szasz, A (1994) *Ecopopulism* (University of Minnesota Press) 151.

Tamanaha, B Z (2004) *On the Rule of Law* (CUP).

Taylor, P (1986) *Respect for Nature* (Princeton UP).

UN (2007) Commentary on the Bangalore Principles of Judicial Conduct (Office on Drugs and Crime).

UN (2012) *The Future We Want* (UN).

UN (2015) *Waste Crimes, Waste Risks: Gaps and Challenges* (UNEP).

UNEP (2005) *UNEP Global Judges Programme* (UNEP).

UNEP (2007) *A Guide to Afghanistan's 2007 Environment Law* (UNEP).

UNEP (2015) *Putting Rio Principle 10 into Action: An Implementation Guide for the UNEP Bali Guidelines for the Development of National Legislation on Access to Information, Public Information and Access to Justice in Environmental Matters* (UNEP).

United Church of Christ (1987) *Toxic Wastes and Race in the United States* (Commission for Racial Justice).

Walzer, M (1983) *Spheres of Justice* (University of California Press).

Wiener, J B (2000/2001) 'Something borrowed for something blue: legal transplants and evolution of global environmental law' 27 *Ecology Law Quarterly* 1295–1372.

Woolf, H (1992) 'Are the judiciary environmentally myopic?' 4(1) *Journal of Environmental Law* 1–14.

Young, I (1990) *Justice and the Politics of Difference* (Princeton UP).

2 Genesis and establishment of the National Green Tribunal

Social and economic justice is at the heart of the Constitution of India. It places a duty on the judiciary to protect the rights of citizens so that each might live a life of dignity and well-being.[1] However, the human and geographical scale of India is gargantuan as are its internal issues, specifically population growth, poverty, illiteracy and corruption (see Introduction). Nevertheless, India has undergone immense transformation as a result of its rapid economic growth. However, it remains a nation of stubborn paradoxes. 'Shining India' is reserved for the select few: the rich and the powerful.

It is against this background of systemic inequality that the senior Indian judiciary assumes seminal importance. The tripartite checks and balances of the relationship between Parliament, the executive and the judiciary, so beloved in western common law constitutionalism and bequeathed to independent India in 1947, continue to experience limited success. The ineffectiveness of both political leadership and administrative authorities to discharge their constitutional roles and statutory duties, coupled with widespread public sector inefficiency and corruption, has cast the Indian judiciary, particularly the Supreme Court, as protector of the interests of the disadvantaged in matters of public concern. Social and economic inequality affects millions of people and for these reasons the judiciary has adopted the proactive role of providing redress through the innovative process commonly called 'public interest litigation' (PIL) or 'social action litigation' (Baxi 1985).[2]

The creation of PIL in the 1980s ushered in a new era of judicial activism aimed at addressing basic violations of human rights affecting marginalised sections of society. The traditional adversarial process of cause of action, person aggrieved and individual litigation experienced an innovative addition (Ministry of Law, Justice and Company Affairs (MLJCA) 1977). This development envisaged that those citizens traditionally excluded from courts by virtue of poverty, ignorance, isolation, fear or caste would be able to enforce their fundamental human rights through law either personally or via a court-recognised 'friend'. The use of PIL as a broad-based, people-oriented approach envisioned access to justice as a 'wheel of transformation' through judge-fashioned processes and remedies.[3] In *Anirudh Kumar v MCD* (2015) 7 SCC 779 the court stated:

Our current processual jurisprudence is not of individualistic Anglo-Indian mould. It is broad-based and people-oriented, and envisions *access to justice* through 'class actions', 'public interest litigation' and 'representative proceedings'. Indeed, Indians in large numbers seeking remedies in courts through collective proceedings, instead of being driven to an expensive plurality of litigations, is an affirmation of participative justice in our democracy. We have no hesitation in holding that the narrow concept of 'cause of action' and 'person aggrieved' and individual litigation is becoming obsolescent in some jurisdictions.

(At 780, emphasis added; see also *Akhil Bhartiya Soshit Karamchari Sangh (Railway) v Union of India* (1981) 1 SCC 246, 281)

The development of PIL in India can be traced through three phases (*State of Uttaranchal v Balwant Singh Chaufal* (2010) 3 SCC 402; see also Dam 2005: 115–116; Deva 2009: 27). The first phase, or golden era, was in the 1970s and early 1980s when the courts entertained cases concerning the enforcement of the fundamental rights of marginalised and deprived sections of the society. The rule of *locus standi* was amended and the procedural meaning of aggrieved person was broadened to provide legal access to large sections of society previously excluded. In terms of the right to life (Article 21 Constitution of India), the courts relaxed the rule of *locus standi* and expanded the definition of aggrieved person by permitting public-spirited citizens, institutions, NGOs and other parties to file petitions on behalf of those unable to act for themselves. In *S P Gupta v Union of India* 1981 Supp SCC 87, Justice Bhagwati stated:

> ...where a legal wrong or a legal injury is caused by a person or to a determinate class of persons by reason of violation of any constitutional or legal right or any burden is imposed in contravention of any constitutional or legal provision or without authority of law or any such legal wrong or legal injury or illegal burden is threatened and such person or determinate class of persons is by reason of poverty, helplessness or disability or socially or economically disadvantaged position, unable to approach the Court for relief, any member of the public can maintain an application for an appropriate direction, order or writ in the High Court under Article 226 and in case of breach of any fundamental right of such person or determinate class of persons, in this Court under Article 32...

(At 201)

Liberalising the procedure to file writ petitions, creating or expanding fundamental rights, overcoming evidentiary problems and evolving new remedies were other fruitful innovations in legal doctrines and techniques to 'have to do with "justice" in the most impoverished sense of the word' and are 'truly marginal' (see Baxi 1985: 110; see also Trubek and Trubek 1981: 119; Cooper 1993: 616–632; Sripati 1997: 118–125; Shah 1999: 467–473; Jain 2003: 51–52; Shankar and Mehta 2008: 146; Singh 2008: 310–322). Examples of successful

PIL applications include the Supreme Court's intervention in *Citizens for Democracy* v *State of Assam* (1995) 3 SCC 743 where patient–prisoners in hospitals were tied and handcuffed. In *Anil Yadav* v *State of Bihar* (1981) 1 SCC 622, the pre-trial accused detained in prison was similarly bound. *Munna* v *State of UP* (1982)1 SCC 545 involved the sexual exploitation by adult prisoners of juveniles awaiting trial. The Supreme Court also stopped custodial violence against female prisoners in Bihar and addressed the issue of child labour, as well as workplace female sexual harassment (see Baxi 1985: 115–116).

The second phase started in the 1980s when the judiciary earned public respect and increased credibility through innovative and creative judicial craftsmanship structured to protect ecology and the environment.[4] The Supreme Court through its Forest Bench (renamed in 2013 as the Green Bench) regularly passed orders and directions regarding forest cover, illegal mining, destruction of marine life and wildlife and pollution-related matters. To quote from *State of Uttaranchal v B S Chaufal* (2010) 3 SCC 402:

> The scale of injustice occurring on the Indian soil is catastrophic. Each day hundreds of thousands of factories are functioning without pollution control devices. Thousands of Indians go to mines and undertake hazardous work without proper safety protection. Everyday millions of litres of untreated raw effluents are dumped into our rivers and millions of tons of hazardous waste are simply dumped on the earth. The environment has become so degraded that instead of nurturing us it is poisoning us. In this scenario, in a large number of cases, the Supreme Court intervened in the matter and issued innumerable directions.
>
> (At 437)

The third phase saw the expansion of the jurisdictional ambit of PIL to include cases dealing with exposing corruption and maintaining probity and morality in state governance. Probity in governance is a *sine qua non* for an efficient system of administration and for the country's development. An important requirement for ensuring probity in governance is the absence of corruption. In *M C Mehta v Union of India* (2007) 1 SCC 110 the Supreme Court froze the prestigious Taj Heritage Corridor Project initiated by the government of Uttar Pradesh. The project involved the diversion of the river Yamuna and the reclamation of 75 acres of land between Agra Fort and the Taj Mahal to construct food plazas, shops and amusement facilities. The court questioned the role of the Uttar Pradesh government ministers – the Minister for Environment and the Chief Minister – and directed registration of a first information report and further detailed investigation.

Thus, PIL became a 'wheel of transformation' to protect the powerless and address matters of collective concern. It emerged as a procedural tool 'redressing public injury, enforcing public duty, protecting social, collective, "diffused" rights and interests or vindicating public interest' (Sathe 2002: 217; also see *Kesavananda Bharathi v State of Kerala* (1973) 4 SCC 225). This chapter traces the growth and usage of PIL in environmental matters. It also identifies short-comings, particularly its overuse in courts that lacked the technical expertise to fully appreciate and adjudicate environmental disputes. This led to a national debate and eventual establishment of a specialised ET: the NGT.

Public interest litigation and environmental protection

In recent years, India's environmental policies and laws have been drafted more comprehensively and stringently, particularly as a consequence of the 1984 Bhopal industrial tragedy (Divan and Rosencranz 2001: 2–3). However, contra-dictions and gaps in institutional mechanisms have resulted in the ineffective implementation of environmental legislation. Factors such as negligence or underperformance by enforcement authorities, multilayered corruption, political interference or indifference and a lack of will to tackle ensconced industrial and commercial interests contribute to poor environmental administration (South Asian Human Rights Documentation Centre 2008: 423). In *Indian Council for Enviro-Legal Action v Union of India* 1996 (5) SCC 281, the court recognised:

> If the mere enactment of laws relating to the protection of environment was to ensure a clean and pollution free environment, then, India would, perhaps, be the least polluted country in the world. But, this is not so. There are stated to be over 200 Central and State statutes which have at least some concern with environmental protection, either directly or indi-rectly. The plethora of such enactments has, unfortunately, not resulted in preventing environmental degradation which, on the contrary, has increased over the years.
>
> (At 293)

The state's failure to prevent environmental degradation has resulted in the increased public standing of the judiciary because of its innovative efforts to protect ecology and the environment. In India, there is no direct articulation of the right to environment, either in the Constitution of India or, for that matter, in statute law. Environmental PIL is a product of the higher judiciary's response to the inaction of the state or failures of state agencies to perform their statutory duties resulting in endangering or impairing people's quality of life as guaranteed by the constitution.[5] This has prompted environmentalists, NGOs and affected citizens to approach the courts, particularly the higher judiciary, for remedial action. In this context, PIL is transformative in that it provides access to justice to victims of environmental degradation. In the past two decades the courts have locked together human rights and the environment and entertained PIL petitions from various quarters seeking remedies, including guidelines and direc-tions in the absence of legislation (Gill 2014; see also Sathe 2002: 210). The proactive judiciary acting as '*amicus* environment' has developed a new environ-mental jurisprudence. In the *Indian Council for Enviro-Legal Action* case, the court stated:

With rapid industrialisation taking place, there is an increasing threat to the maintenance of the ecological balance ... Even though, laws have been passed for the protection of the environment, the enforcement of the same has been tardy, to say the least. With the governmental authorities not showing any concern with the enforcement of the said Acts, and with the development taking place for personal gains at the expense of environment and with disregard of the mandatory provisions of law, some public spirited citizens have been initiating public interest litigations ... The primary effort of the court, while dealing with environmental-related issues, is to see that the enforcement agencies, whether it be the State or any other authority, take effective steps for the enforcement of laws ... Even though, it is not the function of the court to see the day-to-day enforcement of the laws, that being the function of the executive, but because of the non-functioning by the enforcement agency, the courts as of necessity have had to pass orders or direction to the enforcement agencies to implement the law for the protection of the fundamental rights of the people.

(At 300–301)

The use of PIL in the interpretation of three constitutional provisions (Articles 48A, 51A(g) and 21) has produced a major change to India's environmental landscape. Article 48A, a directive principle of state policy, mandates the state to protect and improve the environment and safeguard forests and wildlife. The policy prescription has assumed the legal status of imposing an obligation not only on government but also on courts to protect the environment. Article 51A(g) imposes a fundamental duty on every citizen to protect and improve the natural environment including forests, lakes, rivers and wildlife and to have compassion for living creatures. The social obligation under Article 51A(g) has broadened the scope of 'citizen' to permit public-spirited citizens, interested institutions and NGOs to file and advance PILs for environmental protection.

Importantly, the apex court gave effect to Articles 48A, 51A(g) and 21 by citing them as mutually complementary and, in appropriate cases, has issued necessary directions in environmental cases. A duty cast on the state under Article 48A is to be read as conferring a corresponding right on citizens under Article 51A(g), though couched in the language as 'duty' and, therefore, the right under Article 21 at least must be read to include the same within its ambit. In *Intellectuals Forum, Tirupathi v State of AP* (2006) 3 SCC 549, the Supreme Court observed:

...the environmental protection and conservation of natural resources has been given a status of a fundamental right and brought under Article 21 of the Constitution of India. This apart, Articles 48A and 51A(g) are fundamental in the governance of the country and require the state to apply these principles in making laws and further these two articles are to be kept in mind in understanding the scope and purport of the fundamental rights guaranteed by the Constitution including Article 21.

(At 576)

In the context of environmental discourse, the Supreme Court has rendered justice by resorting to Article 32 Constitution of India which confers jurisdiction on the court to issue directions for the enforcement of fundamental rights, i.e. Article 21 right to life. 'Violation of a fundamental right is sine qua non of the exercise of the right conferred by Article 32. A right without a remedy is a legal conundrum of a most grotesque kind. Article 32 confers one of the highly cherished rights' (Pal and Pal 2011: 1429). Article 32 confers power to the court to enforce fundamental rights and lays down an obligation to protect the fundamental rights of the people. Consequently, the Supreme Court has all incidental and ancillary powers to enforce the fundamental rights, including the power to forge new remedies and fashion new strategies (M C *Mehta v Union of India* (1987) 1 SCC 395, at 405; see also *Bandhua Mukti Morcha v Union of India* (1984) 3 SCC 161).

To promote environmental discourse, the Supreme Court expanded the constitutional provisions and combined human rights and the environment in order to develop a new environmental jurisprudence. The expansionist method is a result of collaborative effort built on innovative substantive and procedural approaches, often novel and contrary to the traditional judicial process in human rights and the environment (Gill 2015: 130). Substantive changes include the extension of fundamental rights, particularly the right to life, the derivative application of principles of international environmental law and strict compliance with regulations and standards. Associated procedural expansion has provided a platform for the implementation of these substantive rights. It includes a broader understanding of *locus standi*, interpreting letters written to the court as petitions, appointing fact-finding commissions and implementing directions as continuing mandamus (Divan and Rosencranz 2001: at 133; Leelakrishanan 2005; Rajamani 2007; Sahu 2008; Faure and Raja 2010; Gill 2014: 203–204).

Substantive approach

Henry Shue pioneered the use of the 'linkage argument' to defend the right to subsistence: 'no one can fully ... enjoy any right that is supposedly protected by society if he or she lacks the essentials for a reasonably healthy and active life' (Shue 1996: 24–25). Shue defines subsistence as meaning 'unpolluted air, unpolluted water, adequate food, clothing, adequate shelter and minimal preventive care' (ibid.). Orend's definition is similar: 'material subsistence means having secure access to those resources one requires to meet one's biological needs – notably a minimal level of nutritious food, clean water, fresh air, some clothing and shelter, and basic preventative health care' (Orend 2001; Nickel 2007: 139). The interlinkage between the right to life and a healthy environment concerns ensuring the conditions, negative and/or positive, of a minimally good life. The normative focus is 'on the individual – in the dignity and worth of the human person' (Rajamani 2007: 414; see, generally, Boyle 1996; McGoldrick 1996). The Supreme Court has developed its case law for environmental protection by providing an expansive interpretation of the term 'life' under Article 21 Constitution of India: it being a fundamental right. The Supreme Court held that life does not simply mean physical existence, but extends to include quality of life. In *Francis Coralie v Delhi* AIR 1981 SC 746, Justice Bhagwati stated:

> We think that the right to life includes the right to live with human dignity and all that goes along with it, namely, the bare necessities of life such as adequate nutrition, clothing and shelter over the head and facilities for reading, writing, and expressing oneself in diverse forms.
>
> (At 753)

In *Virender Gaur v State of Haryana* (1995) 2 SCC 577, the court declared that a healthy environment is one free from environmental pollution, stating:

> Article 21 protects the right to life as a fundamental right. Enjoyment of life ... including the right to live with human dignity encompasses within its ambit, the protection and preservation of the environment, ecological balance free from pollution of air and water, sanitation, without which life cannot be enjoyed. Any contra acts or actions would cause environmental pollution. Environmental, ecological, air and water pollution, etc ... should be regarded as amounting to a violation of Article 21. Therefore, a hygienic environment is an integral facet of the right to a healthy life and it would be impossible to live with human dignity without a human and healthy environment ... There is a constitutional imperative on the State Government and the municipalities, not only to ensure and safeguard a proper environment but also an imperative duty to take adequate measures to promote, protect and improve both the man made and the natural environment.
>
> (At 580–581; also see *Charan Lal Sahu v Union of India* (1990) 1 SCC 613)

The Supreme Court endorsed the *ratio* of right to environment as a part of the fundamental right to life in *Municipal Corporation of Greater Mumbai v Kohinoor CTNL Infrastructure* (2014) 4 SCC 538, saying:

> ...it must be noted that the right to a clean and healthy environment is within the ambit of Article 21, as has been noted in *Court on its Own Motion v Union of India* reported in 2012 (12) SCALE 307 in the following words: – The scheme under the Indian Constitution unambiguously enshrines in itself the right of a citizen to life under Article 21 of the Constitution. The right to life is a right to live with dignity, safety and in a clean environment. The right to a clean and pollution free environment is also a right under our common-law jurisprudence, as has been held by this Court in *Vellore Citizen's Welfare Forum v Union of India*...
>
> (556)

Within the urban environment, extremely unsanitary conditions resulting from non-performance of statutory duties by the municipality fall within the meaning of right to life. Maintenance of health, preservation of sanitation and care of the environment are covered by Article 21 because, if neglected, they adversely affect citizen's lives.[6] The right to enjoy unpolluted air and clean water is covered by Article 21.[7] Again, compulsory exposure of unwilling persons to dangerous and disastrous levels of noise amounts to an infringement of the constitutional guarantee of right to life under Article 21 (*In re Noise Pollution* AIR 2005 SC 3136).

Thus, the judicial lexicon of interpretation has preserved the link between life and a healthy environment and successfully placed human rights within environmental discourse. However, the 'recognition of a right' does not necessarily entail its enforcement (Boyle 1996; Korsah-Brown 2002: 81; Kiss and Shelton 2003: 393; Rajamani 2007). Studies reveal a grim account of the effectiveness of the legally binding right to an environment. The increasing impact of air pollution reflecting the decline in air quality across India has resulted in a sharp rise in cases of chest and throat disease. India is home to 13 of the world's 20 most-polluted cities. According to India's National Health Profile 2015, there were almost 3.5 million reported cases of acute respiratory infection in that year, a 30 per cent increase since 2010[8] (Burke 2015).

The 2014 Yale Environmental Performance Index ranked India as 174th out of 178 countries for air pollution (*New York Times* Editorial 2014). According to this report, more people die of asthma in India than anywhere else. Automobile sales in India have boomed, diesel being the fuel of choice. Many industries pollute, defying existing environmental laws and regulations and pollution monitoring is haphazard. The World Bank says environmental degradation costs India US$80 billion annually and accounts for 23 per cent of child mortality (World Bank 2013: 1).

Similarly, a BBC report. 'Is this the city with the loudest car horns?' states that:

> ...noise pollution is so serious in Delhi that it is having a measurable impact on people's health. Seven million cars jostle for space on Delhi's roads. Beside the revving of engines and squealing of brakes, ear drums are hammered by the continuous blast of automobile horns. The noise pollution is not only affecting school children and hospital patients it is also contributing to increased stress and heart disease and causing the onset of age-related deafness 15 years earlier than normal.
>
> (Anand 2014)

These illustrations show the widespread reality that produces disturbing short-comings and continuing challenges. Public health is defined in a tangible form to include a safe, healthy and wholesome environmental milieu, free from pollution. However, a pollution-free environment is unrealistic. Pollution can be reduced, not eliminated, which in turn, raises the issue of the establishment of standards. The quantification of a safe and healthy environment is difficult. Establishing and adopting quality standards demands extensive research and debate involving public participation and impact studies. Resorting to approximation based upon pollution levels, availability of pollution-control technology, technological capabilities, the efficacy of existing legal norms and costings are prime considerations for setting standards – an exercise relying on relative experience, not absolute targets (Agarwal 1996: 51). This aspirational right to an environment through judicial interpretation ascribes a value or status to an entitlement unlikely to be implemented.

The substantive approach also includes the derivative application of principles of international law into the right to a healthy environment. Environmental principles such as the polluter-pays principle, the precautionary principle, intergenerational equity and the public trust doctrine have been adopted by the Supreme Court and are considered an essential part of the reach of Article 21. In *Intellectual Forum, Tirupathi* v *State of AP* (2006) 3 SCC 549, the Supreme Court accepted that 'all human beings have a fundamental right to a healthy environment commensurate with their well-being ... ensuring that natural resources are conserved and preserved in such a way that present as well as the future generation are aware of them equally' (at 84). This ruling fortifies both the public trust doctrine and intergenerational equity which are derivatives of Article 21. Similarly, in *Research Foundation of Science (18)* v *Union of India* (2005) 13 SCC 186, the court invoked the polluter-pays principle and stated:

> ... the polluter pays principle basically means that the producer of the goods or other items should be responsible for the cost of preventing or dealing with any pollution that the process caused.
>
> (At 200–201)[9]

The precautionary principle has been affirmed as a legal principle providing action to avert risks of serious or irreversible harm to the environment or human health in the absence of scientific certainty about that harm.[10]

Although the principles underpinning international environmental law have been absorbed, yet 'the Court [has] neither been followed consistently nor [have its rulings] been institutionalised to make a long-term impact for the environmental jurisprudence process' (Sahu 2008: 385). For example, polluters abuse the court system by repeatedly filing applications to avoid compliance with Supreme Court orders or judgments. Although the polluter-pays principle is applied in the courts, delays are common, as in *Indian Council for Enviro-Legal Action* v *Union of India* AIR (1996) 3 SCC 212, for example. A group of chemical industries established plants to produce hydrochloric acid and related chemicals for export. Although the production of hydrochloric acid is prohibited in European countries, there remains a need for it. Thus, a remote village in India – Bichhri – became a site for production of this lethal chemical. 'Rogue industries' commenced production without obtaining appropriate no objection certificates from pollution control authorities. The factories' waste products amounted to between 2400 and 2500 tonnes. They were highly toxic. Iron, gypsum sludge and other chemicals were disposed of negligently within the Bichhri area. The waste was randomly dumped on the surface, toxic substances percolated into aquifers and entered the water-table. The damage occurred within a timescale of four months, causing serious harm to land and the water supply and resulted in widespread disease, death and economic damage to the local community. At least 400 farmers and their families in 11 villages were directly affected by groundwater pollution. The Supreme Court decided that absolute liability rested with the rogue industries. It ordered them to compensate for the harm caused to the villagers, the soil and underground water and take all necessary measures to remove sludge and other pollutants and defray the costs of remedial measures required to restore the land and underground water. The court invoked the polluter-pays principle and empowered central government to determine and recover the cost of remedial measures from the industries. The application of Article 21 and the polluter-pays principle makes the case a landmark judgment, yet it simultaneously illustrates the limitations faced by those seeking redress through the courts. Relativity of time is no better illustrated than by comparing the daily lives of the impoverished villagers, living with and dying of the consequences of environmental pollution, and the Supreme Court in Delhi which has taken 23 years to fail to provide social and economic justice for Bichhri. The assessment of compensation, its payment and the remedial measures were delayed and thus became a prohibitive feature of the legal route for those seeking social justice. Litigation expenses were another. From a monetary perspective, the costs of successful litigation are steered by the resource capacity of the parties. The polluters were relatively resource-rich while the villagers were indigents. Thus, the polluters were able to file a series of interlocutory applications aimed at exhausting the resources, energy and determination of the local community (Gill 2012: 213–216).

Another issue is that of the conservation of nature based on current needs, as opposed to those of future generations (Boyd 2012). This tension between 'now and later' is not unique to India, but it nevertheless remains unresolved. The result is that compliance is disappointingly low and environmental pollution is both common and increasingly frequent.

Procedural approach

The Supreme Court has devised new procedures applicable to PIL to provide access to environmental justice to people who otherwise would be denied it. In *Mumbai Kamgar Sabha v Abdulbhai Faizullabhai* (1976) 3 SCC 832, the court, while making a conscious effort to improve judicial access, observed 'procedural prescriptions are handmaidens, not mistresses, of justice and failure of fair play is the spirit in which courts must view (processual) deviances' (at 837). The relaxation of the rule of *locus standi* is a major procedural innovation. Justice

Krishna Iyer, one of the most socially aware and concerned judges in independent India, stated:

> ...the truth is that a few profound issues of processional jurisprudence of great strategic significance to our legal system face us. We must zero in on them as they involve problems of access to justice for the people beyond the blinkered rules of 'standing' of the British-India vintage. If the centre of gravity of justice is to shift, as the Preamble of the Constitution mandates, from the traditional individualism of locus standi to the community orientation of public interest litigation, these interests must be considered.
>
> (*Municipal Council, Ratlam v Vardhichan* (1980) 4 SCC 162, at 163)

Traditional *locus standi* was modified in two ways: representative standing and citizen standing. Representative standing allows any member of the public, acting bona fide, to advance claims against violations of the human rights of victims who, because of their poverty, disability or socially or economically disadvantaged position, cannot approach the court for judicial enforcement of their fundamental rights. NGOs and environmental activists working, for example, on behalf of poor and tribal people have entered the courts through this procedure. The tension between tribal rights, environmental rights and the exigencies of the development of the protection of forest lands and livelihood are cases covered under representative standing. Citizen standing provides a platform to seek redress for a public grievance affecting society as a whole rather than an individual (see, generally, Baxi 2000; Bhushan 2004; Pal and Pal 2011: 1449; Gill 2015: 131; *RLEK v State of UP* AIR 1985 SC 652 (*Doon Valley* case)). The *Judges Transfer* case (*S P Gupta v President of India* AIR 1982 SC 149) lays out the scope of citizen standing:

> ...in public interest litigation undertaken for the purpose of redressing public injury, 'diffused' rights and interests or vindicating public interest, any citizen who is acting bona fide and who has sufficient interest has to be accorded standing. What is sufficient interest to give standing to a member of the public would have to be determined by the Court in each individual case. It is not possible for the Court to lay down any hard and fast rule or any strait-jacket formula for the purpose of defining or delimiting 'sufficient interest'.
>
> (At 192)

The cases of *Urban and Solid Waste Management* (*Almitra H Patel v Union of India* Writ Petition No 888 of 1996) and *The Taj Mahal* (M C Mehta v Union of India AIR 1997 SC 734) were heard as a result of an application through citizen standing, whereby public-spirited citizens sought to make the state accountable for its inaction or wrongdoing.

The new meaning of *locus standi* introduced a transformative process being polycentric, participatory and democratic. An empirical study by Sahu (2014) argues that the general findings by Marc Galanter in 1974 do not apply to subsequent Indian environmental cases. Galanter established that the 'haves' are more successful than the 'have nots' when it comes to access to justice in India (Galanter 1974). Sahu documents that the environmental judgments delivered between 1980 and 2010 reflect that weaker parties, including NGOs and activists, have been relatively successful as court petitioners when bringing actions against the Union of India, state governments and industry. The courts are not meant exclusively for the 'haves' (federal and state governments and the business groups), but also exist for the 'have nots' (individuals, communities and NGOs). Social and economic justice is the essence of the Indian Constitution, which in turn places a duty on the judiciary to protect the rights of every citizen, particularly the vulnerable sections of society.

However, according to Sahu, in matters of public infrastructure, such as the construction of dams and power stations, the Supreme Court has on occasions abandoned its strong environmental position to allow economic development based on national economic needs (Sahu 2014: 55). Several judges known for their pro-environment positions have opted for non-confrontation with the state regarding such petitions, allowing such projects to proceed despite social and environmental concerns and negative consequences. This is problematic because large infrastructure projects reflect two highly relevant and important trends (Bhushan, 2009; Gauri 2009). First, environmental protection clashes with powerful vested commercial and corporate interests. Second, the distributional impact on the affected poor and marginalised is both significant and disproportionate.

Prashant Bhushan's analysis preceded but supports Sahu's conclusion. Bhushan observed:

> ... the right to environmental protection has thus been whimsically applied by individual judges according to their own subjective preferences usually without clear principles guiding them about the circumstances in which the court could issue a mandamus for environmental protection. It appears that when socio-economic rights of the poor come into conflict with environmental protection the court has often subordinated those rights to environmental protection. On the other hand, when environmental protection comes into conflict with what is perceived by the court to be 'development issues' or powerful commercial, vested interests, environmental protection is often sacrificed at the altar of 'development' or similar powerful interests.
>
> (Bhushan 2009: 35)

Sahu's and Bhushan's data analyses are illustrated by contrasting judicial decisions reflecting environmental bias and inconsistency. On 23 November 2007, the Supreme Court in *T N Godavarman Thirumulpad v Union of India* and *In the matter of Vedanta Aluminium Limited* 2008 2 SCC 222, barred the construction of an alumina and bauxite mining project in the state of Orissa by Vedanta Company and its Indian subsidiary M/S Sterlite Ltd. The alumina refinery depended on mining the Niyamgiri Hills, a reserved forest area and habitat of the Dongria Kodha tribe. The mining amounted to the forcible eviction of the poor tribal people from their homes and causing extensive damage to the environment. Although mining is an important revenue-generating industry, it cannot be placed in the hands of companies lacking an ethical business model that recognises and balances profitability and sustainability alongside the historic rights and current livelihood expectations of the affected tribal communities. Accordingly, the Supreme Court decided that it might consider granting clearance to the project provided a rehabilitation package (including tribal development in the project area, taking into consideration requirements for health, education, communication, recreation, livelihood and cultural lifestyle; setting aside 5 per cent of its profit before tax for reinvestment in the tribal community, compensatory afforestation and a comprehensive wildlife management plan) was agreed by the project proponents and state of Orissa. The Supreme Court accorded its approval on 8 August 2008 after the rehabilitation package was accepted by the project proponents.[11]

Subsequently this legal challenge continued in *Orissa Mining Corporation v MoEF* (2013) 6 SCC 476 where the Supreme Court directed the Gram Sabhas, the basic level of local governance, to use their powers and take a decision on whether the Vedanta Group's $1.7 billion bauxite mining project in Odisha's Niyamgiri Hills could go forward. The Gram Sabhas were directed to take a decision within three months having considered the forest dwellers' various claims, including cultural, religious, community and individual rights. The landmark judgment was a result of a damaging 2010 Government of India report known as the Saxena Committee Report.[12] The Committee found that the Vedanta Company consistently violated Indian environmental laws and showed blatant disregard for the rights of the Donria Kodha tribe, for example, the company's act of illegally enclosing and occupying at least 26.123 hectares of village forest lands within its refinery thereby depriving tribal people and other rural poor of their rights. This high-profile case illustrates how the Supreme Court safeguarded the rights of the tribals by involving them in environmental decision-making process and thereby protecting the fragile ecology of the Niyamgiri Hills.

The Delhi Commonwealth Games case illustrates the judicial trend of favouring 'infrastructure development' by condoning misplaced priorities and erroneous decisions of local authorities (Gill 2014). The Supreme Court was faced with choosing between a controversially sited urban development or ecological protection (*DDA v Rajendra Singh* AIR 2010 SC 2516). The construction of the Commonwealth Games Village (CWGV) on a legally protected floodplain of the river Yamuna was challenged on the ground that it was in violation of Environmental Protection Agency regulations which stipulated that no permanent structures could be built on the riverbanks. The hosting of the games for India in 2010 was a matter of national pride, providing opportunities for economic profit, urban regeneration and international exposure, showcasing Delhi as a 'world class city' and India as Asia's new superpower. However, the games' development was, in reality, disturbingly different. The social and environmental impact was considerable. The displacement of the 'invisible common poor' from their homes to create building space was large scale: over 100,000 families were moved. Beggars and homeless people were arrested and arbitrarily detained in the 'no tolerance zone' (Housing and Land Rights Network Report 2010: 3). The Delhi Minister for Social Welfare, Mangat Ram Singhal, declared:

> ...beggars are a nuisance and begging has to be stopped. When we make Delhi a world class city, it will be compared with other class capitals. One does not come across beggars in other countries. Why should there be beggars in Delhi? We must make the city free of them.
>
> (Mahaprashasta 2010)

The environmental impacts of constructing the CWGV on the floodplain of the Yamuna, the 'lifeline of Delhi and a source of major supply of water to the city' (Misra 2010: 71), impaired the water recharging function of the floodplain eco-system and damaged natural resources, migratory avifauna and the wetland to which the Yamuna floodplain area belonged.

Despite these negative impacts, the Supreme Court did not halt construction, declaring that the site was not located on the floodplain, despite the concerned observation of the Delhi High Court that the matter should be further investigated by an expert committee. As soon as the games concluded, the then Prime Minister of India, Manmohan Singh, established a High Level Committee under V K Shunglu to examine issues concerning the Commonwealth Games with special reference to the CWGV. As a result, various games officials were charged with corrupt practices and the selection of the site was severely criticised (High Level Committee 2011). The former Environment and Forest Minister, Jairam Ramesh, was asked in 2011 whether EC should have been granted for the CWGV. Ramesh stated that it should not as he felt that riverbed had been devastated by its construction. Was the CWGV located on the floodplain? (*Hindu* 2011). The Yamuna provided its own answer in August and September 2010 when the CWGV was flooded by monsoon rain. This case illustrates the tensions that face the Supreme Court when it is subjected to powerful political and economic interests, both in the private and public sectors. The court's minimalist responses at key points in the planning and construction of the CWGV were ultimately to the detriment of the Yamuna and India's environmental jurisprudence.

Thus, a climate of inconsistency and uncertainty exists with reference to entertaining and rejecting environmental PILs. This has become a serious concern among public-spirited citizens who see the court as the last resort for protecting the environment and citizens' rights.

In addition, the liberal interpretation of *locus standi* has been criticised because it promotes litigation within an already litigious society. Cases are lodged in a system already groaning under the weight of its caseload. Trial time in India challenges and possibly surpasses *Jardine v Jardine* in Dickens' *Bleak House*. If justice delayed constitutes justice denied, then India's justice quota continues to be severely constrained. Delay is not a recent phenomenon and can be traced back to the time of the Raj. It is a result of court-clogging, adjournments, missing papers, absent witnesses and conscious delaying tactics by both lawyers and parties (Galanter 1989; Moog 1992; Singh 2008). The Law Commission of India in its 77th report stated that: 'delay is a product of too much business for too few judges and the demand simply exceeds the supply of resources' (1978). The Indian legal profession operates on the economic belief that litigation is its prime purpose and largest income-generator. An over-supply of advocates has resulted in fierce competition for clients, particularly at the lower-level, more traditional sector of the legal services market. Consequently, services such as planning, negotiation, settlement or arbitration are not considered as a substitute for court appearances fees nor do they reflect legal training and the advocate's perceived role. Court appearances can be the basis of billing clients and therefore encourage time extensions through adjournments, application-filing, revisions, reviews and appeals. An already litigious public is egged on through the courts by a well-organised Bar. In 1981, Supreme Court Judge D A Desai wrote: 'The members [advocates] may organise in groups to protect their interest, to advance their position and to secure benefits for the group. This appears to be the only role the legal profession is fulfilling.' For example, in the *Delhi Vehicular Pollution* case (M C Mehta v *Union of India* WP Civil No 13029 of 1985), the original writ was filed in 1985. The case remains active to this day, despite the court passing many interim orders and directions.

Further, the relaxation of the *locus standi* in PIL has also been exploited through bogus litigation that is collusive, profiteering or speculative. Manipulative litigants may seek to damage rivals or competitors through this procedure (Sahu 2010; Desai and Muralidhar 2013: 181). The Supreme Court has shown its annoyance at the taking of every conceivable public interest issue to its door as court time, energy and resources are wasted, thus causing further strain on the court list. With the passage of time, there is a growing belief that PIL has a tendency to become 'publicity' or 'private' interest litigation and is counterproductive (*BALCO Employees' Union v Union of India* (2002) 2 SCC 333). In *State of Uttaranchal v Balwant Singh Chaufal* (2010) 3 SCC 402, the court observed:

> ...unfortunately, of late, it has been noticed that such an important jurisdiction which has been carefully carved out, created and nurtured with great care and caution by the courts, is being blatantly abused by filing some petitions with oblique motives. We think the time has come when genuine and bona fide public interest litigation must be encouraged whereas frivolous public interest litigation should be discouraged...
>
> (409–410)

For example, in *Neetu v State of Punjab* AIR 2007 SC 758, the Supreme Court concluded that it is necessary to impose exemplary costs to ensure that the message is understood that petitions filed with unequitable motives do not have the courts' approval.[13]

The expansion of the 'standing rule' has opened the courts to the possibility of 'forum-shopping', whereby justice according to law is more personality-driven than institutionalised adjudication. Some judges have become known as 'green judges', 'pro-poor' or 'progressive', thereby promoting the cult of individualism that, in turn, reduces the certainty factor in judicial decisions. Precedent is neither based upon the whim of the individual nor the randomness of the trial courtroom (Srikrishna 2005; Sahu 2008: 7).

Another novel procedural feature is the court's power to appoint 'fact-finding commissions or committees', usually comprising environmental experts (Divan and Rosencranz 2001; Desai and Muralidhar 2013: 165–167).[14] PIL has been affected by complex scientific and technical issues relating to the environment. The commission or expert committee reports are treated as prima facie evidence of facts and collected data. The power to appoint is an inherent power of the court under Article 32 Constitution of India (*Bandhua Mukti Morcha* at 816, 817 and 849). For example, in the *Doon Valley* case (at 653), the court appointed D N Bhargav, for the purpose of inspecting the limestone quarries mentioned in the writ petitions and the list submitted by the government of Uttar Pradesh. On the basis of the committee report, certain mining operations were ordered to be closed immediately, and others in a phased manner. The courts treat the opinions of these committees with great deference. Again, in the *Shriram Gas Leakage* case (*M C Mehta v Union of India* (1986) 2 SCC 176), the Nilay Choudhary Committee was appointed to advise the court on whether Shriram's hazardous plant should be allowed to recommence operations in view of the environmental dangers and threat it posed to the neighbourhood.

However, there are issues associated with appointment of the expert committees and their ability to resolve disputes. One problem is contradictory or divided findings, which place further evidential burdens on the judiciary (*AP Pollution Control Board v M V Nayudu I* (1999) 2 SCC 718). Another problem, as Sahu identifies, is their functioning and composition often bears witness to a strong inclination to forward particular departmental agendas (for example, conservation) without taking a holistic view of the environmental problem:

> ...the members of the Central Empowered Committee set up by the Court consists entirely of wildlife conservationists who have traditionally prioritised wildlife over people, and officers of the Ministry of Environment and Forests, with their strong inclination to enlarge the territory under forest department control. There is no representative of tribal people, the Ministry of Tribal Affairs or the Constitutional Authority of the Commissioner, Scheduled Castes and Scheduled Tribes.
>
> (2008: 387)

Further, these committees have acquired a permanent status in the form of statutory authorities thereby 'creating a parallel power structure within the governance frame' (ibid.).

'Judicial notice of facts' is another procedural innovation adopted by the court to simplify the evidentiary burden of the petitioner in environmental disputes. Traditionally, 'facts generally known with certainty by all the reasonably intelligent people in the community' and 'facts capable of accurate and ready determination by resort to sources of indisputable accuracy' qualify for judicial notice (Onstott 2007: 471). Reliance on academic writings and scientific data brought to the court's notice would lead the judge to assume that 'such injuries either had occurred or were likely to occur, and proceed to issue remedial directions' (Divan and Rosencranz 2001: 144).

Continuing mandamus is another procedural process used by the Supreme Court to implement and monitor its PIL directions (ibid.). In environmental cases, judgments are relatively few as compared with interim directions that have a broad-based, ongoing impact. Through such processes, the court has moved from being exclusively an adjudicator to embracing the role of policymaker and, thereafter, superior administrator. The Supreme Court can respond specifically to each situation and, backed by the power of contempt proceedings and penalties, exert pressure on inefficient state agencies.

This judicial activism is not without its critics who see the courts adopting responsibilities traditionally exercised by Parliament and the executive. The hoary jurisprudential chestnut of the appropriateness of judicial law-making is no better illustrated than in India where the Supreme Court through PIL has been charged with being a hyperactive law-making body (Baxi 1983; Dam 2005). The judges are accused of breaching the doctrine of separation of powers by trespassing upon areas traditionally and properly occupied by the executive and legislature. It has been suggested that the court is guilty of populism as well as adventurism, thereby in violation of the doctrine of separation of powers. The court, however, has denied any such usurpation. In its pronouncements, it has justified its actions either under a statutory provision or as an aspect of its inherent powers (Sahu 2008: 391).

The expansion of judicial activism through environmental cases, in particular, is widely debated and discussed in India. The legitimacy of environmental PIL through judicial activism has to be weighed as there are theoretical objections against pragmatic considerations, particularly when basic human rights are underrated or ignored due to legislative or executive inaction. A step-by-step purposive interpretation which takes society forward by redressing public wrongs, protecting collective diffused rights and interests, and balancing competing interests between environment and development would never find the judiciary guilty of transgressing its limits and violating the time-honoured doctrine of separation of powers. In *Chameli Singh v State of UP* AIR 1984 SC 802, the court stated:

In any organised society, the right to live as a human being is not ensured by meeting only the animal needs of man. It is secured only when he is assured of all facilities to develop himself as freed from restrictions which inhibit his growth. All human rights are designed to achieve this object.

Right to life guaranteed in any civil society implies the right to food, water, decent environment, education, medical care. These are basic human rights known to any civilised society.

(At 842)

Judicial activism is not an aberration (Sathe 2002: 310). It is not governance by judiciary, but action within the judicial process and restraint in legitimising its actions causes the public to repose faith in them. Such faith, respect and reverence provides legitimacy to the court and judicial activism. Fairness, integrity, impartiality and objectivity infuse the court's legitimacy. Justice Ahmadi, in a public lecture, stated:

The most important quality of law in a free society is its power to command respect, acceptance and support from the community. This quality which has been called 'the power of legitimacy' is attached to those commands of established organs of the government, which are perceived as flowing from the lawful exercise of their functions. In engaging in constitutional adjudication, the Supreme Court thwarts powerful interest, arouses the deepest of political emotions, often runs against the executive, sets aside the will of the legislature and also dictates the two wings of the government. Not being armed by the purse or sword, the court is uniquely dependent upon the power of legitimacy for the compliance of its orders. Therefore to ensure the continuance of legitimacy the court should issue directions only after assessing ground realities and analysing the prospect of their being successfully implemented.

(Ahmadi 1996)

Thus, environmental PIL both promoted and experienced an expansionist approach from the Supreme Court. It has widened the frontiers of fundamental rights (particularly Article 21) and opened its doors to public-spirited citizens for judicial redressal. 'Collaborative approach, procedural flexibility, judicially supervised interim orders and forward-looking relief' (Rajamani 2007: 1) have by and large received strong public support and acquired social legitimacy. It is a 'testament to Indian democracy' (ibid.: 12) in recognising and addressing governmental distrust and inaction. The environmental governance process has become more complex through such judicial intervention and innovations. Nevertheless, it is important that judicial activism arising from PIL simultaneously recognises the importance of judicial discretion. A former Chief Justice of India, A S Anand, rightly cautioned against the excessive use of PIL stating: '...care has to be taken to see that PIL essentially remains public interest litigation and does not become either political interest litigation or personal interest litigation or publicity interest litigation or used for persecution' (Sathe 2002: 308; Jain 2003: 86).

The environmental court debate

Within the context of the expansion of PIL, the quest for an environmental court – the foundations of which were laid by a proactive judiciary through innovative and creative efforts to protect the environment – assumed importance. The concept was a result of concern within the Supreme Court regarding the complexity and uncertainty underpinning the scientific evidence presented to it. Complete scientific certainty is the exception, not the norm. It is no longer possible to have so-called technical standards that express the facts in a definitive manner. Uncertainty, resulting from inadequate data, ignorance and indeterminacy, is inherent in science.[15] Such evidence generated tensions, usually between claimants' fears and assurances given by defendants. Uncertainty becomes a problem when scientific knowledge and claims are institutionalised into policy-making as a basis for courts' decision-making. Scientists may refine, modify or discard variables or models as more information becomes available. However, agencies and courts must make choices based on existing scientific knowledge. In addition, evidence presented in a scientific form may prove difficult to test or refute. Therefore, inadequacies in the record arising out of uncertainty or insufficient knowledge may not be properly acknowledged or considered (Gill 2010: 463). As the US Supreme Court stated in its landmark judgment of *Daubert v Merrel Dow Pharmaceuticals* 509 US 579 (1993),[16] when referring to the difficult goals of science and law in the establishment of truth: 'there are important differences between the quest for truth in the court room and the quest for truth in the laboratory. Scientific conclusions are subject to perpetual revision. Law, on the other hand, must resolve disputes finally and quickly' (596 and 597).

The setting up of an environmental court was posited for the first time in the case of M C Mehta v Union of India (1986) 2 SCC 176. The case involved the leakage of oleum gas from the premises of Shriram Foods and Fertilizers Ltd, one of India's major corporations. A significant number of people were affected, including both employees and the public. One person died from inhaling oleum gas. The leakage occurred after a tank containing the gas burst when the structure on which it was mounted collapsed, resulting in panic among local residents. The incident happened on 4 December. The Supreme Court indirectly acknowledged the right to live in a pollution-free environment as part of the fundamental right to life under Article 21 Constitution of India. Importantly, the Supreme Court advocated the establishment of environmental courts, stating:

> ...we would also suggest to the Government of India that since cases involving issues of environmental pollution, ecological destruction and conflicts over national resources are increasingly coming up for adjudication and these cases involve assessment and evolution of scientific and technical data, it might *be desirable to set up environment courts on a regional basis* with one professional judge and two experts, keeping in view the expertise

required for such adjudication. There would be a right to appeal to this court from the decision of the environment court.

(Ibid.: 202, emphasis added)

Another influential judgment reflecting judicial environmental concern and growing interest in a new environmental court was the *Indian Council for Enviro-Legal Action v Union of India* (1996) 3 SCC 212 which involved serious damage to the environment by toxic-chemical-producing industries. Thousands of villagers were adversely affected and between 1989 and 1994, a number of orders were passed by the court. They included a request to establish an expert committee to examine the situation in the affected area and provide recommendations for short and long-term remedial action. The court seized the opportunity to highlight the importance of specialised environmental courts, stating:

> The suggestion for the establishment of environment courts is a commendable one. The experience shows that the prosecutions launched in ordinary criminal courts under the provisions of Water Act, Air Act and Environment Act never reach their conclusion either because of the workload in those courts or because there is no proper appreciation of the significance of the environment matters on the part of those in charge of conducting of those cases. Moreover, any orders passed by the authorities under Water, Air or Environment Acts are immediately questioned by the industries in courts. Those proceedings take years and years to reach conclusion. Very often, interim orders are granted meanwhile which effectively disable the authorities from ensuring the implementation of their orders. All these point to the need for creating environment courts which alone should be empowered to deal with all matters, civil and criminal, relating to the environment. These courts should be manned by legally trained persons/judicial officers and should be allowed to adopt summary procedures. This issue, no doubt, requires to be studied and examined in depth from all angles before taking any action.
>
> (At 252)

The case for environmental courts was supported again in *AP Pollution Control Board v M V Nayudu* (1999) 2 SCC 718 and (2001) 2 SCC 62. The Supreme Court had the claims of the party tested by experts. The question was whether the industry was hazardous and whether, in case it became operational, the chemical ingredients produced would sooner or later percolate into the substratum of the earth and pollute underground water feeding two huge lakes, Osman Sagar and Himayat Sagar, the main sources of drinking water to the twin cities, Hyderabad and Secunderabad. The Supreme Court repeated earlier dicta:

> Of paramount importance was the need to establish environmental courts, authorities and tribunals for providing adequate judicial and scientific inputs rather than leaving such complicated disputes to be decided by officers

drawn from the executive. There is an urgent need to make appropriate amendments so as to ensure that at all times, the appellate authorities or tribunals consist of judicial and also technical personnel well versed in environmental laws.

(At 736)

The Supreme Court was of the opinion that an environmental court would benefit from expert advice from environmental scientists and technically quali-fied persons as part of the judicial process. It suggested that the Law Commission should examine the matter.

In India some initial legislative support for creating a NGT existed in the form of the National Environment Tribunal Act 1995. However, despite its suc-cessful passage through Parliament, it remained unimplemented. The 1995 Act provided for strict liability for damages arising out of any accident occurring while handling any hazardous substance and for the establishment of a tribunal for effective and expeditious disposal of cases arising from such accidents, with a view to giving relief and compensation for damages to person, property and the environment. The liability for compensation was based on the no-fault principle and claimants were not required to establish the wrongful act, neglect or default of any person. The composition of the tribunal consisted of a chairperson with membership including vice-chairpersons, judicial members and technical members as the central government deemed fit. It could sit in benches, each consisting of a judicial and technical member. The members were required to have adequate knowledge and experience in or capacity to deal with adminis-trative, scientific or technical aspects of problems relating to the environment, including judicial experience. Appeals could be made to the Supreme Court on questions of law. The 1995 Act was specialised legislation to deal with environ-mental issues and compensation. Unfortunately, it was not notified 'due to the sheer neglect and/or lack of political will to take the risk on the part of the executive to pave the way for the establishment of such a specialized environ-ment tribunal' (Desai and Sidhu 2010: 103). Thus, the environment tribunal was not constituted.

The National Environmental Appellate Authority (NEAA) Act 1997 pro-vided for the establishment of the NEAA to hear appeals with respect to restric-tion of areas in which any industries, operations or processes shall be carried out or not subject to safeguards under the Environment (Protection) Act 1986. Expertise or experience in administrative, legal, management or technical aspects of problems relating to environmental management law or planning and development were essential qualifications for persons to be appointed to the NEAA. The NEAA was established on 9 April 1997 to address grievances regarding the process of EC and implement the precautionary and polluter-pays principles.[17]

However, the NEAA did little work because its role was limited to the exam-ination of complaints regarding ECs. After the first chairperson's term expired no further appointment was made (Desai and Sidhu 2010: 104). In *Vimal Bhai v*

Union of India High Court of Delhi CM 15895/2005 in WP(C) 17682/2005, the court expressed concern that the government was unable to find qualified members to fill positions in the NEAA. The posts of chairperson and vice-chairperson remained vacant from July 2000 until the 1997 Act was repealed by the National Green Tribunal (NGT) Act 2010.[18] Thus, both ETs were or became non-operational. This background helps contextualise the various interventions and *dicta* by the Supreme Court during this period.

Following the powerful observations made by the Supreme Court, the Law Commission undertook a study. As an active and influential participant in legal reform, in its 186th Report *Proposal to Constitute Environment Courts*, it strongly advocated the establishment of 'Environment Courts' (2003: 142), keeping in mind the following considerations:

a   the uncertainties of scientific conclusions and the need to provide, not only expert advice from the Bar but also a system of independent expert advice to the Bench itself;
b   the present inadequacy of the knowledge of Judges on the scientific and technical aspects of environmental issues, such as, whether the levels of pollution in a local area are within permissible limits or whether higher standards of permissible limits of pollution require to be set up;
c   the need to maintain a proper balance between sustainable development and control/regulation of pollution by industries;
d   the need to strike a balance between closure of polluting industries and reducing or avoiding unemployment or loss of livelihood;
e   the need to make a final appellate view at the level of each State on decisions regarding 'environmental impact assessment';
f   the need to develop a jurisprudence in this branch of law which is also in accord with scientific, technological developments and international treaties, conventions or decisions; and
g   to achieve the objectives of Articles 21, 47, 48A and 51A (g) of the Constitution of India by means of a fair, fast and satisfactory judicial procedure (at 8–9).

In this context, the Law Commission posed further questions, namely:

a   Should there be one Environment Court in each State?
b   Should these Courts oust the jurisdiction of the High Courts/Supreme Court or should it be left to the discretion of these superior Courts to direct parties to first exhaust (seek) the effective alternative remedy before the proposed Environmental Courts? Should the jurisdiction of normal civil and criminal courts be totally ousted?...
c   What should be the nature of the jurisdiction of the State Environmental Courts, – should it be only appellate jurisdiction against orders of administrative or public authorities and government but also original jurisdiction, so as to reduce the burden of PILs in the High Courts?

d   What should be the composition of the Courts and qualification of the Members?

e   What should be the procedure of these Environmental Courts?

f   Should public interest or class actions cases be allowed before these Courts?

g   What relief these Courts should be able to grant – ad interim, final, injunctions (permanent and mandatory), appointment of receivers, grant of compensation/damages etc?

h   Should they exercise civil as well as criminal jurisdiction?

i   What is the mode of execution of the orders?

j   Should the Court have power to punish wilful disobedience of its orders by exercising power of contempt of Court?

k   Should the National Environment Tribunal Act, 1995 and the National Environment Appellate Authority Act, 1997 be repealed and powers and jurisdiction of the tribunals thereunder be vested in the proposed State Environmental Courts? (ibid.: 9–10).

Against this backdrop, the Law Commission examined the questions by reviewing the technical and scientific problems that arise before courts. Citing the work of Alyson C Flournay (1991: 333–335) regarding the reasons for scientific inaccuracies, it observed:

> The inadequacies of science result from identification of adverse effects of a hazard and then working backwards to find the causes. Secondly, clinical tests are performed, particularly where toxins are involved, on animals and not on humans, that is to say, are based on animal studies or short term cell-testing. Thirdly, conclusions based on epidemiological studies are flawed by the scientists' inability to control or even accurately assess past exposure of the subjects. Moreover, these studies do not permit the scientists to isolate the effects of the substance of concern. The latency period of many carcinogens and the toxins exacerbates problems of later interpretation. The timing between exposure and observable effect creates intolerable delays before regulation occurs.
>
> (Law Commission 2003: 13)

It further observed: '... it is quite clear that the opinions as to science which may be placed before the Court keep the judge always guessing whether to accept the fears expressed by an affected party or to accept the assurances given by a polluter' (ibid.).

The Law Commission's concern was in relation to the technical and scientific problems arising before the courts in a variety of ways at various stages. One instance offered by the Law Commission is in the field of pollution prevention and control, where it was accepted that health and environmental damage might arise at the stage of the initial establishment of an industry or during its subsequent operation. Decisions on whether the industry needs to be closed, relocated or allowed to continue to function but with enhanced environmental safeguards could involve significant costs. These might include the laying-off of employees, loss of excise duty and sales taxes to the government, or economic and environmental costs of provision of alternative sites. On the other hand, the lack of appropriate action might pose serious danger to the health and well-being of local people.

The Law Commission was persuaded that, in seeking a balanced decision in such cases, 'Environmental Courts' with scientific as well as legal inputs would be better placed to reach a determination. Such courts could have wide powers to make on-the-spot inspections and hear oral evidence from resident panels of environmental scientists. In addition, it was suggested that the establishment of Environmental Courts would reduce the burden on the High Courts and Supreme Court, given the growth of PIL, often involving complex and technical environmental issues. To quote:

> It is true that the High Court and Supreme Court have been taking up these and other complex environmental issues and deciding them. But, though they are judicial bodies, they do not have an independent statutory panel of environmental scientists to help and advise them on a permanent basis. They are prone to apply principles like the Wednesbury Principle and refuse to go into the merits. They do not also make spot inspections nor receive oral evidence to see for themselves the facts as they exist on ground. On the other hand, if Environmental Courts are established in each state, these Courts can make spot inspections and receive oral evidence. They can receive independent advice on scientific matters by a panel of scientists.
>
> (Law Commission 2003: 21)

The Law Commission referred to specialised environmental courts in Australia and New Zealand staffed by judges and expert commissioners, generally, persons with expert knowledge in environmental matters. However, particular reference was made to the UK and the words of Lord Woolf and the 23rd Report of the Royal Commission. In his lecture 'Are the judiciary environmentally myopic?' (1992; see also Woolf 2001), he highlighted the problems of increasing specialisation in environmental law and the difficulties facing the courts. Discussing the benefits of an ET, he said:

> Having a tribunal with general responsibility for overseeing and enforcing the safeguards provided for the protection of the environment. The tribunal could be granted a wider discretion to determine its procedure so that it is able to bring to bear its specialist experiences of environmental issues in the most effective way.
>
> (Woolf 1992: 13)

Woolf envisaged 'a multi-faceted and multi-skilled body', a one-stop shop combining the adjudication services provided by existing courts, tribunals and inspectorates in the environmental field. The resulting resolution of disputes was envisaged as faster, cheaper and more effective than the existing overburdened system and the forum more appropriate to specialist disputes. Woolf saw this as 'an exciting project' with a new, more fluid role for judges (ibid.: 14). It was a vision shared to some degree by the UK Royal Commission on Environmental Pollution in its 23rd Report (2002), which recommended the establishment of ETs to handle appeals under environmental legislation other than the town and country planning system:

> ... there is a great deal of inconsistency at present, both in whether there is a right of appeal on merits and in who decides any such appeal. Some appeals are made to the Secretary of State. Others, such as those concerning contaminated land or statutory nuisances, are made to the Magistrate's Courts, which often lack the expertise to handle the considerable technicalities involved. In many contexts, for example, the granting of consents in relation to genetically modified organisms, there is no right of appeal on merits. Procedures have grown up haphazardly with no apparent underlying principle, and we consider they fail to provide a system appropriate for contemporary needs. We recommend the establishment of Environmental Tribunals to handle appeals under environmental legislation other than the town and country planning system, including those now handled by planning inspectors.
>
> (Para 5.36)

In its view, establishing an ET would be a significant contribution to a more coherent and effective system of environmental regulation. As to its constitution, and scope of appeals from it, the Royal Commission said:

> We envisage such a Tribunal would consist of a legal chairperson and members with appropriate specialized expertise. It would rapidly develop the authority and understanding needed to handle complex environmental cases ... On points of law, there would be a right of appeal from the Tribunal to the High Court. Applications for judicial review or environmental matters would not be considered by the High Court unless the applicant had exhausted any remedy available from the Environmental Tribunal or from other sources.
>
> (Para 5.377)

Ultimately, the Indian Law Commission explicitly recommended the establishment of environmental courts for accessible and speedy justice. It stated that environmental courts should be staffed only by persons with judicial or legal experience assisted by persons with scientific qualifications and experience in the field of environment. The proposed environmental courts would consist of a chairperson and at least two other members. It was suggested that these should either be retired judges of the Supreme Court or High Court, or have at least 20 years' experience as practising advocates in any High Court. Appointments would be for five years. Importantly, the three judicial members were to be assisted by at least three scientific or technical experts known as commissioners.

Each commissioner must have: a degree in environmental sciences, with at least five years' experience as an environmental scientist or engineer; or adequate knowledge of, and experience in dealing with, various aspects of problems relating to the environment and, in particular, the scientific or technical aspects of environmental problems, including the protection of the environment and EIAs. However, the commissioners' role was to be advisory only, to independently assist the court in analysing and assessing scientific or technological issues. A quorum for hearing a case was to be two members, including the chairperson (Law Commission 2003: 165–166).

The proposed court would have original and appellate jurisdiction. The original jurisdiction would cover all civil cases where a substantial question relating to 'environment', including enforcement of any legal or constitutional right relating to environment, was involved. The appellate jurisdiction was in respect to all appeals under four environmental legislations and rules made thereunder: the Environment Protection Act 1986; the Water (Prevention and Control of Pollution) Act 1974; the Air (Prevention and Control of Pollution) Act 1981; and the Public Liability Insurance Act 1991 (with power given to central government to include any other environment-related enactment under the said jurisdiction).

The proposed court would follow the principle of strict liability in cases of hazardous substances, the polluter-pays, precautionary and preventive principles and doctrines of public trust, intergenerational equity and sustainable development. The proposed court could pass all kinds of orders, final or interlocutory. It could also award damages, compensation and grant injunctions (permanent, temporary and mandatory) (Law Commission 2003: Chapter 9).[19]

Following the strong judicial pronouncements and recommendations of the powerful Law Commission of India, the NGT Bill 2009 was introduced in the Lower House (Lok Sabha) on 31 July 2009. It was also referred to the Parliamentary Standing Committee on Science and Technology, Environment and Forests for examination and reporting.[20] Based on the critique and recommendations of Parliament and the standing committee, the then Minister of Environment and Forests, Jairam Ramesh, introduced changes to the Bill in direct response to issues raised on the floor of the House saying:

> The members have made important suggestions. Even though their exact demands may not be part of the official amendment moved by the government but I am open to their suggestions. I will remove all objectionable clauses or sections in the proposed law and keep the window of discussion open.
>
> (Madhavan 2011)

Accordingly, the Bill was amended seven times to introduce necessary changes. Its principal features included:

- setting up specialised environmental courts thereby replacing the NEAA;
- hearing initial complaints as well as appeals from decisions of authorities;

- composition of the tribunal to consist of a minimum number of full-time judicial and expert members being not be less than 10 with a maximum of 20;
- the tribunal to hear substantial questions relating to the environment;
- a broadened definition of 'person aggrieved' to include not only a person who sustained injury or an owner of property to which damage had been caused or the legal representatives of the deceased where death resulted from environmental damage, but also, with the permission of the Tribunal, a representative body or organisation functioning in the field of the environment, making the provisions sufficiently wide to allow enforcement by NGOs of all legal rights relating to the environment;
- the decisions of the tribunal to be subject to appeal to the Supreme Court of India;
- application of the foundational principle, namely, sustainable development, precautionary principle, polluter-pays principle and intergenerational equity;
- and the chairperson of the tribunal as the authority to break the deadlock in case there is a deadlock.[21]

According to the former Environment Minister, Jairam Ramesh, the tribunal was 'one element' of a reformist approach to environmental governance. To quote from the Parliamentary debate:

> There are 5,600 cases before our judiciary today relating to environment. I am sure the number of cases will increase. We need specialised environmental courts. The Supreme Court has said this. The Law Commission has said this. India will be one of the few countries which will have such a specialised environmental court. I believe Australia and New Zealand are the two countries that have specialised tribunals.[22]

Consequently, the government proposed the creation of a circuit system for the new tribunal. The main bench was to be situated at Bhopal in recognition of the city's disastrous industrial history.[23] The government proposed four regional benches across the country. According to the Minister:

> The main bench of the tribunal will be in Bhopal. This way the government and parliament could show some sensitivity to the people of Bhopal, the site of the worst industrial disaster. We can never obliterate that tragedy from our memories but by setting the national green tribunal in Bhopal, I think we would send a signal that we mean business. A circuit approach would be followed to enable access for people. The court will go to the people. People would not come to the court. I assure you this.[24]

The Bill was passed by the Lok Sabha on 23 April 2010 and Rajya Sabha on 5 May 2010. The NGT Act 2010 received presidential assent on 2 June 2010 and formally came into existence.[25] The NGT Act implements India's commitments, made in the Stockholm Declaration of 1972 and at the Rio Conference of 1992, to take appropriate steps for the protection and improvement of the human environment and provide effective access to judicial and administrative proceedings, including redress and remedies. This also includes the development of national laws regarding liability and compensation for the victims of pollution and other forms of environmental damage. In consequence, the Act provides for the establishment of the NGT which decides cases relating to environmental protection and conservation of forests and other natural resources, including enforcement of legal rights relating to the environment, and gives relief and compensation for damage to persons and property.[26]

The NGT was established on 18 October 2010 and became operational on 5 May 2011 with New Delhi ultimately selected as the site for the Principal Bench.[27] Justice Lokeshwar Singh Panta, former judge of the Supreme Court of India, was appointed as its first chairperson.[28] The Principal Bench exercises jurisdiction in the states of Uttar Pradesh, Uttarakhand, Punjab, Haryana, Himachal Pradesh, National Capital Territory (NCT) of Delhi and Union Territory of Delhi. Subsequently, regional benches were established in Bhopal, the central zone,[29] covering Madhya Pradesh, Rajasthan and Chattisgarh. Pune is the western zone base and covers Maharashtra, Gujarat and Goa with Union Territories of Daman and Diu and Dadar and Nagar Haveli. The southern zone is located in Chennai and serves Kerala, Tamil Nadu, Andhra Pradesh, Karnataka, Union Territories of Puducherry and Lakshadweep. The fifth area, the eastern zone, is based in Kolkata and is responsible for West Bengal, Orissa, Bihar, Jharkhand and the seven sister states of the northeastern region, Sikkim, Andaman and the Nicobar Islands. Additionally, in order to become more accessible, especially in remote areas, the NGT follows the circuit procedure of 'courts going to people and not people coming to the courts'. Shimla has received circuit benches from Delhi[30] as has Jodhpur from the central zone,[31] Meghalaya from the eastern zone[32] and Kochi from the southern zone.[33] The Principal Bench and regional benches are now operational.[34] Nevertheless, at the initial stages the benches received a mixed reception from both central and regional governments.[35]

Conclusion

This chapter has traced the creation, successes and limitations of PIL through time and case law. However, increasing pressure on court lists and the inability to appreciate and evaluate scientific evidence in complex environmental disputes has further limited the ability of courts to progress and reach appropriate environmental decisions. Recognition of the need for expansive change in the form of specialised ETs came from the Supreme Court and ultimately from the Law Commission. The Law Commission also acquired illustrative support and direction from Australia, New Zealand and a UK Royal Commission. The chapter has followed the passage of the NGT Act and the earliest days of the

Principal Bench and regional benches. The initial establishment of these benches required the involvement of the Supreme Court and in turn raised questions, addressed in Chapter 7, about the NGT's future role, success and relationship with powerful external interests.

Notes

1 See *Dalmia Cement (Bharat) Ltd v Union of India* (1996) 10 SCC 104; *M Nagaraj v Union of India* (2006) 8 SCC 212; *Consumer Education and Research Centre v Union of India* (1995) 3 SCC 42; *Madhu Kishwar v State of Bihar* (1996) 5 SCC 125; In *Bihar Legal Support Society v Chief Justice of India* (1986) 4 SCC 767 the Supreme Court stated that

> the majority of people of our country are subjected to denial of 'access to justice' and overtaken by despair and helplessness. They continue to remain victims of an exploitative society where economic power is concentrated in the hands of few and it is used for perpetuation of domination over large masses of human beings … The strategy of public interest litigation has been evolved by this court with a view to bringing justice within the easy reach of the poor and disadvantaged sections of the community.
>
> (768–769)

See, generally, Shankar 2009; Shankar and Mehta 2008.

2 Baxi argued that, whereas PIL in the United States has focused on 'civic participation in governmental decision making', the Indian PIL discourse was directed against 'state repression or governmental lawlessness' and was focused primarily on supporting the rural poor. See also Bhagwati, 1984; Cunningham 1987; Vandenhole 2002.

3 *Fertilizer Corporation Kamagar Union v Union of India* AIR 1981 SC 344; *Jasbhai Motibhai Desai v Roshan Kumar* (1976) a1 SCC 671; *Bar Council of Maharashtra v MV Dasholkar* (1976) 1 SCR 306.

4 A detailed discussion of environmental PIL follows later in this chapter.

5 Article 21 Constitution of India states: 'No person shall be deprived of his life or personal liberty except according to procedure established by law.'

6 *Delhi Jal Board v National Campaign for Dignity and Rights of Sewerage and Allied Workers* (2011) 8 SCC 574; *State of Uttaranchal v Balwant Singh Chaufal* (2010) 3 SCC 402; *Chhetriya Pradushan Mukti Sangharsh Samiti v State of Uttar Pradesh* AIR 1990 SC 2060; *Subhash Kumar v State of Bihar* AIR 1991 SC 420; M C *Mehta v Kamal Nath* (2000) 6 SCC 213.

7 *Narmada Bachao Andolan v Union of India* AIR (2000) 10 SCC 664; *M C Mehta v Union of India* (2007) 1 SCC 110.

8 'India's doctors blame air pollution for sharp rise in respiratory diseases' *Guardian*, 23 September 2015 www.theguardian.com/world/2015/sep/23/india-doctors-air-pollution-rise-respiratory-diseases-delhi.

9 See also *Deepak Nitrate v State of Gujarat* (2004) 6 SCC 402; *Indian Council for Enviro-Legal Action v Union of India* (1996) 3 SCC 212.

10 *Vellore Citizen Welfare Forum v Union of India* AIR 1996 SC 2715; *AP Pollution Control Board v Nayudu I* (1999) 2 SCC 718; *Narmada Bachao Andolan v Union of India* (2000) 10 SCC 664.

11 Also see *Banwasi Seva Ashram v State of Uttar Pradesh* AIR 1987 SC 374; *Karjan Jalasay YASAS Samiti v State of Gujarat* (1986) Supp SCC 350.

12 Report of the Four Member Committee for Investigation into the Proposal submitted by the Orissa Mining Company for Bauxite Mining in Niyamgiri (16 August 2010) at 9.

13 Also see *Charan Lal Sahu v Giani Zail Singh* AIR 1984 SC 309.

14 The court also held that the power to appoint commissioners is not constrained by the Code of Civil Procedure or Supreme Court Rules (Order XXVI Civil Procedure Code and Order XLVI Supreme Court Rules 1966).
15 For a detailed discussion on scientific evidence and the role of scientists as NGT bench members, see Chapter 6.
16 See also *Ohio v Wyandotte Chemicals Corporation* 401 US 493 (1971) and *State of Washington v General Motors Corporation* 40 USLW 4437 (US 24 April 1972).
17 For a detailed discussion see *AP Pollution Control Board v M V Nayudu I* (1999) 2 SCC 718.
18 NGT Act 2010 section 38(1) (repealing the National Environment Tribunal Act 1995); see Ministry of Environment and Forests (MoEF) www.envfor.nic.in.
19 For detailed discussions of these principles, see Chapters 4 and 6.
20 www.prsindia.org/billtrack/the-national-green-tribunal-bill-2009-740/.
21 See, generally, Vital Statistics, PRS Legislative Research www.prsindia.org/bill-track/the-national-green-tribunal-bill-2009-740/. PRS Legislative Research, a unit of the Centre for Policy Research, New Delhi, is an independent research initiative which works with MPs across party lines to provide research support on legislative and policy issues. It is the only organisation that tracks the functioning of Parliament.
22 Statement by Jairam Ramesh, former Minister of Environment and Forests, Indian Parliament, 30 April 2010.
23 See Chapter 1.
24 See n 19 above.
25 Gazette of India Extraordinary (No 19 of 2010); National Environment Tribunal Act No 27 of 1995 www.envfor.nic.in/legis/others/tribunal.html.
26 Preamble NGT Act.
27 MoEF Notification 5 May 2011 SO 1003 E.
28 MoEF Notification 18 October 2010, SO 2570(E) and 2571(E).
29 MoEF 17 August 2011 SO1908 (E).
30 NGT/PB/157/2013/331 20 December 2013 [office order].
31 NGT/PB/266/2013/281 2 December 2013 [office order].
32 NGT/PB/Pr/CB/97/2014/M78.
33 NGT/PB/266/2015/299.
34 Additionally, each bench is supported by a Registrar's Court that deals with minor and administrative matters. See section 7 NGT (Practices and Procedure) Rules 2011.
35 See Chapter 7 for a fuller account of this period.

References

Agarwal, A (1996) *Slow Murder: The Deadly Story of Vehicular Pollution in India* (Centre for Science and Environment).

Ahmadi, Justice A M (1996) 'Judicial process: social legitimacy and institutional validity' 4 *Supreme Court Cases Journal* section 8–9.

Anand, A (2014) 'Is this the city with the loudest car horns?' BBC News www.bbc.co.uk/news/magazine-25944792.

Baxi, U (1983) 'How not to judge the judges: notes towards evaluation of the judicial role' 25 *Journal of the Indian Law Institute* 211.

Baxi, U (1985) 'Taking suffering seriously: social action litigation in the Supreme Court of India' 4(1) *Third World Legal Studies* 107–109.

Baxi, U (2000) 'The avatars of Indian judicial activism: explorations in the geographies of (in)justice' in S K Verma and K Kumar (eds), *Fifty Years of the Supreme Court of India* (OUP).

Bhagwati, P N (1984) 'Judicial activism and public interest litigation' 23 *Columbia Journal of Transnational Law* 561.

Bhushan, P (2004) 'Supreme Court and PIL' 39(18) *Economic and Political Weekly* 1770–1774.

Bhushan, P R (2009) 'Misplaced priorities and class bias of the judiciary' 44(14) *Economic and Political Weekly* 32–37.

Boyd, D R (2012) *The Environmental Rights Revolution* (University of British Columbia Press).

Boyle, A (1996) 'The role of international human rights law in the protection of the environment' in A Boyle and M Anderson (eds), *Human Rights Approaches to Environmental Protection* (OUP).

Burke, J (2015) 'India's doctors blame air pollution for sharp rise in respiratory diseases' *Guardian*, 23 September.

Cooper, J (1993) 'Poverty and constitutional justice' 44 *Mercer LR* 611.

Cunningham, C D (1987) 'Public interest litigation in Indian Supreme Court' 29(4) *Journal of Indian Law Institute* 494–523.

Dam, S (2005) 'Law-making beyond lawmakers: understanding the little right and the great wrong (analysing the legitimacy of the nature of judicial law-making in India's constitutional dynamic)' 13 *Tulane Journal of International and Comparative Law* 109.

Desai, A (1981) 'Role and structure of the legal profession' 8 *Journal of the Bar Council of India* 112.

Desai, A H and Muralidhar, S (2013) 'Public interest litigation: potential and problems' in B N Kirpal, A H Desai, G Subramanium, R Dhavan and R Ramachandran (eds) *Supreme But Not Infallible* (OUP) 159.

Desai, B H and Sidhu, B (2010) 'On the quest for green courts in India' 3(1) *Journal of Court Innovation* 79.

Deva, S (2009) 'Public interest litigation in India: a critical review' 28(1) *Civil Justice Quarterly* 19–40.

Divan, S and Rosencranz, A (2001) *Environmental Law and Policy in India* (OUP).

Faure, M G and Raja, A V (2010) 'Effectiveness of environmental public interest litigation in India: determining the key variable' 21 *Fordham Environmental LR* 225.

Flournay, A C (1991) 'Legislating inaction: asking the wrong questions in protective environmental decision making' 15 *Harvard Environmental Law Review* 327.

Galanter, M (1974) 'Why the "haves" come out ahead: speculations on the limits of legal change' 9(1) *Law and Society Review* 95–160

Galanter, M (1989) *Law and Society in Modern India* (OUP).

Gauri, V (2009) 'Public interest litigation in India: time for an audit' *India in Transition* http://casi.ssc.upenn.edu/iit/gauri.

Ghosh, S (2012) 'A new era for environmental litigation in India' *India in Transition* https://casi.sas.upenn.edu/iit/ghosh.

Gill, G N (2010) 'A Green Tribunal for India' 22(3) *Journal of Environmental Law* 461–474.

Gill, G N (2012) 'Human rights and the environment in India: access through public interest litigation' 14 *Environmental LR* 201.

Gill, G N (2014) 'Environmental protection and development interests: a case study of the River Yamuna and the Commonwealth Games, Delhi 2010' 6(1–2) *International Journal of Law in the Built Environment* Special Issue 69–90.

Gill, G N (2015) 'Human rights and environmental protection in India: a judicial journey from public interest litigation to the National Green Tribunal' in A Grear and

E Grant (eds), *Thought, Law, Rights and Action in an Age of Environmental Crisis* (Edward Elgar) 123–154.

High Level Committee (2011) *High Level Committee Report on Commonwealth Games Chair V K Shunglu* (Government of India).

Hindu, The (2011) 'River Regulation Zone Coming: Jairam' 7 January www.thehindu. com/news/national/river-regulation-zonecoming-jairam/article1063315.ece.

Housing and Land Rights Network Report (2010) *The 2010 Commonwealth Games: Whose Wealth, Whose Commons?* (Housing and Land Rights Network/South-Asia Regional Programme Habitat International Coalition).

IANS (2013) 'SC asks states to provide offices to green tribunal' TwoCircles.net http:// twocircles.net/2013mar15/sc_asks_states_provide_offices_green_tribunal.html#.Vuqq vuaHjdM.

Jain, M P (2003) 'The Supreme Court and fundamental rights' in S K Verma and K Kusum (eds), *Fifty Years of the Supreme Court of India* (OUP) 22–37.

Juneja, S (2014) 'Environment ministry failed to monitor forest diversion: CAG' Down-ToEarth www.downtoearth.org.in/news/environment-ministry-failed-to-monitor-forest-diversion-cag-42131.

Kiss, A and Shelton, D (2003) *International Environmental Law* (UNEP) 393.

Korsah-Brown, D (2002) 'Environment, human rights and mining conflicts in Ghana' in Lyuba Zarsky (ed.), *Human Rights and the Environment* (Earthscan).

Law Commission of India (1978) *Delay and Arrears in Trial Courts* 77th Report.

Law Commission of India (2003) *Proposal to Constitute Environment Courts* 186th Report http://lawcommissionofindia.nic.in/reports/186th%20report.pdf.

Leelakrishanan, P (2005) *Environmental Law in India* (Butterworths).

Legal India (2012) 'SC slams poor facilities for green tribunal' www.legalindia.com/news/ sc-slams-poor-facilities-for-green-tribunal.

Madhavan, M R (2011) 'In Parliament' Pragati http://pragati.nationalinterest.in/2011/02/ in-parliament-10.

Mahapatra, Dhananjay (2013) 'Kolkata may lose green tribunal bench to Guwahati or Ranchi' *Times of India* http://timesofindia.indiatimes.com/city/kolkata/Kolkata-may-lose-green-tribunal-bench-to-Guwahati-or-Ranchi/articleshow/20996616.cms.

Mahaprashasta, A A (2010) 'War on Beggars' *Hindu* 19 June–2 July 27, 13.

McGoldrick, D (1996) 'Sustainable development and human rights: an integrated conception' 45(4) *International and Comparative Law Quarterly* 796.

Misra, M (2010) 'Dreaming of a blue Yamuna' in B Chaturvedi (ed.), *Finding Delhi: Loss and Renewal in the Mega City* (Penguin Viking).

MLJCA (1977) *Report on the National Juridicare: Equal Justice–Social Justice.*

Moog, R (1992) 'Delays in Indian courts' 16(1) *Justice System Journal* 19–36.

New York Times Editorial (2014) 'India's Air Pollution Emergency' *New York Times* www.nytimes.com/2014/02/14/opinion/indias-air-pollution-emergency.html?_r=1.

Nickel, J W (2007) *Making Sense of Human Rights* (Blackwell).

Onstott, C (2007) 'Judicial notice and the law's "scientific" search for truth' 2(3) *Akron LR* 465–491.

Orend, B (2001) *Human Rights: Concept and Context* (Broadview Press).

Pal, Justice R and Pal, S (2011) *M P Jain Indian Constitutional Law* 6th edn (LexisNexis/ Butterworths).

Rajamani, L (2007) 'Public interest litigation in India: exploring issues of access, participation, equity, effectiveness and sustainability' 19(3) *Journal of Environmental Law* 293.

Rajamani, L (2010) 'The increasing currently and relevance of rights-based perspective in the international negotiations on climate change' 22(3) *Journal of Environmental Law* 409.

Royal Commission on Environmental Pollution (2002) *Environmental Planning* 23rd Report Cm 5459 (HMSO).

Sahu, G (2008) 'Implications of Indian Supreme Courts' innovation for environmental jurisprudence' 4(1) *Law, Environmental and Development Journal* 3–19.

Sahu, G (2010) 'Implementation of environmental judgments in context: a comparative analysis of Dahanu Thermal Power Plant Pollution Case in Maharashtra and Vellore Leather Industrial Pollution Case in Tamil Nadu' 6(3) *Law, Environment and Development Journal* 335.

Sahu, G (2014) 'Why the underdogs came out ahead: an analysis of the Supreme Court's environmental judgments, 1980–2010' 49(4) *Economic and Political Weekly* 52–57.

Sathe, S P (2002) *Judicial Activism in India* (OUP).

Shah, S B (1999) 'Illuminating the possible in the developing world' 32 *Vanderbilt Journal of Transnational Law* 435.

Shankar, S (2009) *Scaling Justice: India's Supreme Court, Anti-Terror Laws, and Social Rights* (OUP).

Shankar, S and Mehta, P B (2008) 'Courts and socioeconomic rights in India' in V Gauri and D M Brinks (eds), *Courting Social Justice: Judicial Enforcement of Social and Economic Rights in the Developing World* (CUP) 146–182.

Shrivastava, K S (2012) 'Green tribunal gets short shrift' Down To Earth www.downto earth.org.in/news/green-tribunal-gets-short-shrift-38426.

Shue, H (1996) *Basic Rights* (Princeton UP).

Singh, P (2008) 'Protecting the rights of the disadvantaged groups through public interest litigation' in M P Singh, H Goerlich and M von Hauff (eds), *Human Rights and Basic Need* (Universal Law).

South Asian Human Rights Documentation Centre (2008) *Human Rights and Humanitarian Law: Developments in Indian and International Law* (OUP).

Srikrishna, B N (2005) 'Judicial activism – judges as social engineers: skinning a cat' 8 *Supreme Court Cases Journal* S3.

Sripati, V (1997) 'Human rights in India fifty years after independence' 26 *Denver Journal of International Law and Policy* 93.

Trubek, L G and Trubek, D M (1981) 'Civic justice through civil justice: new approach to public interest advocacy in the United States' in M Cappelletti (ed.), *Access to Justice and the Welfare State* (Le Monnier).

Vandenhole, W (2002) 'Human rights law, development and social action litigation in India' 3(2) *Asia Pacific Journal on Human Rights and the Law* 136–210.

Woolf, Lord (1992) 'Are the judiciary environmentally myopic' 4(1) *Journal of Environmental Law* 1–14.

Woolf, Lord (2001) 'Environmental risk: the responsibilities of law and science' 13 *Environmental Law and Management* 131 (Environmental Law Foundation's Professor David Hall Memorial Lecture) 24 May.

World Bank Report (2013) *India-Diagnostic Assessment of Select Environmental Challenges: An Analysis of Physical and Monetary Losses of Environmental Health and Natural Resources* Report No 70004-IN, volume 1, 5 June 5.

3 The National Green Tribunal Act 2010

Interpretation and application

The NGT is a creation of a statute and thus, its jurisdiction, powers and proced-ures are bound and controlled by the provisions of the statute i.e. the NGT Act 2010. The successful establishment of the NGT encouraged the Supreme Court to review its PIL environmental caseload and consider its limited environmental expertise. In 2012, in a PIL case, the Supreme Court transferred all environmental cases, both active and prospective, to the NGT to render expeditious and special-ised judgments and to avoid the likelihood of conflicts of orders between High Courts and the NGT. Further, the High Courts were advised by the Supreme Court, at their discretion, to transfer to the Tribunal those environmental cases filed and pending prior to the coming into force of the NGT Act.[1] This chapter focuses on the meaning and interpretation of the key sections of the NGT Act. It draws on illustrative case law that demonstrates how the NGT has given liberal content and meaning to the statute in order to promote environmental justice.

Preamble

A preamble 'walks in front' of a statute (Davis and Lemezina 2010: 261; Twomey 2011). The preamble of a statute is an admissible aid to the construc-tion aimed at expressing the scope, object and purpose of the Act more compre-hensively than the long title. It may recite the ground and cause of making the statute, the evils sought to be remedied or doubts which may be intended to be settled. It may not strictly be an instrument for controlling or restricting a stat-ute's provisions, but it certainly acts as a precept to gather legislative intention and help give prudent interpretation to achieve the Act's objective.[2] In *Wacando v Commonwealth* (1981) 148 CLR 1, the court observed:

> It has been said that where the enacting part of a statute is clear and unam-biguous it cannot be cut down by the preamble. But this does not mean that a court cannot obtain assistance from the preamble in ascertaining the meaning of an operative provision. The particular section must be seen in its context; the statute must be read as a whole and recourse to the pre-amble may throw light on the statutory purpose and object.
>
> (Mason J at 23)

The NGT Act provides for the establishment of the NGT for the effective and expeditious disposal of cases relating to environmental protection, conservation of forests and other natural resources, including enforcement of environmental legal rights, giving relief and compensation for damages to persons and property, and for matters connected or incidental. India's commitment to international conventions – stemming from the UN Conference on the Human Environment 1972 and UN Conference on Environment and Development 1992 – is recognised within the Preamble, to take appropriate steps for environmental protection and improvement and provide effective access to judicial and administrative proceedings, including redress and remedy by states.[3]

The Preamble recognises the judicial exegesis of the right to a healthy environment as part of the right to life. Recognition of the right to an environment, an emotive entitlement, has influenced the development of law within nations, thereby affecting constitutions, legislation and jurisprudence. Principle 1 Stockholm Declaration 1972 recognises the right of individuals to an adequate environment, but stops short of proclaiming the right to an environment. The right to an environment was neither explicitly included nor endorsed in either the Rio Declaration 1992 or the World Summit on Sustainable Development 2002, thus indicating uncertainty and leaving room for debate (Boyd 2012: 90). The right to an environment is deeply problematic given that it is characterised by 'an undefined content, variable and constant changing technical requirements, complicated temporal and geographical elements, vast territorial scope and objectivity claims' (Kiss and Shelton 2003: 394–395 and 402–404; see also Boyle 1996; Korsah-Brown 2002: 81; Rajamani 2010). Despite the variability of implementation demands, the right to an environment has been hegemonic in terms of its inclusion in more than 100 national constitutions and has been increasingly applied in national court systems (Boyd 2012: 45–77).

In light of the language used in the Preamble, the NGT, in *M/S Sterlite Industries Ltd v Tamil Nadu Pollution Control Board* (Judgment 8 August 2013), stated:

> Article 21 of the Constitution of India … is interpreted to include in the right to life the right to a clean and decent environment. It is in the form of right to protect the environment, as by protecting environment alone can we provide a decent and clean environment to the citizenry. The most vital necessities, namely air, water and soil having regard to the right to life under Article 21 cannot be permitted to be misused or polluted so as to reduce the quality of life of others. Risk of harm to the environment or to human health is to be decided in public interest.
>
> (Para 113)[4]

The legislative 'recognition of a right' does not necessarily result in its enforcement or practical execution. As stated in Chapter 2, recent studies reveal a grim, realistic picture of India that questions the legally binding right to a wholesome environment. A World Health Organization (WHO) report states that 13 of the top 20 most-polluted cities are in India.[5] Air pollution slashes life expectancy by 3.2 years for the 660 million Indians living in cities, including Delhi. The WHO states that fine particles of less than 2.5 micrometres in diameter (PM2.5) should not exceed 10 micrograms per cubic metre. Delhi had 153 micrograms of PM2.5 per cubic metre. Not far behind are Patna (149 micrograms), Gwalior (144 micrograms) and Raipur (134 micrograms). Other listed Indian cities include Ahmedabad, Lucknow, Kanpur, Firozabad, Amritsar and Ludhiana.

India's water is also at serious risk. An alarming 80 per cent of India's surface water is polluted, according to Wateraid. Domestic and untreated sewerage flowing into water bodies has almost doubled in recent years. This leads to an increase in vector-borne diseases such as cholera, dysentery, jaundice and diarrhoea.[6] Delhi, for instance, uses 4346 million litres of water daily of which 87 per cent returns as waste of which Delhi has the capacity to treat only 61 per cent. The 51 class I cities in Maharashtra together consume three times as much as Delhi, turn 80 per cent into sewage and treat less than half their waste-water. The statistics are far worse for class II cities.[7] This data illustrates that the right to a healthy environment through statutory declaration or judicial action ascribes a value or status to an entitlement, but does not ensure its implementation.

Composition

A remarkable feature of the NGT is its composition of both judicial and expert members which reflects the specialist nature of environmental law and the multidisciplinary issues relating to the environment (see Chapter 2). This multifaceted and multi-skilled body encourages a coherent and effective institutional mechanism to adjudicate complex laws and principles in a consistent manner while simultaneously reshaping the approach to environmental problem-solving rather than being limited to predetermined remedies.[8]

The NGT Act states that the minimum number of full-time judicial and expert members will not be less than 10 with a maximum of 20.[9] The chairperson of the Tribunal is appointed by central government in consultation with the Chief Justice of India.[10] Members are appointed on the recommendation of a selection committee in such manner as prescribed by central government.[11] The judicial members, including the chair, are (or were) judges of the Supreme Court, High Court Chief Justices or High Court judges.[12] The technical experts include persons from life sciences, physical sciences, engineering or technology with 15 years' experience in the relevant field or administrative experience, including five years' practical experience in environmental matters in a reputed national-level institution, or central or state government. Interestingly, there is no room for social scientists with appropriate specialisation or familiarity with environment or occupational risk.[13] The 'administrative experience of 15 years' clause raises significant issues based on the historic field performance of government officers. The mismanagement and frequent failure to enforce relevant legislative norms concerning environmental protection has contributed significantly to the backlog of complaints and current state of environmental indifference. Had enforcement officials proved diligent and effective in their duties, the need for a new procedure and Tribunal might not have been so urgent. The present rigorous qualifications and selection process to the NGT ensures that there is expertise, transparency and accountability in Tribunal membership.

Aggrieved persons and participation

A broad understanding of environmental justice involves participation in environmental controversies. Participatory mechanisms can help meliorate issues of inequality, recognition and the larger question of capabilities and functioning of individuals and communities (Schlosberg 2007: 25–29). 'Parity of participation' comes with the satisfaction of two conditions: 'that institutionalized cultural patterns of interpretation and evaluation express equal respect for all participants and ensure equal opportunity…' and 'the resources to enable participation' (Fraser 2001: 29–30).

Participatory parity in Indian environmental discourse evolves from the concept of broad and liberal litigant 'standing' in environmental matters facilitated by PIL. The proactive Supreme Court acting as '*amicus* environment' through representative and citizen standing has promoted dynamism and capability, thereby providing victims of environmental degradation with a way to access justice in a participatory manner.[14] With the implementation of the NGT Act, 'standing' has been reformulated in terms of an 'aggrieved person' who has access to the Tribunal to seek relief or compensation or settlement of environmental disputes.

According to section 18(2) NGT Act, an application for grant of relief, or compensation or settlement of a dispute may be made to the Tribunal by a person who:

a   has sustained an injury;
b   is the owner of the property to which damage has been caused;
c   is the legal representative in the case of death resulting from environmental damage;
d   is a duly authorised agent;
e   represents a state agency; or
f   is an aggrieved person, including any representative body or organisation.

Section 18(2) NGT Act has wide coverage which also allows any aggrieved person and legal representatives of the various categories to file an application for grant of relief or compensation or settlement of dispute. Participatory parity has been addressed in the NGT by providing an expansive interpretation of the term 'aggrieved person'. The NGT, in *Jan Chetna v Ministry of Environment and Forests* (MoEF) (Judgment 9 February 2012) explained the scope and ambit of the term. The court stated:

…the expression aggrieved person cannot be considered in a restricted manner. A liberal construction and flexible interpretation should be adopted. In environmental matters, the damage is not necessarily confined to the local area where the industry is established. The effects of environmental degradation might have far reaching consequences going beyond the local areas. Therefore, an aggrieved person need not be a resident of the local area. Any person whether he is a resident of that particular area or not, whether aggrieved or not, can approach this Tribunal. In such a situation, it is necessary to review the credentials of the applicants/appellants as to their true intention or motives.

(Paras 21–22)

The liberal approach of the Tribunal is evidenced in the cases of *Amit Maru v MoEF* (Judgment 1 October 2014), *Goa Foundation v Union of India* (Judgment 18 July 2013) and *Vimal Bhai v Ministry of Environment and Forests* (Judgment 14 December 2011). There are two reasons for this approach. The first is the inability of persons living in the vicinity of proposed projects to understand the scientific detail, coupled with the effects of the ultimate project and any disaster it may cause. India continues to live in the countryside.[15] Uneducated and under-educated villagers may be unaware of environmental matters and possible negative consequences, leaving aside statutory obligations such as project clearances or EIAs. In such situations, any individual, persons or body of individuals can challenge proposed projects and the scientific aspects already approved by granting authorities. Thus, there is a citizen's right to approach the Tribunal regardless of whether or not they are directly affected or a resident of affected area. Second, the subservience of the provisions of the NGT Act to the constitutional mandate of Article 51A(g) establishes a fundamental duty of every citizen to protect and improve the natural environment.[16]

The judgment that further expands the already liberal definition of person aggrieved is the case of *Betty C Alvares v State of Goa* (Judgment 14 February 2014). The word 'person' was construed to include 'an individual', whether an Indian national or a person who is not a citizen of India. The proceedings related to an environmental dispute raised by Betty Alvares (not an Indian citizen) and was admitted. The Tribunal held that it is not necessary that an individual has personally suffered any loss on account of damage caused to the environment by acts of illegal construction and encroachment of beaches thereby violating coastal zone regulations. It was sufficient to ascertain whether there was a substantial environmental question and that such a question arose out of the implementation of enactments in Schedule I, appended to the NGT Act. Therefore, the application was allowed because Betty Alvares fell within the definition of 'person' as defined in section 2(1)(j) NGT Act. The court has opened its doors globally to each and every person, including incorporated bodies that consider themselves 'aggrieved' within the jurisdictional boundaries of India subject to the enactments specified within Schedule I.

The person aggrieved does not have to show personal interest, damage or injury. The concept of personal injury is applicable to applicants invoking the jurisdiction of the Tribunal under sections 15 and/or 17, but it is not so under sections 14 and/or 16. It is sufficient that a person states that the environment of the area has been adversely effected, the protection of which, is of his or her interest. The expression 'person aggrieved' is given a wide connotation and any person directly or indirectly affected or even interested is permitted to ventilate grievance in an application or appeal.[17]

Participatory parity also extends to the recognition and consideration of nature and inanimate objects within the NGT's ecological justice mandate. This is an emerging area whereby a nature-centred approach is accepted as a legitimate party. The NGT, in its judgment *Tribunal on its Own Motion v Secretary of State* (Judgment 4 April 2014), recognised this approach by reiterating the Supreme Court judgment in *Centre for Environment Law, WWF-I v Union of India* (IA No 100 in Writ Petition (Civil) No 337 of 1995).

> Anthropocentrism is always human interest focussed thinking that non-human has only instrumental value to humans, in other words, humans take precedence and human responsibilities to non-human are based on benefits to humans. Eco-centrism is nature-centred, where humans are part of nature and non-humans have intrinsic value. In other words, human interest does not take automatic precedence and humans have obligations to non-humans independently of human interest. Eco-centrism is, therefore, life-centred, nature-centred where nature includes both humans and non-humans. *Article 21 of the Constitution of India protects not only the human rights but also casts an obligation on human beings to protect and preserve a species becoming extinct, conservation and protection of environment is an inseparable part of right to life.*
>
> (Paras 32 and 33, original emphasis)[18]

Environmental dispute litigation is not simply adversarial in nature. It is quasi-adversarial, quasi-investigative and quasi-inquisitorial in nature for effective participatory parity and involvement of the person aggrieved.[19] Spot inspections by judicial and expert members of the NGT and appointing expert committees and *amicus curiae* to represent victims are some initiatives that expand the existing procedure of relief, compensation or settlement for participatory involvement. For this, the NGT regulates its own procedure which is guided by the principles of natural justice (PNJ), while exercising its jurisdiction.[20]

In *Forward Foundation v State of Karnataka* (Judgment 10 September 2015), the NGT ordered expert members to visit the site in question to gain an informed interpretation of facts and the actual situation at the site and place their findings before the Tribunal. In *MoEF v Nirma Ltd* (Order of the Supreme Court 4 August 2014), the Supreme Court found nothing wrong with the procedure adopted by the NGT requiring two of its technical members to visit the site and make a report after carrying out a personal inspection.

In *Krishna Kant Singh v National Ganga River Basin Authority* (Judgment 16 October 2014), the NGT examined an application jointly filed by a public-spirited citizen and an NGO with respect to water pollution in the River Ganges due to discharge of highly toxic effluents by the sugar factories and distilleries. The contamination was so high that it not only polluted the canal and the river but also threatened the life of endangered aquatic species. It also polluted village groundwater. The water became harder, oily and greasy and unfit for human consumption. On 24 March 2014, the NGT directed its expert members to visit and inspect the site to assess the adequacy and appropriateness of all anti-pollution measures taken by the industries. Three expert members of the Tribunal visited the site on 29 March 2014 to ensure the expeditious review of the environmental issues.

The case of *Environment Support Group v Union of India* (Judgment 27 August 2014) is illustrative of the appointment of expert committees to understand the nature of environmental problems and issues around them. An application was filed by an environmental organisation against the diversion of a grassland ecosystem known as Amrit Mahal Kaval for non-forest purposes involving proposed industrial, infrastructure and defence development projects. In order to ascertain the ground reality, the Tribunal constituted a fact-finding committee (FFC) of eminent persons to report back to the Tribunal since the parties disagreed regarding the factual position in respect of Amrit Mahal Kaval. The terms of reference for the FFC included a field study and submission of a report focused on the issues including historical information in respect of the ecological nature and demographic features of the landscape, biodiversity of the region, local dependence on the grasslands ecosystem sought to be diverted to non-forest purposes, likely impacts of the proposed projects on human settlements and related issues.

In the *Chemfab Unit* case, the NGT constituted a team of experts to inspect an industrial unit run by Chemfab Alkalis Ltd at Kalapet. The team comprised of representatives from the Central Pollution Control Board, the National Environmental Engineering Research Institute, Nagpur, the MoEF, the member secretary of Puducherry Pollution Control Committee and IIT Delhi.[21]

In both, *Mahalaxmi Bekar v SEIAA, Mumbai* (Order 27 February 2015) and *A Concerned Villager from Nerul Village (Bardez-Goa) v State of Goa* (Order 19 September 2014), the Tribunal appointed a lawyer as *amicus curiae* on behalf of the poor applicants on a pro bono basis.

The availability of 'resources to enable participation' (Fraser 2001: 29–30) promotes participatory parity. The NGT rules provide for an application or appeal where no compensation has been claimed to be accompanied by a fee of Rupees 1000 (£10).[22] Where compensation is claimed the fee is equivalent to 1 per cent of that compensation, subject to a minimum of Rupees 1000 (£10).[23] Thus, the low fees reflect the NGT's open-door commitment to be open to both the poor and the wealthy.

In contrast, the Tribunal has discouraged litigation where persons with vested interests indulge in misusing the judicial process either by force of habit or for improper motives. Litigious petitioners are not entertained and costs are imposed to deter such people from filing frivolous applications. *Rana Sengupta v Union of India* (Judgment 22 March 2013) demonstrates the strict ruling of the NGT concerning applications filed by a person deemed a 'busy body and their motives ulterior'. The applicant, Rana Sengupta, claimed to be a public-spirited citizen working for the welfare of people, particularly those who might otherwise remain unrepresented. Sengupta challenged the EC granted by the respondent, the MoEF, to M/S Rashmi Metaliks, the project proponent, for the expansion of an existing steel plant on the grounds of illegal and improper EIAs and the concealment of information. The MoEF refuted the allegations and contended the report was produced according to law and there was no factual concealment by the project proponents. The ministry challenged the *locus standi* of the appellant on the ground that he was a busy-body and had no experience of working with iron and steel industries. The NGT decided that the appellant had not approached the Tribunal with clean hands and thus could not be called a 'person aggrieved'. There was no tangible evidence to show that the appellant was an expert in the field of iron and steel with knowledge of the impact of these industries on the ecology, environment or local inhabitants. His self-proclaimed 'public-spirited citizenship' was false. There was no record to show that the applicant had participated in a public consultation process or raised any issue regarding environmental or socio-economic adverse impacts. Accordingly, the Tribunal imposed costs of Rupees 15,000 (£150) on the applicant to discourage litigation without proper cause and declared that he was not an aggrieved party.[24]

A review of the above-mentioned judgments reflects the judicial approach of allowing persons aggrieved to initiate proceedings before the NGT in order to 'assert diffused and meta-individual rights' (Sahu 2008: 379). The NGT provides an expansive and inclusive broad-based forum to both human and non-humans to voice their concerns and claims against environmental degradation.

Jurisdiction

The NGT Act is a self-contained code that lays down the forum, procedure, limitation, functions and powers of the Tribunal. The rationale of the legislation is to prevent and protect against environmental pollution and to provide for and make accessible the administration of environmental justice. Accordingly, the NGT has wide original, appellate and special jurisdiction in relation to environmental matters.[25]

Original jurisdiction

The original jurisdiction under section 14 NGT Act empowers the Tribunal to entertain original applications covering civil cases involving substantial environmental questions that arise from enactments specified in Schedule I.[26] In *Sachin v State of Maharashtra* (Judgment 25 March 2014), the Pune NGT refused to examine the question of declaring an area as a reserved sanctuary for the great Indian bustard as it was covered under the Wildlife (Protection) Act 1972 and not a part of the enactments stated in Schedule I appended to the NGT Act.[27] In *Tribunal on its Own Motion v Secretary of State* (Judgment 4 April 2014), the Bhopal NGT acknowledged the Wildlife (Protection) Act 1972 is not listed under Schedule 1 of the NGT Act and therefore the Tribunal had no jurisdiction to adjudicate matters related to wildlife. However, the Tribunal carved out an exception by entertaining the matter relating to movement of tigers and operation of mining activities in close proximity to their wildlife habitats. The Tribunal was of the opinion that wildlife in a particular ecosystem is a part of the 'environment'[28] and any action that causes damage to the wildlife, or that is likely to lead to damage to wildlife, cannot be excluded from the purview of the Tribunal. Therefore, movement of tigers in a particular locality which is proximate to the protected area requires measures to be taken for their protection under the Tribunal's jurisdiction.

Civil cases

The content of an original application should be a civil case. The expression 'all civil cases' is of a pervasive nature and, therefore, cannot be given restrictive meaning.[29] The wording 'civil cases' involves all legal proceedings except criminal cases which are governed by the provisions of the Criminal Procedure Code. In *MP Pollution Control Board v Commissioner Municipal Corporation Bhopal* (Judgment 8 August 2013), the Tribunal observed:

> ...once the legislature restricts the jurisdiction of the Tribunal only to civil cases, then that jurisdiction is incapable of being expanded to the cases which are patently and substantially criminal in nature and are controlled or have been instituted under the provisions of criminal procedure code. This Tribunal is a creation of a statute and thus, its jurisdiction will have to be construed with reference to the language of its provisions.
>
> (Para 7)

In this case the NGT declared its jurisdictional inability to try, adjudicate and punish the accused persons who were defaulters for their failure to manage and dispose of municipal solid waste (MSW) in accordance with the MSW (Management and Handling) Rules 2000.

Substantial question relating to environment

The original jurisdiction covers cases where a substantial question relating to environment is involved. It relates to questions not previously settled and must have a material bearing on the case and its issues relating to the environment. The word 'substantial' implies the real and tangible rather than the imaginary and is a term that does not demand a strictly quantitative or proportional assessment.[30] Section 2(m) NGT Act classifies 'substantial question relating to environment' under two heads: first, where there is a direct violation of a statutory duty or environmental obligation which is likely to affect the community; and, second, where the environmental consequences relate to a specific activity or a point of source. The following case law demonstrates the trend and approach adopted by the Tribunal in its interpretation of the term 'substantial question'.

A Direct violation of a specific statutory environmental obligation

Cases that involve a direct violation of a specific statutory environmental obligation fall into three categories:

1   where the community at large other than an individual or group of individuals is affected or likely to be affected by the environmental consequences; or
2   the gravity of damage to the environment or property is substantial; or
3   the damage to public health is broadly measurable.

1 *Environmental consequences affecting the community at large*

Environmental consequences that affect communities are widespread in India. For example, MSW, one of the major and continuing challenges in India, is illustrative of a 'substantial question of law' where the community is affected as a consequence of violation of a specific environmental obligation. It is estimated that 62 million tonnes of solid waste is generated by 377 million people in urban India annually. Managing waste is a major concern. Delhi produces 10,000 tonnes of waste every day,[31] followed by Mumbai at 7025 tonnes,[32] Bengaluru at 4500[33] and Ahmedabad at 4000.[34]

Massive mounds of noisome MSW sit in the back streets of every city. The Union of India through the MoEF gazetted the MSW Rules 2000, making local city administration responsible for collecting, segregating and scientifically disposing of waste. More than 80 per cent of the waste is disposed of indiscriminately causing serious health and environmental degradation. For disposal of municipal waste, landfills were considered the best options. However, if the current annual 62 million tonnes continues to be dumped without treatment, it will need 340,000 cubic metres of landfill space every day.[35] In many municipalities landfill sites have not been identified and in several they are exhausted.[36] Noise, odour, smoke, dust and wind-blown litter are common on landfill sites. As biological material decomposes, it gives off heat that can cause spontaneous combustion and constitute a fire risk. Poorly maintained landfills attract birds, vermin and insects. They are hazardous to health by contaminating the air, soil and water. Very few urban local bodies have prepared long-term plans for effective solid waste management. The municipal authorities are responsible for managing MSW under the MSW Rules 2000, but are often unable to perform their statutory duties effectively. The official agency, the Central Pollution Control Board, in its report stated 'by and large, hardly we can see any city/town complying with the MSWs (Management and Handling) Rules, 2000 in totality' (2015: 1). MSW treatment issues include the absence of comprehensive short and long-term municipal treatment plans in accordance with the rules. The majority of municipal authorities are unable for financial reasons to set up waste-processing and disposal facilities. Studies from various cities report that inappropriate bin locations, badly designed community bins, poor condition of collection vehicles, inadequate labour for collection and transportation, and lack of waste treatment and disposal facilities are the major reasons for inadequate solid waste management (Rana *et al.* 2015: 1548–1549).

In *Satpal Singh v Municipal Council Gardhiwala* (Judgment 25 April 2013), an application was filed by Satpal Singh and others, the residents of Gardhiwala town, concerning the failure of the municipal council and Punjab Pollution Control Board to implement and monitor the provisions of the MSW Rules 2000 and Punjab Municipality Act 1911, sections 154 and 168. The applicants required the removal of dead animals from open places and that paths and roads in the township be kept clean. The NGT allowed the application and observed that the authorities had committed dereliction in discharging their statutory obligations. The inaction on the part of the authorities adversely affected the health and well-being of residents. The foul smell and the presence of stray dogs in the vicinity caused air pollution and amounted to a public nuisance. The authorities failed to ensure the local community's fundamental right to pollution-free air and pure water. The NGT directed the authorities to take immediate action to shift the dumping ground to a suitable place away from the residential area and file a six-monthly affidavit on progress for the next two years.

The case of *Rayons-Enlightening Humanity v Union of India* (Judgment 18 July 2013) also illustrates the MSW issue. An original application was filed by Rayons-Enlightening Humanity, an NGO, against the operation of an MSW management plant at Rzazu-Paraspur, Bareilly. The applicant opposed the operation of the project as being illegal, not in accordance with EC regulations and based on arbitrary decisions by the municipal authorities. The plant was established in an area very close to residences, educational institutions, hospitals and water bodies, thereby resulting in environmental harm. The major part of the plant was in the open air and its basin pits had not been prepared in compliance with the schedule to the MSW Rules 2000. The NGT allowed the application and observed that:

> The site in which the plant is located, is bound to cause pollution of ground water, which is relatively at a higher level, by leaches. Therefore, the contaminated water is bound to seep into the underground water and affect the adjoining water bodies and irrigation water. The foul smell arising from the dumping at the site is bound to pollute the air quality and affect the health

of the residents in the vicinity of the site ... they would be exposed to diseases like asthma, emphysema or even cancer. Thus, the adverse effects of permitting the plant to carry on its activities at the site in question are bound to cause irretrievable damage to public health and environment.

(Para 47)

In *People for Transparency through Kamal Anand v State of Punjab* (Judgment 25 November 2014), the Principal Bench of the NGT sought to execute the MSW management plan 2014 in the state of Punjab in the larger public interest. The NGT approved the project for the establishment of a solid municipal waste plant. The collection and disposal of MSW was needed within a time-bound programme. The plan should have included the segregation and processing of MSW at the site and what scientific methods were being adopted to ensure proper MSW management in accordance with MSW Rules. The NGT stated that the project must become operational by December 2016 in relation to all phases. The authorities must ensure that there is no pollution, public nuisance nor environmental degradation resulting from the operation of the plant. According to the NGT:

> We do express our concern that in our country there is not even a single city as of now that has the capacity to provide for total scientific methods for collection and disposal of MSW. Such a facility if fully established and made optimally operative, would not only help the public at large but would largely serve the purpose of environmental protection.

(Para 25)

On 2 September 2014, the Supreme Court transferred a writ petition, *Almitra H Patel v Union of India* (WP(C) No 888 of 1996), to the Delhi Bench NGT (*Almitra H Patel v Union of India* Order 15 January 2015). The Supreme Court directed the NGT to deal with the MSW matter expeditiously at the national level and provide adequate measures for proper collection, transportation and disposal of the MSW in accordance with the MSW Rules 2000.

The Supreme Court passed this direction recognising the serious health hazards associated with MSW and causing pollution.

The matter had been pending in the Supreme Court since 1996.[37] It was admitted by the NGT as original application number 199 of 2014. On 20 December 2014 and 20 March 2015, the NGT passed orders directing the states to file comprehensive affidavits on collection, storage and disposal of MSW in their respective states within four weeks. The Tribunal expressed concern that the matter was being unduly delayed due to non-filing of documents by the states. The NGT warned of imposing a cost of Rupees 50,000 (£500) each on the defaulting states, union territories boards and concerned secretaries, which would be recovered personally from the concerned officer in case of any violation of the order. The litigation is ongoing wherein the NGT hopes to replicate the *People for Transparency through Kamal Anand* case (Judgment 25 November

2014) of establishing the MSW plant. The centralised MSW plants can be operationalised more effectively, would be technically and economically viable and in the larger interest of the public and the environment.

Although the NGT is focused on evolving an effective MSW management plan, apathetic and corrupt enforcement procedures blunt its rulings. In reality, the rules are frequently violated. It has been alleged that there exists a well-oiled nexus of 'mafia-type business' between elected representatives and private contractors responsible for collecting waste. Faking bills and falsifying the number of trips and the amount of waste deposited at the dumpsites contribute to significant irregularities and illegalities.[38] Private contractors may be relatives of elected representatives and are unaccountable. For example, the Ahmedabad Municipal Corporation unearthed a garbage scam at the Pirana landfill site where private contractors were dumping mud and stones in place of garbage and claiming payments for the entire false weight deposited in the landfill.[39] Again, news reports state that the Bengaluru Mayor was in trouble in December 2015 after the garbage mafia, invoking his name, threatened residents of an upscale city apartment complex for outsourcing waste collection to a private agency.[40] These instances demonstrate the challenges faced by the NGT in implementing its decisions.

2 Damage to environment or property

This category includes situations where there is substantial damage to the environment or property. In *Rohit Chaudhary v Union of India* (Judgment 7 September 2012), the NGT allowed an application of infringement of law around the area of Kaziranga National Park in the State of Assam. Kaziranga National Park is not only a national park and tiger reserve under the provisions of the Wildlife (Protection) Act 1972, but also a United Nations Educational, Scientific and Cultural Organization (UNESCO) World Heritage Site. Kaziranga National Park is the home of three-quarters of India's rhinos and contains the largest single concentration of endangered species and wild animals, including swamp-deer, wild buffalo, elephants, tigers and gangetic dolphins. It is the only park of its kind with a viable lowland grassland ecosystem in South Asia. The issue before the NGT was the flagrant violation of government of India MoEF notification dated 5 July 1996 under the Environment (Protection) Act 1986. The rules framed thereunder declared no expansion of industrial areas, townships, infrastructural facilities and activities leading to pollution and congestion within any No Development Zone (NDZ) except with the prior approval of the central government. The applicant, Rohit Choudhary, a local resident, approached the NGT to pass directions to the concerned authorities, particularly, the MoEF and state of Assam, to safeguard the eco-sensitive zone of Kaziranga against unregulated quarrying and mining activities permitted in and around the NDZ of Kaziranga National Park. The expansion of stone-crushing units, brick kilns, tea factories and miscellaneous industries (fuel-dispensing stations, a saw mill, an oil tanker-making unit, mustard oil mills, a flour mill, concrete-making units and a restaurant) were established indiscriminately. These anthropogenic activities caused air, water and land pollution thereby endangering forest, gene-pool reserves, vegetation and living creatures. Interestingly, the state government of Assam had previously issued a notification on 19 January 1996 declaring a NDZ in and around Kaziranga National Park. The NGT came to the conclusion that the MoEF and the state government of Assam had failed in their legal duties. In a strongly worded observation, it stated that the callous and indifferent attitude by the authorities and infringement of law had led to the establishment of polluting industries in and around the national park that threatened the biodiversity, eco-sensitive zone, ecology and environment. The Tribunal directed the authorities to close illegal industrial units with immediate effect or shift them outside the NDZ. It also directed the MoEF and government of Assam to deposit Rupees 100,000 (£1000) each for the conservation and restoration of the ecology and environment of Kaziranga National Park.

The case of *Goa Foundation v Union of India* (Judgment 18 July 2013) is another illustration of a 'substantial question relating to environment'. A case was filed by two NGOs: the Goa Foundation and the Peaceful Society, Goa. They sought directions requiring the state government to take steps for the conservation and protection of another World Heritage Site, the Western Ghats, as requested by the high-powered panel, the Western Ghats Ecology Expert Panel (WGEEP). The Western Ghats are a treasure trove of biological diversity and are recognised as a global 'hotspot of biodiversity'. They are considered to be a repository of endemic, rare and endangered flora and fauna. The Ghats are areas of major plantations including tea, coffee, rubber and various spices. The Union of India maintained that the case could not be entertained by the Tribunal. It argued that the NGT lacked jurisdiction to issue directions as the WGEEP report was pending for consideration before the MoEF. Accepting the contention of the NGOs, the Tribunal observed that the authorities were required to maintain and ensure environmental equilibrium. Non-performance of the statutory obligation attracted the jurisdiction of the Tribunal under the NGT Act.

It is argued that the state took a position detrimental to the conservation and protection of the Western Ghats. Instead of opposing the petition on the ground of jurisdictional error, the state should have used it as an opportunity to develop and apply the principle of ecocentrism as opposed to anthropocentrism. Thus, the adoption of an ecocentric approach and a related ecological ethic would have prioritised and encouraged the development and enforcement of species protection law in the discourse of environmental justice, or what some scholars and green environmentalists term 'ecological justice' (Jessup 2012: 65).

In *Forward Foundation v State of Karnataka* (Judgment 7 May 2015), the NGT entertained an application filed by an NGO, the Forward Foundation, interested in protecting the environment and ecology, particularly, in the State of Karnataka. The principal grievance related to commercial projects that were being developed by the respondents without prior EC on the wetlands and catchment areas of the water bodies – the Agara and the Bellandur Lakes. The EIA notification 2006 requires that without grant of EC, no project can commence. This restriction applies not only to operationalisation of the project but also for the purposes of establishment. Construction of a large-sized, mixed-use development project/building complex, including setting up of a special economic zone park, hotels, residential apartments and a mall, covering approximately 80 acres on the valley land immediately abutting the Agara Lake and, more particularly, identified as lying between Agara and Bellandur Lakes, exposed the entire ecosystem to severe threat of environmental degradation and consequential damage.

The NGT admitted the application as the multi-purpose projects caused unfavourable environmental and ecological impact, particularly on the water bodies. The scientific reports and Google satellite images reflected a definite possibility of the environment, ecology, lakes and wetlands being adversely affected. Ecological and environmental implications in terms of land use change, loss of drainage network, alteration in land topography and loss of shoreline, appeared to be the imminent threats faced by the wetland and catchment area in question. The Tribunal observed:

> ...wetlands are amongst the most productive ecosystems on the earth, and provide many important services to human society. However, they are also ecologically sensitive and adaptive systems. 'Free' services provided by wetlands are often taken for granted, but they can easily be lost as wetlands are altered or degraded in a watershed.
>
> (Para 56)

Accordingly, the NGT restrained the respondents from creating any third-party interests or parting with the possession of the property in question or any part thereof, in favour of any person. The plea that construction was nearing completion and huge amounts of the respondents' money, including investments made by various land and other purchasers, was at stake was rejected by the Tribunal. It observed: 'We are not impressed with this contention at all. The respondents have started the construction even prior to the grant of environmental clearance and instigated the public to invest money. They cannot be permitted to take advantage of their own wrong' (para 80).

These judgments reflect the pragmatic discourse of environmental and ecological justice embraced by the NGT by not compromising the ecological impact, especially where resources are non-renewable or where the end result would be irreversible.

3 Broad damage to public health

Public health is defined as a safe, healthy and wholesome environment, free from pollution. The duty of the state is to protect the social collective diffused rights and interests of the public by establishing and adopting quality standards for a healthy existence.[41] Any violation or non-compliance on the part of state authorities that amounts to degradation of the environment having adverse impacts on public health amounts to a 'substantial question relating to environment'. Pollution cases are covered under this category.

The case of *Supreme Court Group Housing Society through its Secretary v All India Panchayat Parishad* (Judgment 18 December 2012) illustrates the 'damage to public health' aspect. The main issue was the ineffective implementation of the Noise Pollution (Regulation and Control) Rules 2000. It is the obligation of the state and the state pollution control boards to enforce these provisions and ensure a clean and decent environment. Rules 4 and 8 state that it is the responsibility of the authorities to enforce noise pollution control measures and prohibit continuance of music sound-systems or noise. The use of loudspeakers, music and public-address systems during weddings, receptions and parties until late at night, without obtaining prior permission from concerned authorities, was disturbing to local residents. It was argued that noise pollution affected the health and limited the sleep of residents, particularly infants and the aged. It not only caused annoyance but also led to significant adverse health consequences including raised blood pressure, hearing impairment and neurological disorders. Children are most susceptible to noise pollution which may impair the development of their mental capacity. The NGT decided that the Noise Pollution (Regulation and Control) Rules 2000 were observed more in breach than compliance. The Tribunal stated:

> The effect of noise on health is a matter which has not yet received the full attention which it deserves. Noise can be regarded as a pollutant because it contaminates environment with high decibel noise intensity, causes nuisance and affects the health of a person and would therefore offend Article 21 of the Constitution if it exceeds a reasonable limit.
>
> (Para 6)

Keeping public health in mind, the Tribunal directed the authorities, especially the sub-divisional magistrate and local police, to ensure that the Noise Pollution Rules 2000 are strictly observed, failure in respect of which should be considered a serious violation of law justifying action against the officer, including disciplinary action. The Tribunal also required a strategy and suggested an action plan involving various departments to mitigate noise pollution problems in the city. These included: establishing and running a 24/7 call centre for citizen complaints; the requirement for complaints to be attended by the police and a sub-divisional magistrate within 24 hours; and providing adequate noise meters to all police stations to enable them to check noise levels emanating from various sources. There should also be periodical surveys in different parts of Delhi, especially in sensitive areas – such as hospitals, educational institutions, courts and those located close to heavy traffic intersections – and educational and noise pollution awareness programmes should be established.[42]

The NGT judgment is well intentioned and policy-oriented, but ground-level reality reveals considerable shortcomings and continuing challenges. Scientific evidence shows that noise pollution is gripping Delhi and triggering presbycusis (age-related hearing loss) at the age of 60. This normally sets in after the age of 75. The rules and orders remain on paper. The quintessential Delhi-ites' spirit is loud and unaware of the health hazards associated with noise. Put simply, Indians are socially active and collectively noisy! (Chandra 2013; Lalchandani 2013; Nandi 2013).

In *D B Nevatia v State of Maharashtra* (Judgment 9 January 2013), the Tribunal expressed concern over vehicular noise caused by unrestricted use of sirens and multi-tone horns with unspecified standards, including by ambulances and government and police vehicles. The noise pollution has an adverse impact on the health and well-being of the public. Noise has both auditory and non-auditory effects depending upon its intensity and duration. Accordingly, the Tribunal directed both the federal and state government authorities to take corrective steps. The federal government, namely the Ministry of Road Transport and Highways, Government of India, was directed to provide source-specific standards for sirens and multi-tone vehicles within a period of three months from the date of the order for compliance with the ambient air quality standards under the Noise Pollution (Regulation and Control Rules) 2000. The State of Maharashtra's Transport Department and Pollution Control Board was required to take steps to enforce these standards within one month of the date of notification from the Ministry of Road Transport and Highways.

Administrative delay is one of the biggest challenges facing India's environmental governance, causing frustration and inaction, thereby jeopardising environmental justice. Ironically, while the NGT wanted the pollution regulators to frame guidelines for sirens and multi-tone horns at the earliest opportunity, the pollution regulators failed to respond within the stated timescale. Instead, they delayed their first meeting for a year. The meeting finally took place on 14 January 2014. However, directives were issued in June 2014 in which the state government ordered ambulances, police vans and other vehicles operating during an emergency not to use sirens or multi-tone horns between 10 p.m. and 6 a.m., barring exceptional circumstances. The directives further stated that the sound level of the sirens should be as per the stipulated standards and, in case of any violation, the administration should take action including the removal of the siren.[43]

Finally, the Principal Bench of the NGT, in *Indian Spinal Injuries Hospital v Union of India* (Judgment 27 January 2016), expressed concern over the government's failure to establish environmental norms on noise pollution in residential areas near airports. The application was filed by residents of Vasant Kunj, Bijwasan and the Indian Spinal Injuries Centre (ISIC), a super-speciality hospital located near the Indira Gandhi International (IGI) Airport. The applicants alleged that the noise created by aircraft at the airport affected the health of local residents. The ISIC argued that aeroplane noise was usually between 75 and 94 decibels and exceeded the standards laid down under the Noise Pollution (Regulation and Control) Rules 2000. As a result of engine thrust patients suffered unacceptable noise pollution, routine lack of sleep, and doctors performing surgery complained of distraction.

The air pollution problem in India's capital Delhi is a threat to the city's inhabitants as well as the flora and fauna of the city. It was named as the most-polluted city in the world by the WHO in 2014.[44] Various studies have reported that weather, energy-consumption culture, the growing urban population, increased use of vehicles and industrial production combine to elevate concentrations of air pollutants, including ultra-fine particles that are harmful to health. A study on air pollution in Delhi by researchers led by the University of Surrey states 'the truth is that Delhi is a toxic pollutant punchbowl with myriad ingredients, all of which need addressing in the round'.[45] A report by the Centre for Science and Environment, titled 'Body Burden 2015: State of India's Health' claims air pollution is responsible for 10,000 to 30,000 deaths annually in Delhi and is the fifth leading cause of death in India.[46] 'A four city Breathe Blue 15' conducted between 31 March and 30 April 2015 revealed that 40 per cent of children between 8 and 14 years of age in Delhi have weak lungs; 21 per cent have poor lung capacity; and 19 per cent show lung capacity that can be termed bad.[47]

In 2014, a young lawyer and environmentalist, Vardhman Kaushik, filed a petition (*Vardhman Kaushik v Union of India* Application 21 of 2014) before the Principal Bench of the NGT with a limited pleading to identify and curb the sources of rising air pollution in the NCT of Delhi. The petition has escalated into one of the most important NGT cases. Taking serious note of the air pollution problem, the Principal Bench admitted the petition under section 14 NGT Act as it involved a 'substantial question relating to environment' affecting public health. The litigation is presently ongoing with important directions emerging. The NGT has adopted a 'consultative approach'[48] and provides leverage for deliberations with the stakeholders and authorities responsible for resolving an issue of such wide magnitude and/or of greatest public welfare that is seriously affecting the environment.[49]

In its order dated 26 November 2014, the Tribunal stated that the mere consideration of the air pollution problem at different levels would not resolve the issue. It is a constitutional and statutory duty of all authorities and ministries to provide clean air. It is a fundamental right and it cannot be subjected to limitation by the state and should not be lost sight of in the realm of planning and anticipated actions. According to the NGT, dust, burning of plastic and other materials, including leaves, in the open and vehicular pollution are three major carcinogenic contributors to air pollution. These three sources introduce high particulate matters, hydrocarbon, oxides of sulphur and nitrogen, benzene and ozone into the air, thereby causing health hazards. The Tribunal decided preventive and restorative directions need to be passed to ensure attainment of improved ambient air quality in NCT Delhi. Individual rights must be conceded in favour of public rights.

Justice Swatanter Kumar, the NGT Chairperson, was critical of ministries and Delhi government departments involved in addressing the problem: 'Government officials sit in air-conditioned offices and do not realise the problems faced by the common man on the roads. Those with respiratory disorders are suffering, new cases are emerging each year and a whole generation of children is being destroyed.'[50]

On 26 and 28 November 2014, the NGT issued an action plan to the Delhi and Central government to clear the toxic air. The action plan included:

- banning 15-year-old vehicles or older (diesel and petrol);
- banning the burning of plastic or any other material in the open, including leaves;
- banning polluting trucks entering Delhi (diesel vehicles);
- avoiding congestion on the roads by restricting parking by banning it on footpaths and allowing it only on one side of roads;
- reducing dust from construction sites;
- implementing a dust-management plan;
- installing air-purifiers at market places;
- banning loading vehicles in busy places;
- checking Delhi transport buses for emissions beyond prescribed limits; and
- installing weighbridges on six entries into Delhi.

In furtherance of its earlier directions, the NGT, in its order of 19 January 2015, analysed the site-monitoring location report with regard to ambient air quality in NCT Delhi submitted by the regulatory authorities. The NGT expressed deep concern over the deteriorating air quality and observed:

> The prescribed parameters are found to be much in excess to the National Ambient Air Quality Standards. For instance, Nitrogen Dioxide (NO_2) which is expected to be 80 microgram per cubic meter is found to be 146 and even 218 ug/m3 at Delhi. The particulate matters as against the permissible limit of PM10 ug/m3 is found to be 484. Similarly the particulate matter, sized less than and equal to 2.5 (PM2.5), is excessively volatile in Delhi and is going to the extent of 1284 as against 60 ug/m3. Ozone (O_3) in Delhi against is found to be 223 ug/m3. Carbon monoxide against permissible limit of 2 mg/m3 is found to be 7.81 at Delhi. From the above data, it is clear that ambient air quality in Delhi NCR is highly polluted. Obviously it is dangerous to human health and environment. These statistics clearly show that drastic measures need to be taken, if the residents of NCR Delhi are to be protected against health hazards arising from air pollution. We direct that all the directions issued by the Tribunal, particularly in relation to the vehicular pollution shall be carried out by all the concerned agencies without delay and default.
>
> (*Vardhman Kaushik v Union of India*, para 3)

On 7 April 2015 the NGT again expressed its frustration that, with increasing air pollutants, Delhi is becoming more and more vulnerable to various diseases and the greatest sufferers from these pollutants are young children. The casual attitude of the authorities of the state government is exhibited by the fact that air pollution has reached an alarming level. There is no concerted effort on the government's part to deal with the problem nor to implement the earlier directions. The NGT also observed that no checks on the emission of dust resulting from construction and allied activities were being carried out by the responsible agencies and there was blatant violation of the earlier order to take preventive steps where such activities were being carried out. The NGT also expressed grave concern over the increase of diesel vehicles:

> ...it is reported further that as many as 80,000 trucks enter Delhi every night and sleeping population is compelled to inhale high particulate matters resulting in serious health hazards as diesel fuel can damage the lungs, brain and even cause cancer. It has been pointed out that diesel is the prime source for bringing serious air pollution in Delhi particularly and children are even finding it difficult to breathe. The situation is so alarming that medically it is being advised that for recovery, people should leave Delhi.
>
> (Ibid.: para 3)

Further directions in the wider interest of the public and improving public health were passed by the NGT on 13 April 2015. These included: a cap on the number of vehicles to be registered in NCT Delhi, with reference to sources of energy/fuel; incentives to be provided to members of the public who adopt pool commuting/travel; benefits or concessions that can be provided to the transferor/transferee of prohibited vehicles; concession/benefits available to persons scrapping vehicles as a result of any or all of the restrictions in terms or orders of the Tribunal. Additionally, public transport vehicles should be given priority at all the locations with high levels of commercial activity, markets or industrial areas; and an imposition of a higher registration fee and other charges, including congestion charges, particularly in relation to the families who own more than one vehicle.

A review of the above-mentioned orders reflects that the NGT has passed diverse directions to prevent and control pollution and improve Delhi's air quality. Unfortunately, their implementation remains a major cause for concern. Table 3.1 shows the implementation status of the NGT's directions issued[51] in November 2014 to tackle air pollution:

Implementing the Tribunal's orders and combating Delhi's toxic air needs strong political will to take bold decisions and make changes at the micro-level. The deteriorating air quality necessitates that stringent measures are taken and directions implemented expeditiously by regulatory authorities. The Delhi government has proposed some measures to clean the toxic air. It introduced the odd–even car policy scheme from 1–15 January 2016 and 15–30 April 2016 on a trial basis, to restrict the number of vehicles on the road. For the first phase in January 2016, overall the odd–even rule was a success in terms of reducing congestion and traffic, but there is no definitive evidence on whether pollution levels reduced during the period.[52] The data was not recorded properly and

Table 3.1 Implementation status of NGT directions

Direction	Status
Banning 15-year-old vehicles or older	Stayed by Supreme Court
Banning the burning plastic or any other material in the open, including leaves	Partially implemented
Banning polluting trucks entering Delhi	Partially implemented
Banning parking on footpaths and allowing it only on one side of roads	Not implemented
Reducing dust from construction sites	Not implemented
Implementing a dust management plan	Not implemented
Installing air-purifiers at market places	Not implemented
Banning loading of vehicles in busy places	Implemented
Checking Delhi transport buses for emissions beyond prescribed limits	Inspection carried out but NGT dissatisfied with the report. Report to be filed again.
Installing weighbridges on six entries into Delhi	Under consideration

Source: compiled by the author from the articles in n. 51.

hence disputed. The initial reports indicated that the second phase was a failure. A relatively low compliance rate, large numbers of people opting for alternatives such as second car (old or new), fake clear natural gas stickers, disputed and scarce data, and meteorological factors have all contributed towards the unsuccessful implementation of the experiment.[53]

Augmentation of public transport by adding 10,000 more buses was another proposal adopted by the Delhi government. The proposal came under criticism from the NGT which questioned the rationale behind it. Delhi has one of the highest road densities in the world at 21.19 km of road per square km of area. The total road length is around 30,000 km. In its order dated 7 August 2015, the Tribunal observed:

> Delhi is adding 1,000 cars every day. It takes 1 hour to travel 10 kms today. If you introduce buses simultaneously what would be the status of roads? Will you be able to move an inch? Have you thought about this? Encourage public transport but what is your scheme on this? Why do you expect every court to pass orders for any work to get it done? When we pass orders we are accused of judicial activism. For the last two months you have not given clear answers. We are trying to find out ways and means to curb pollution.[54]

The federal government (MoEF) has also pledged to help clear the toxic air. The former Minister of Environment, Forest and Climate Change, Prakash Javadekar stated: 'the truth is Delhi's air quality is bad. The government is not in denial. It accepts the problem as it is. We are committed to cleaning city's air and we seek everyone's cooperation'.[55] Prime Minister Modi on 6 April 2015 launched the Air Quality Index[56] and joined a global league of nations which includes the USA, France, China and Mexico that have implemented such an alert system. The system gives details of air quality and information on its likely health implications for city-dwellers. Further, the Minister of Environment, Forest and Climate Change on 10 February 2016 announced that the government plans to introduce euro-VI standards emissions, vehicles and fuel norms by 2020.[57]

The present attempts to curb air pollution are well intentioned but need vigorous commitment going beyond the orders of the NGT. A wider set of restrictions by road-mapping, short and long-term strategies at structural, regulatory and behavioural levels need to be in place. Measures that could act as catalysts for purer air include: encouraging efficient and robust public transport and renewable transportation (incentives for scrapping old vehicles and buying electric ones and generation of bio-fuel); leapfrogging euro-VI emission norms; making diesel less attractive by higher tolls and road tax and removing the price difference between petrol and diesel; increasing charges (registration, congestion, parking); demarcating parking zones; and public awareness (CSE *Annual Reports* 1999–2015).

Environmental assaults on people's health are identifiable and most are measurable. A review of the above-mentioned judgments reflects the judicial approach of supporting health promotion, protecting individuals and populations from hazards, and overall health improvement for present and future generations.

B Specific activity or point of source of pollution

The second heading of a substantial question relating to environment identifies the environmental consequences relating to specific activity or a point of source of pollution.[58] In *Vijay G Vaidya v Union of India* (Judgment 21 October 2014), the NGT allowed an application where air pollution was caused by coal depots handling large quantities of coal in an unscientific and improper manner and adversely impacting on school children nearby. The storage and handling activities produced higher levels of ambient dust and small-particle concentration than prescribed norms. The NGT directed the state pollution control board to adopt precautionary measures for these uncontrolled coal-transportation activities. These included the spraying of water and the creation of rubber-clad buffer walls of sufficient height to stop dust from coal-handling activities reaching school premises.[59]

In *P Chandrakumar v Chairman Tamil Nadu Pollution Control Board* (Judgment 20 March 2014), the NGT allowed an application filed by a farmer alleging groundwater pollution caused by 15 to 20 dyeing factories. These operated without proper treatment plants and discharged untreated, coloured trade effluent into the canal and onto vacant land located within the dyeing units. Due to seepage and percolation, the untreated effluent polluted underground and surface water and the quality of the applicant's well-water. The NGT ordered the state pollution control board to take necessary action against the units and close any units not complying with the directions.

In *Neel Choudhary v State of Madhya Pradesh* (Judgment 6 May 2014), the NGT admitted an application regarding problems with the running of marriage gardens, function halls and similar venues for holding parties in and around the city of Bhopal, resulting in environmental pollution, in particular around Bhopal's lakes into which the owners or management of these premises discharged untreated solid waste and sewerage. Further, the use of generator sets for electrification and decoration within the premises and road traffic congestion due to inadequate parking space resulted in traffic jams and consequential noise and air pollution. The NGT ordered the closure of 24 marriage gardens for causing environmental degradation.[60]

Disputes and cause of action

The Tribunal hears and settles disputes arising from a substantial environmental question covered under scheduled enactments of the NGT Act.[61] The NGT is mandated to pass orders, decisions or awards in conformity with sustainable development, precautionary and polluter-pays principles, while deciding a substantial environmental question.[62] In *Manoj Misra v Union of India* (Judgment 13 January 2015), the NGT observed:

> these principles are the very foundation of the determinative process before the Tribunal. In fact, all three principles i.e. the Precautionary Principle, the Polluter-Pays Principle and the Principle of Sustainable Development have to be collectively applied for proper dispensation of environmental justice.
>
> (Para 68)

Section 14(3) mandates that no application for adjudication of disputes under section 14(1) shall be entertained by the Tribunal unless made within six months from the date on which the cause of action for such a dispute first arose. However, the Tribunal for sufficient cause can condone a delay in making the application for a period not exceeding 60 days. The expression 'sufficient cause' is sufficiently flexible to include attendant circumstances and other factors to be taken into consideration by the Tribunal while dealing with the question of condonation of delay.[63]

The phrase 'cause of action' involves all facts that give rise to an enforceable claim. In *Forward Foundation v State of Karnataka* (Judgment 7 May 2015), the NGT stated:

> Under the provisions of the NGT Act cause of action should essentially have nexus with the matters relating to environment. If such [a] dispute leading to cause of action is alien to the question of environment or does not raise a substantial question relating of environment, it would be incapable of triggering prescribed period of limitation under the NGT Act, 2010. A cause of action which is complete in all respects gives the applicant a right to sue. An applicant has a right to bring an action upon a single cause of action while claiming different reliefs. Rule 14 of the National Green

Tribunal (Practice and Procedure) Rules, 2011, shows the clear intent of the framers of the Rules that multiple reliefs can be claimed in an application provided they are consequential to one another and are based upon a single cause of action.

The multiple cause of action again would be of two kinds. One that arises simultaneously and the other arise at a different or successive point of time. In the first kind, cause of action accrues at the time of completion of the wrong or injury. In the latter, it may give rise to cause of action or if the statutes so provide when the cause of action first arose even if the wrong was repeated. Where the injury or wrong is completing at different times and may be have similar and different nature, then every subsequent wrong depending upon the facts of the case may give rise to a fresh cause of action.

(Paras 24 and 29)[64]

In summary, the NGT's willingness to locate key statutory terms such as 'environment', 'substantial question' and 'person aggrieved' within the wide social and economic context has expanded the jurisdictional reach of the Tribunal. However, the 'environment-plus cases', as Sanjay Upadhyay states, remains a grey area. For instance, if a Coastal Regulation Zone (CRZ) violation is filed, it may also involve town-planning or special economic zone regulations. Similarly, forest cases would invariably involve wildlife.[65] A further delineation in the environment-plus cases would be helpful in redefining the parameters of the original jurisdiction.

Thus, the Tribunal interprets serious and complex environmental harms not as individual-centric but socio-centric, thereby acknowledging the larger interest of society, public health and protection and preservation of the environment for posterity. Importantly, it requires public authorities to address the huge environmental problems facing India and is taking a determined stand by ordering them to abandon their denial mode and move to an acceptance-of-solution mode.

Appellate jurisdiction

Section 16 NGT Act entitles a person aggrieved to file an appeal before the Tribunal.[66] 'Appeal' is defined as the transference of a case from an inferior to a higher court or tribunal in the hope of reversing or modifying the decision of the former.[67] An appeal is a creation of a statute and it cannot be created by acquiescence of the parties or by order of the court.[68] If the statute does not provide an appeal against a specific order, no appeal can be entertained. In M/S *Ahuja Plastics v State of Himachal Pradesh* (Judgment 13 January 2015), the NGT refused to entertain an appeal under the Mines and Minerals (Development and Regulation) Act 1957 and the Mineral Concession Rules 1960 as it was not part of Schedule I NGT Act.[69] The appellate jurisdiction of the NGT can only be invoked provided the appellant has exhausted all appeal forums in the Act under which the order was passed. *M/S P Manokaran Power Loom v Tamil Nadu Pollution Control Board* (Judgment 15 February 2012) illustrates this point. An order was passed by the pollution control board against M/S P Manokaran Power Loom, the appellant, under section 31A Air (Prevention and Control of Pollution) Act 1981 for the closure of the unit and stoppage of electricity for certain violations under the said Act. The appellant approached the NGT under section 16 NGT Act without first approaching the Appellate Authority under section 31A Air Act 1981. The NGT refused to entertain the appeal as it amounted to allowing the appellant to jump the statutory appeal requirement.[70]

EC is an important area attracting appellate jurisdiction under the NGT Act. EC regulations are set rules governing the procedure of the grant or rejection of EC to projects and activities enumerated therein. It is designed to dispense justice to local affected persons, the public at large and the project proponent, keeping in mind material environmental concerns. Screening, scoping, public consultation and appraisal are the four material stages for the grant of EC. However, incentivising development imperatives at the cost of some dilution of the processes has increased judicial intervention. The following cases illustrate this point.

In *Prafulla Samantray v Union of India* (Judgment 30 March 2012) (the POSCO case), the issue before the NGT was opposition to the proposed POSCO project, involving the construction of an integrated steel plant with a service sea-port at Paradip in the Jagatsinhpur district of the state of Orissa. The government of Orissa agreed to facilitate the project and assist the POSCO multinational steel company, based in South Korea, to obtain a no objection certificate and EC in the minimum time. The POSCO port was to be located at the mouth of an estuary, one of the most dynamic and fragile coastal ecosystems. In order to create a channel for ships to enter, POSCO intended to dump sand at the mouth of the Jatadharmohan creek and demolish a sand-spit. To build the port, it also planned to level sand dunes protecting the coast from storm surges. Each one of these drastic activities is prohibited as the area enjoys the highest protection under the CRZ Notification.[71] The construction of the proposed plant and port threatened the area's unique biodiversity and anticipated dislocation and displacement of the long-standing forest-dwelling communities.

The appellant, a social and environmental activist, challenged the project regarding the way appraisal was undertaken – starting from preparation of the EIA report, through conduct of the public hearing to the examination by the MoEF EAC. The appellant alleged that the MoEF had not only failed to consider the environmental and social implications of the proposed project but also not completed its statutory process for EC. Instead, it had incorrectly relied on misleading assurances from POSCO. The MoEF and POSCO denied the appellant's allegations and contended that the prescribed procedure was followed in both letter and spirit.

The NGT allowed the matter and observed:

> we have kept in mind the need for industrial development, employment opportunities created by such projects that involve huge foreign investment,

but at the same time we are conscious that any development should be within the parameters of environmental and ecological concerns and satisfying the principles of sustainable development and precautionary measures. A close scrutiny of the entire scheme revealed that a project of this magnitude particularly in partnership with a foreign country has been dealt with casually, without there being any comprehensive scientific data regarding the possible environmental impacts. No meticulous scientific study was made on each and every aspect of the matter leaving lingering and threatening environmental and ecological doubts unanswered.

(POSCO case: para 7)

Accordingly, the NGT suspended the approval granted to POSCO and directed the MoEF to conduct a fresh review. Factors should include the siting of the project, present pollution levels, impact on surrounding wetlands and mangroves and their biodiversity, risk assessment with respect to the proposed port project, impact of source of water requirements under competing scenarios, and evaluation of the zero discharge proposal. The Tribunal required a comprehensive and integrated EIA based on at least one full year of baseline data, especially considering the magnitude of the project and its likely impact on various environmental attributes in the ecologically sensitive area. The initial clearance was set aside as 'arbitrary and illegal' and 'vitiated in the eyes of law'.[72]

The Tribunal's verdict was welcomed especially as P Chidambaram, the former Minister of Finance, and Manmohan Singh, the former Prime Minister, were known to have encouraged A Raja, the former Minister of Environment and Forests, to fast-track necessary clearances for POSCO. In fact, on 15 May 2007, his second-last day as minister, Raja had granted environmental approval for the POSCO port.[73] Ironically, the Tribunal's decision came within a week of the former Prime Minister Manmohan Singh's assurance in Seoul regarding the progress of the troubled project: 'I recognize that sometimes our processes can be slow but there are effective mechanisms for resolution of problems and differences and a strong rule of law. The government is keen to move forward with the POSCO project.'[74] POSCO was the largest direct foreign investment in India wherein state machinery and influential political power were used hastily and improperly to grant clearances.

In *K L Gera v State of Haryana* (Judgment 25 August 2015), the NGT quashed the EC granted to a speciality hospital on the ground that the project proponent did not take into consideration the impact of the existing project on the environment and ecology. The measures to handle and dispose of different kinds of waste (bio-medical, hazardous and MSW), prevention and control of water and air pollution, and instituting a cumulative impact assessment study to provide data analysis and reports were ignored by the project proponent. According to the NGT, the order granting EC by the regulatory authorities, namely the State Environment Impact Assessment Authority and State Environment Assessment Committee, was a mere formality. The EC order was 'arbitrary, without application of mind, contrary to law … authorities have not only acted with undue haste, but, in fact, their entire approach was casual and they having abrogated their entire functions…' (para 59).

In *Jan Chetna v MoEF*, the NGT allowed an appeal against the MoEF for the grant of EC for expansion of a steel and power plant without following the mandatory requirement of a public hearing. A public hearing in environmental projects is not just a procedural formality but is meant to ensure that the decision is based on proper assessment, evaluation of the pros and cons including the cost and benefits in general, and takes into account the needs and living conditions of locals. In a sweeping judgment, the Tribunal identified a public hearing as a *sine qua non* for not only environmental matters but also in accordance with good governance based on transparency and accountability.

The above-mentioned case law suggests that the granting of EC requires proper and independent application of mind. It involves the evaluation of all relevant material in order to establish whether an EC grant is merited.

The appellate jurisdiction also covers the legality and correctness of the orders passed by the regulatory authorities on grounds of natural justice. Despite the fact that PNJ do not have statutory force, adherence to them is fundamental when evaluating compliance with statutory rules. Violation of PNJ has the effect of vitiating the action, be it administrative or quasi-judicial, in so far as it affects the rights of a third party. Flexibility in the process of natural justice is an inbuilt feature of this doctrine. Three principles – *audi alteram partem* (right to be heard), *nemo judex in re sua* (rule against bias) and *speaking orders* (reasoned decision) – are deeply and indelibly ingrained to ensure law is applied impartially, objectively and fairly by statutory regulatory authorities.[75]

In *Rajasthan Rajya Vidyut Utpadan Nigam Ltd Jaipur v Cess Appellate Committee* (Judgment 20 August 2015), the appellant challenged the order of the Cess Appellate Committee constituted under section 13 Water (Prevention and Control of Pollution) Cess Act 1977 of not providing a hearing before passing the assessment order holding the appellant liable for payment of the cess. The Tribunal allowed the appeal and stated that the PNJ have to be complied with by the authority assigned to take the decision even in quasi-judicial matters.

In *P S Vajiravel v Chairman Tamil Nadu Pollution Control Board* (Judgment 26 March 2015), an appeal was filed by the appellant against the closure order issued to the respondent. The appellant obtained consent to operate a dyeing unit under the Air (Prevention and Control of Pollution) Act 1981 and Water (Prevention and Control of Pollution) Act 1974. The consent was renewed periodically. However, a closure order was passed against the appellant on 28 October 2012 without an enquiry. The respondent alleged that a number of deficiencies in prevention and control measures in respect of pollution were found during inspection. The NGT set aside the closure order on the ground of violation of PNJ. The appellant was not served with a show cause notice nor given adequate opportunity to make a representation of his case. The appeal was allowed by the Tribunal.

In *M/S Om Shakthi Engineering Works v Chairman Tamil Nadu Pollution Control Board* Judgment 10 April 2012, the pollution board ordered the closure of the appellant's engineering workshop on the ground of noise pollution under the Environment (Protection) Act 1986 and Air (Prevention and Control of Pollution) Act 1981. The pollution board directed the electricity authority to disconnect the supply. The appellant was not served with notice nor offered a hearing by the board. The NGT cancelled the closure order and restored the electricity supply as the pollution board had violated the PNJ with arbitrariness and unreasonableness.

Thus, compliance with the PNJ is mandatory when a regulatory authority embarks upon determination of a dispute between parties or when an administrative action involving civil consequences is in issue. The rules are flexible and cannot be contained within a cast-iron formula.

Period of limitation for filing an appeal

Section 16 NGT Act provides that an appeal may be preferred to the Tribunal within 30 days from the date of the impugned order, decision or direction is communicated to the aggrieved person. If the appeal is presented beyond the 30-day period it becomes obligatory upon the applicant to show sufficient cause explaining the delay. Where there is sufficient cause, the Tribunal may allow a further period not exceeding 60 days.

A reading of section 16 indicates three significant expressions:

1 every appeal has to be filed within 30 days from the date on which the order or decision or direction or determination is *communicated to him*;
2 if the Tribunal is satisfied that the appellant was prevented *by sufficient cause* from filing the appeal within the said period; and
3 allow it to file an appeal within a further period *not exceeding 60 days* (emphasis added).

1 Communication

The act of communication requires participation by two persons, one who initiates communication and the other to whom the communication is addressed and who receives it, i.e. the intended receiver. It requires sufficient knowledge of the basic facts constituting the communication. The action of communicating is specifically the sharing of knowledge of the thing communicated one with another. Communication, particularly to the public, has to be by methods of mass communication, like satellites, websites, newspapers and other modes. In *Save Mon Region Federation v Union of India* (Judgment 14 March 2013), the NGT explained the scope of 'communicated to him' as:

It is expected that the order which a person intends to challenge is communicated to him, if not *in personam* then *in rem* by placing it in the public domain. 'Communication' would, thus, contemplate complete knowledge of the ingredients and grounds required under law for enabling that person to challenge the order. 'Intimation' must not be understood to be communication. 'Communication' is an expression of definite connotation and meaning and it requires the authority passing the order to put the same in the public domain by using proper means of communication. Such communication will be complete when the order is received by him in one form or the other to enable him to appropriately challenge the correctness of the order passed.

(Para 17)

The phrase 'communicated to him' is important in appeals relating to orders made after the commencement of the NGT Act granting ECs to industries, operations or processes under section 16(h).[76] Such an appeal has to be preferred within the 30-day period from the date on which the order is communicated to the aggrieved person. There is no provision in the NGT Act which explains how and when the order would be treated as communicated to any aggrieved person. For the purpose of computation of limitation, the NGT has read the provision of section 16(h) in conjunction with para 10 of the EIA Notification 2006. Paragraph 10 places different obligations on stakeholders, namely, project proponents as well as the MoEF or State Environment Impact Assessment Authority. Paragraph 10 contemplates that an order granting EC should be in the public domain and easily accessible and known to the public at large because any person who feels aggrieved has a right to prefer an appeal under section 16, irrespective of whether that person has suffered any personal injury or not. The day the MoEF uploads the complete EC order to its website, and the same can be downloaded without any hindrance, and has also put it on its public notice board, the limitation is reckoned from that date. The limitation may also trigger from the date when the project proponent uploads the EC order with its environmental conditions and safeguards upon its website to be downloaded easily, as well as publishing it in the newspapers. The limitation could also commence when the EC order is displayed by local bodies, panchayats and municipal bodies along with the state government departments concerned displaying the order in the manner indicated. Of the three points from which the limitation commences and is computed, the earliest point in time is the relevant date, determined with reference to the facts of each case.[77]

In *Save Mon Region Federation v Union of India*, the appellant, consisting of citizens of Monpa indigenous community, challenged the legality of the EC made by the MoEF for the construction of the 780-megawatt Naymjang Chhu Hydroelectric Project in Tawang district of Arunachal Pradesh. The appeal was time-barred as it was filed beyond 30 days from the date of communication of the order to the appellant. The appellant prayed for the condonation of delay on the ground that the order was not communicated to him as per the law. The MoEF granted the EC on 19 April 2012 and uploaded the order to its website on 22 May 2012. However, there were errors in the synchronisation of old and new websites. The order could only be downloaded by the appellant from the

MoEF website on 8 June 2012, the date on which the appellant claimed completion of communication. The NGT condoned the delay and directed the appeal to be heard on merit. The Tribunal observed:

> Either the [MoEF] or the State Authority, as the case may be, is obliged to place the Environmental Clearance in public domain on Government portal. The expression 'public domain' will mean anything which is accessible to the public at large and anyone can access that information without any restriction ... The [MoEF] is also to ensure that its order of Environmental Clearance is brought to the notice of the concerned persons as well as to the general public. The regulation clearly provides that the [MoEF] must upload the order on its website. Once it is so provided then it must be complied with in a manner which is flawless and free from ambiguity and uncertainty.

> (Paras 47–48)

2 Sufficient cause

The Tribunal may allow the appellant to institute an appeal after 30 days provided it is satisfied the appellant was prevented by sufficient cause from filing an appeal. The expression 'sufficient cause' implies the presence of legal and adequate reasons. The sufficient cause should persuade the court, in exercise of its judicial discretion, to treat the delay as excusable. These provisions give courts enough power and discretion to apply a law in a meaningful manner, while assuring that the purpose of enacting such a law does not stand frustrated.

In *Nikunj Developers v M/S Veena Developers* (Judgment 14 March 2013), the Tribunal stated:

> ...the term 'sufficient cause' must receive a liberal meaning and has to be incorporated so as to introduce the concept of reasonableness ... the expression 'sufficient cause' be considered with pragmatism in a justice oriented approach rather than the technical detection of sufficient cause for every day's delay.

> (Paras 9–10)

In *Paryavarana Sanrakshan Sangarsh Samiti Lippa v Union of India* (Judgment 15 December 2011), the Tribunal observed:

> The expression 'sufficient cause' used by the legislature is adequately elastic to enable the court to apply the law in a meaningful manner which subserves the ends of justice. There cannot be a straight-jacket formula for accepting or rejecting explanations furnished for the delay caused in taking steps. The Tribunal on the question of limitation should not be hyper-technical.

> (Para 14)

The NGT condoned the 30-day limitation period as there was sufficient cause to entertain an appeal against an order granting forest clearance for the construction of a hydro-electric project in the state of Himachal Pradesh. The NGT allowed that the appellants who lived in the remote interior of Himachal Pradesh had high travel costs and communications difficulties due to the remoteness of the area.

In *S S Parab v State Level Expert Appraisal Committee* (Judgment 17 August 2015), the NGT condoned the delay of six days in filing of appeal under section 16 of the Act. The appellant was involved in the collection of relevant documentation under the Right to Information Act 2005 in order to file an appeal before the Tribunal. According to the NGT, the delay was marginal, unintentional and duly explained in the appeal. The technical barrier of such delay did not hamper the right of the appellant to prefer an appeal under the Act, which is a statutory right.

3 Not exceeding 60 days

Section 16 NGT Act states the power to condone the delay has an inbuilt limitation as it ceases to exist if the appeal is filed in excess of 60 days beyond the prescribed period of limitation of 30 days from the date of communication of such order. In *Sudeip Shrivastava v Union of India* (Judgment 25 September 2014), the NGT refused to condone the delay of more than 90 days and entertain an appeal under section 16 NGT Act. The appellant, a social activist and advocate, challenged the legality and correctness of the EC order for an open-cast coal-mine project. The appeal against the EC order dated 21 December 2011 was instituted in the registry of the Tribunal on 19 March 2013. According to the NGT, the appeal should have been filed within 30 days from that date or at best within the further period of 60 days thereafter and not beyond that.

Thus, the NGT has strictly construed the time-limitation clause in entertaining both the original and appellate jurisdiction. In both cases, where there is a sufficient cause, the Tribunal may allow a further period not exceeding 60 days. The delay must be bona fide and not a result of negligence, intentional inaction or mala fide and must not result in the abuse of process of law. Once these conditions are satisfied, the Tribunal adopts a balanced approach to condone the delay or not in light of the facts.

Special jurisdiction

The NGT is vested with special jurisdiction under section 15 NGT Act which empowers the Tribunal to order relief and compensation to victims of pollution and other environmental damage arising under the enactments specified in the Schedule I. It also allows the Tribunal to pass orders for restitution of damaged property and for restitution of the environment in such area/areas as it considers appropriate. The liability that accrues upon a person from the orders of the

Tribunal in exercise of its powers under section 15 NGT Act is in addition to the liability that may accrue or had accrued under the Public Liability Insurance Act 1991. In terms of section 15(3) NGT Act, such application must be filed within five years from the date on which the cause of action for such compensation or relief first arose. The proviso to section 15(3) NGT Act empowers the Tribunal to entertain applications beyond this period, but not exceeding 60 days thereafter, if sufficient cause is shown. Further, the Tribunal, having regard to the damage to public health, property and environment, may divide the compensation or relief payable under separate heads, as specified under Schedule II, to the claimants and for restitution of the damaged property or environment as it thinks fit.

In a landmark judgment, *Ramdas Janardan Koli v Secretary, MoEF* (Judgment 27 February 2015), the NGT criticised the Jawaharlal Nehru Port Trust (JNPT) for continuing to reclaim land in violation of the CRZ Notification, and ordered the City and Industrial Development Corporation (CIDCO), JNPT and the Oil and Natural Gas Corporation (ONGC) to pay Rupees 951,920,000 (£9,519,200) to 1630 fishermen's families affected by JNPT's project of creating an additional berth at the port in Navi Mumbai. The NGT also directed the respondents to pay Rupees 50 lakhs (£50,000) to the collector, Raigad, as the restoration cost for environmental damage. The Tribunal labelled the case a 'classic example of civil action brought by traditional fishermen' living in *koliwadas* (habitats of the Koli fishermen of Maharashtra), who were seeking compensation under section 15 NGT Act for loss of livelihood due to project activities of the respondents, as well as implementation of rehabilitation of their families, who were unsettled on account of the projects in question.

The principal appellant, a fisherman named Ramdas Janardan Koli, on behalf of the Paramparik Macchimar Bachao Kruti Samiti, a fishers' organisation, argued the case himself. He claimed that 1630 families of traditional fishermen from four localities had been affected due to development projects undertaken by the respondents, particularly CIDCO, JNPT, ONGC and the Navi Mumbai Special Economic Zone. The claim for compensation and right to rehabilitation was based mainly on the fishermen's traditional right to catch fish from sea areas being reclaimed for project activities. These impaired regular tidal-water exchanges and egress and ingress of fishermen's boats to the sea through the creek near the JNPT. They were thus deprived of daily earnings from their traditional rights of access to the sea. The petition further alleged that the reclamation of land, and removal of mangroves in the area, had caused large-scale destruction of surrounding mangrove forests, which had, in turn, substantially reduced or obliterated breeding fish and narrowed the navigational route of the traditional fishing craft, which had also added to the desolation of the fishing communities.

The Tribunal observed:

> We have come to the conclusion that JNPT degraded environment to much extent by destruction of mangroves after and during commencement

of the project activity, preparation of work at the site even prior to grant of EC and conducted the EIA report without proper relief and rehabilitation programme, as well as risks and benefits auditing due to implementation of the project. Loss of ecology, loss of livelihood to the applicants, loss of spawning grounds, loss of species of fishes in the area and de-settlement of the applicants, are significant issues, which require due payment of compensation to them, though it is difficult to relocate them with some kind of facilities, environment and culture.

(*Koli v Secretary*: paras 55 and 68)

In *A G Kajale v M/S Godhavari Bio-Refineries Ltd and Others* (Judgment 19 May 2015), the applicants approached the NGT under sections 14 and 15 NGT Act seeking relief against an industry and regulatory authorities. The applicants, village residents, alleged that the industrial activities of the respondent industry caused groundwater pollution and thereby affected groundwater quality, pollution of the river Godavari and loss of agriculture. The industry generated highly polluting effluents from its distillery unit near Godavari riverbank and, due to the ineffective effluent treatment and disposal system, huge quantities of untreated effluent were stored in temporary lagoons. Untreated effluents discharged from the lagoons resulted in the groundwater pollution and affected agricultural land and soil quality and reduced agricultural yield. The pollution control boards, i.e. the regulatory authorities, were aware of the inadequate effluent management system but did not take any stringent action against the respondent industry. The NGT, based upon sufficient evidence on record, admitted the allegations of the applicants that the unscientific industrial effluent management had caused groundwater pollution. It found that water samples showed high levels of concentrations of nucleophiles which indicated ingress of industrial effluents into groundwater. This mismanagement had resulted in adverse impacts on surrounding ground water quality and agricultural yields.

The NGT concluded that immediate corrective and remedial measures should be initiated to improve groundwater quality and the degradation of the land. Accordingly, it directed the industry to pay and bear all costs of remediation of groundwater and land, including studies and actual execution of remediation works and provide compensation. An initial sum of Rupees 50 lakhs (£50,000) was to be deposited with the collector of the region and Rupees 5 lakhs (£5000) with the pollution control board within four weeks from the date of the order. Further, each applicant was entitled to compensation of Rupees 2 lakhs (£2000) towards affected agricultural lands and polluted water.

In *S K Navelkar v State of Goa* (Judgment 8 April 2015), the Tribunal allowed an application under section 15 NGT Act for the restitution and restoration of environment and also regarding damage to agricultural lands. The applicants, farmers and agricultural tenants, alleged that the respondent mining industry caused damage to the agricultural land and the surrounding environment by dumping mining waste and discharge of untreated water generated during mining operations. The industry disposed of mineral deposits or solid waste material in the area of the appellants' paddy-fields. The documents on record, i.e. the collector's report, indicated that the dumping was spread over an area of 10,752 square metres and the approximate quantity was 21,504 cubic metres. The agricultural fields were silted with fine particles of mine waste. The NGT directed the mining industry to pay Rupees 400,000 (£4,000) as compensation towards loss of agriculture. The loss of agriculture was to be considered in a holistic manner involving remediation measures and additional requirements of fertilisers and nutrients to return the land to its original status. The mining industry was also to pay Rupees 200,000 (£2,000) per hectare of affected land to owners towards cost of remediation and restitution of the land.

In *Kalpavalli Tree Growers Mutually Aided Cooperative Society Ltd v Union of India* (Order 10 July 2013), the issue before the NGT concerned relief under section 15 NGT Act regarding windmills installed by the respondent, Enercon India Ltd, in the forest area. The applicants, a society of tree-growers and affected villagers, alleged that the project had commenced on forest land, a declared biodiversity heritage site. To allow the construction and erection of 55 windmills, roads were made over mountain tops and transmission lines erected. Over 30,000 mature trees were cut and thousands of smaller trees and shrubs destroyed in order to erect the windmills. Plastic and metal debris were also spread over the area. The construction work caused a huge amount of debris to spill into adjacent fields and into tanks and water bodies, thus destroying the water bodies wholly or partially. Overall, there was irreversible long-term ecological damage to the area. The respondent refuted the allegations by stating that the project was not in forest land but wasteland as per revenue records. The respondent also highlighted the importance of wind as a green energy that does not create an environmental hazard. The NGT, on the basis of the evidence, decided the project was in the forest area. Accordingly, it ordered the respondent to pay Rupees 50 lakhs (£50,000) as compensation for the damage and degradation caused to the ecology and environment.

A review of the above judgments shows that section 15 NGT Act has wide jurisdiction to grant relief to victims of pollution and other environmental damage and restitution of damaged property and the affected environment. The corrective and remedial measures require highly skilled and analytical expertise. This process is expensive and time-consuming and involves a co-ordinated effort by all stakeholders. In order to bring objectivity in this area, the Tribunal ensures the regulatory authorities evolve guidelines or identify institutions and experts to scientifically determine relief, compensation and restitution on a case-by-case basis.

Procedural requirements

Powers and procedures

Under section 19 NGT Act, the Tribunal evolves its own procedure in consonance[78] with the PNJ and is not bound by the provisions of the Civil Procedure

Code 1908 (CPC).[79] The intention of the legislature was to avoid procedural impediments and ensure an expeditious final decision in environmental matters. Further, under section 19(4) NGT Act, the Tribunal is vested with the same powers as a civil court under CPC. These include the summoning and attendance of witnesses, discovery and production of documents, receiving evidence on affidavits, requisitioning of public records or documents, reviewing its decision, dismissing an application for default or deciding it *ex parte*, passing interim orders, including injunctions or stays, and any other matter prescribed. Furthermore, all proceedings before the Tribunal are deemed judicial proceedings within the meaning of sections 193, 219 and 228 for the purposes of section 196 Indian Penal Code 1860 and the Tribunal is deemed a civil court for the purposes of section 195 and chapter 26 Code of Criminal Procedure 1973 in terms of sections 19(4) and (5) NGT Act.

As per section 25 NGT Act, an award, order or decision of the Tribunal is executable by the Tribunal as a decree of a civil court and, for this purpose, the Tribunal has the powers of a civil court. In *Goa Foundation v MoEF* (Order 3 February 2016), the Pune Bench found Leading Hotels in contempt of court for violating the status quo on tree-cutting at Terekhol. The NGT also confiscated Rupees 5 lakhs (£5000) deposited by the company pursuant to an earlier order.

However, three important issues have emerged in respect of the procedure and powers of the NGT under section 19 NGT Act. The *first issue* relates to the scope and ambit of 'reviewing its decision'. Through a series of cases, the NGT has clarified that the scope of the review application is limited in nature and cannot be treated as an appeal.[80] The review application can only be entertained when there is mistake or error apparent on the face of the record or when some material fact is brought to the notice of the Tribunal which is bona fide or with any sufficient reason.[81] If such error continues or its perpetration results in miscarriage of justice, then the Tribunal may interfere. A review application cannot be considered favourably merely on the ground that a different view was probable and could have been taken by the Tribunal. Where an applicant seeks the same relief sought at the time of arguing the main matter and refused, then the review is not maintainable as it would amount to rehearing the matter. Thus, the scope of a review petition does not permit re-adjudication of the issues as the scope of review jurisdiction is limited.

The second issue pertains to the NGT exercising *suo motu* power (on its own) for environmental matters. This is a grey area and, in the absence of specific stipulation in the NGT Act, a debatable issue.[82] The NGT has taken *suo motu* cognisance of environmental matters in several cases based upon newspaper reports. Unscientific evacuation of accumulated waste leading to environmental pollution and health problems[83] and attempts made to destroy Kovalam estuary[84] are illustrative of *suo motu* proceedings.[85] As the NGT is empowered to evolve its own procedure, the *suo motu* jurisdiction becomes an integral effective functioning of the institution. The larger interest of public and environmental protection has been the yardstick to initiate proceedings. However, reservations have been expressed about the exercise of this power. Both the MoEF and the

Madras High Court challenged the usage of *suo motu* by the NGT, claiming it is overstepping its statutory powers.[86]

The third issue relates to the NGT conferring upon itself the power of judicial review, it being another contentious issue.[87] The NGT claims widespread authority to enforce environmental rights, clarifying that it has 'the complete trappings of a civil court' and that its power of judicial review is 'implicit and essential for expeditious and effective disposal of the cases'.

The NGT Act gives the Tribunal complete independence to discharge its judicial functions, security of tenure and conditions of service and it is possessed of complete capacity associated with regular courts. In *Wilfred J v MoEF* (Judgment 17 July 2014), the NGT exercised judicial review to examine the constitutional validity of the delegated legislation.[88] The exercise of judicial review has evoked mixed responses. Environmentalists feel a strong message is delivered that the NGT is not only concerned with the merits of the decision, but also the decision-making process. As an independent body, the NGT aims to protect individuals against abuse or misuse of power by the authorities.[89] Some lawyers feel that the

> NGT is trying to acquire the powers of superior courts. NGT cannot strike down a statute. It can only examine the decisions that are taken and consider if they are in compliance with the three principles laid down in Section 20 of the Act.[90]

The government, on the other hand, feels that it amounts to usurping its jurisdiction. It claims that the NGT can only examine decisions, but cannot strike down a statute. This is yet another important conflict being played out between the NGT and the MoEF.[91]

Appeal and bar of jurisdiction

Any person aggrieved by an order or decision of the Tribunal can file an appeal to the Supreme Court within 90 days from the date of communication of the order. The Supreme Court may condone the time-limitation provided it is satisfied that the appellant was prevented by sufficient cause from preferring the appeal.[92] In *Braj Foundation v Government of Uttar Pradesh* (Judgment 5 August 2014), the NGT stated 'under the Act all the awards/decisions are appealable to the Supreme Court on the grounds available under section 100 Code of Civil Procedure 1908, like the second appeal provision which only relates to the substantial questions of law' (para 25). No civil court has jurisdiction to entertain an appeal, settle a dispute or entertain any question relating to environment in respect of any matter which the Tribunal is empowered to determine under the Act. Thus, it implies that civil cases or suits not involving any substantial question relating to environment and not arising out of the implementation of enactments specified under Schedule I NGT Act can be entertained by the civil court.[93]

An important question relating to the scope and ambit of sections 22 and 29 NGT Act, vis-à-vis the jurisdiction of the High Courts has emerged. Is the jurisdiction of the High Court impliedly excluded by virtue of sections 22 and 29 NGT Act? Is a writ petition maintainable under Article 226 Constitution of India challenging the order of the NGT?[94] Section 22 NGT Act provides for an appeal to the Supreme Court against the orders of the NGT. The provision of appeal to the High Court is not specifically mentioned, but neither is it excluded. Section 29 excludes the jurisdiction of the civil courts. In *Kollidam Aaru Pathukappu Nala Sangam v Union of India* (2014) SCC Online Mad 4928, the divisional bench of Madras High Court decided that the High Courts, being the constitutional courts, did have jurisdiction to entertain appeals against the orders of the NGT. The divisional bench stated that section 29 NGT Act deals with bar of jurisdiction of civil courts and the jurisdiction of the High Court under Articles 226/227 is not excluded under the NGT Act. The bench, relying on the Supreme Court judgment *of L Chandra Kumar v Union of India* (1997) 3 SCC 261, held that the jurisdiction bestowed upon the High Courts under Articles 226/227 and upon the Supreme Court under Article 32 is part of the unchallengeable basic structure of the Indian Constitution and cannot be removed. The decision can be challenged before the High Court in the first instance and before the divisional bench and parties need not be forced to file a special leave petition before the Supreme Court. The divisional bench, when referring to an earlier Supreme Court case, *T Sudhakar Prasad v Government of Arunachal Pradesh* (2001) 1 SCC 516, stated:

> ...jurisdiction should not be confused with status and subordination ... there is no anathema to the Tribunal exercising jurisdiction of the High Court and in that sense, being supplemental and additional to the High Court, but at the same time not enjoying the status equivalent to the High Court and also being subject to judicial review and judicial superintendence of the High Court.
>
> (Para 42)[95]

The Bombay High Court, in *Court on its Own Motion v National Highway Authority of India* (2015) SCC Online Bom 6353, concurred with the Madras High Court and stated:

> ...we are in respectful agreement with the view taken by the Division Bench of the Madras High Court. It could thus clearly be seen that it is a settled position of law that the High Court exercise the power of judicial review over all the Tribunals which are situated within its jurisdiction.
>
> (Paras 42–43)

In *Mira Bhaindar Municipal Corporation v Nagri Hakka Sangharsh Samiti* (2015) SCC Online Bom 6992, it was held that the NGT is amenable to the writ jurisdiction of the Bombay Court and as such, therefore, it cannot sit in appeal over the order passed by the High Court.[96]

However, the Madras High Court in two subsequent judgments, *P Sundararajan v Deputy Registrar, NGT, Southern Zone* (2015) SCC Online Mad 10338,[97] refrained from exercising jurisdiction under Article 226 Constitution of India in view of the judgment of the Supreme Court in *Union of India v Major General Shri Kant Sharma* (2015) 6 SCC 773. In the Major General's case, though it pertained to the Armed Forces Tribunal Act 2007, it was observed that the jurisdiction of the High Court under Article 226 Constitution of India may not be circumscribed by the provisions of any enactment, but due regard has to be given to the legislative intent evidenced by provisions of the Acts and courts would exercise their jurisdiction consistent with the provisions of the Acts. When a statutory forum is created by law for redressal of grievances, a writ petition should not be entertained ignoring the statutory dispensation (pages 804–805). Accordingly, the Madras High Court in *P Sundararajan v Deputy Registrar* in relation to the NGT held:

> We do believe that the distinction which the said judgment sought to give was in respect of the two categories of the cases, i.e. conferment of appellate power before the judicial and quasi-judicial forums and the conferment of appellate power before the Supreme Court. If this is the position, we have to restrain our hands while exercising jurisdiction under Article 226 of the Constitution of India.
>
> (Para 8)

In the same case, the court stated:

> …in view of the aforesaid position, we fail to appreciate as to how we would be able to exercise the jurisdiction … It would require reconsideration of the views expressed by the Supreme Court in *Major General Shri Kant Sharma's case* and judicial hierarchy would not permit this Court to embark upon the said exercise.
>
> (Para 4)

In the light of the above discussion, two challenging issues emerge. First, is the existence of an ambiguous jurisdictional relationship between the High Courts and the NGT that needs clarification and, second, the effectiveness and speed of disposal of an appeal before the Supreme Court, given its existing extensive waiting list. According to Supreme Court Judge Madan B Lokur, 'there are 65,000 cases pending in the Supreme Court. Cases are piling up in the courts by the day'.[98] There is a backlog of more than 30 million cases in courts across the country. *Bloomberg Business Week* reported:

> …if the nation's judges attacked their backlog non-stop and closed 100 cases every hour, it would take more than 35 years to catch up. India had

only 15.5 judges for every million people in 2013. The number of pending cases in the Supreme Court was 64,919 on December 1, 2014.[99]

Currently, the NGT is not subject to an untenable caseload that has resulted elsewhere in India's courts in delay and widespread judicial decision-making paralysis. Nevertheless, there is a clear and ominous trend in the growth of cases listed before the NGT which, unless addressed by extra resources and benches, could result in unwanted delay. Official figures indicate that in 2012, the first full year of the NGT's operation, principally in Delhi and Chennai, some 548 cases were listed and 523 were disposed. Thereafter, the remaining regional benches began to function. By the end of 2015 some 6158 cases had been listed in the benches and 2191 were disposed of with 2144 listed as pending.[100]

Costs

The Tribunal has the power to issue cost orders as it considers necessary, including where the claim is not maintainable or is false or vexatious.[101] In *Baijnath Prajapathi v MoEF* (Judgment 20 January 2012), the NGT imposed costs of Rupees 50,000 (£500) against the appellant who engaged in frivolous litigation that amounted to the abuse of the Tribunal process. The Tribunal observed:

> the Tribunal is expected to ensure effective environmental management ... In this regard, the jurisdiction of the Tribunal should not be invoked for frivolous litigation that unnecessarily consumed the time of the Tribunal without serving the purpose for which the Tribunal was constituted.
>
> (Para 7)

In *Vijay Singh v Balaji Grit Udyog* (Judgment 26 September 2013) and *Aadi Properties v State Level Environmental Impact Assessment Committee* (Judgment 25 April 2014), the NGT imposed costs of Rupees 50,000 (£500) and Rupees 10,000 (£100) respectively against the appellant as the case reflected a personal vendetta rather than a matter of public interest.

Penalty

The NGT Act provides a penalty for not complying with the Tribunal's orders against persons, companies and government departments. Failure of compliance on the part of a person attracts imprisonment for three years or a fine of Rupees 10 crores (£1 million) or both. If the failure continues, an additional fine may be imposed of up to Rupees 25,000 (£250) for every day during which such failure continues after the decision of the first such failure.[102] In *Braj Foundation v Government of Uttar Pradesh* (Judgment 5 August 2014), the NGT observed:

> ...this Tribunal has inherent power of not only enforcing its orders but also treating with any person who either disobeys or violates its orders ... Even

otherwise the NGT Act itself confers enormous power on the Tribunal to deal with any person who fails to comply with the order or award either by punishing with imprisonment or to impose a fine under Section 26...

(Paras 23–24)

In this case, the NGT did not find the government of Uttar Pradesh in contempt for implementing a scheme regarding restoration of Vrindavan forests. Delay on the part of the government due to administrative reasons cannot be branded either as wilful disobedience or interference with the administration of justice.[103]

In *Shrushti Paryavaran Mandal v Union of India* (Order 7 September 2015), the NGT's Principal Bench issued notices to the Secretary of Forest and Environment, State of Maharashtra; Chief General Manager of the National Highway Authority of India (NHAI), State of Maharashtra, and Chief Conservator of Forest, State of Maharashtra, to show cause as to why their properties be not attached and/or be not committed to the civil prison under section 26 NGT Act. The NGT initiated contempt proceedings regarding violation of earlier NGT orders not to fell trees on National Highway-7 between Mansar and Khawasa.

After the NGT order on contempt, the beleaguered NHAI and forest department moved to the High Court of Bombay, pleading for protection from the contempt proceedings as they were following High Court orders on tree-felling along the highway. In a strongly worded judgment, *Court on its Own Motion v National Highway Authority of India*, the High Court of Bombay stayed all the proceedings of the NGT as it fell under its territorial jurisdiction. The Principal Bench of the NGT had no jurisdiction to entertain any matters wherein a cause of action arose within the State of Maharashtra:

we find that the continuation of contempt proceedings against the applicants before us would not be in the interest of justice, in as much as the said officers would be required to face undue hardship and that too for following the directions issued by a constitutional court.

(Para 64)

The case illustrates yet another instance of the jurisdictional struggle between the High Court and NGT.

The 186th Law Commission report advised that the NGT be awarded contempt powers. Thereafter, the Parliamentary Standing Committee that reviewed the NGT Bill took a similar stance on NGT powers. However, the central government chose not to include contempt powers in the final draft of the Bill. Instead penal provisions, as addressed above, were added to the Act. Nevertheless under section 19(4) the NGT has assumed and exercises the power of contempt on the basis of being a civil court.[104] The NGT's Chairperson, Justice Swatanter Kumar stated: 'the Tribunal has power to punish the people disobeying its orders. Section 19(4) of the NGT Act vests the power of Civil Courts in us. We can issue contempt notices'.[105]

However, the NGT has previously issued various contempt notices. They included against: the Delhi Pollution Control Board for non-compliance with its order to stop illegal mining carried out in the Yamuna riverbed in the Wazirabad and Jagatpur Bund areas;[106] the Chief Minister of Madhya Pradesh Shivraj Singh Chouhan in the Kaliasot green belt case;[107] Andhra Pradesh government for violation of NGT directives to stop work at Amaravati;[108] and against the Delhi government for defying its orders not to cut trees, as the NGT had expressed concern over the alleged felling of nearly 400 trees in a residential colony in northeast Delhi.[109]

Corporate bodies are punishable by a fine of Rupees 25 crores (£2.5 million) and relevant company officials may face personal liability.[110] The adequacy of corporate liability here needs re-examination in an era of corporate crime. Twenty-five crores may be an insufficient deterrent in relation to irreparable environmental damage, biodiversity loss or serious injury to public health. In a situation similar to Bhopal, a fixed penalty of Rupees 25 crores, unless accompanied by strict remediation conditions, may dilute the very purpose of the Act which seeks to penalise offending companies in proportion to the damage caused to present and future generations. The NGT is empowered under section 28 NGT Act to punish with imprisonment and/or fine and proceed against government departments or officials if they are in breach of environmental laws.

Conclusion

The NGT's jurisdiction and powers, either expressly provided or by necessary implication, are wide and unrestricted, relating to a substantial question of environment and the enactments covered under Schedule I NGT Act. The NGT has expanded its jurisdictional ambit by not only adjudicating disputes in strict compliance with the statutes in Schedule I, but, through expansive rationale and innovative judgments, it has also gone beyond the 'courtroom door'. This has had far-reaching social and economic implications. In exercise of its jurisdiction, one feature of the NGT is its ability both to fast-track and decide cases within six months of application or appeal. Nevertheless, with a rapidly increasing workload, delay might become a serious issue for the NGT.[111] Challenges include: the increase in the number of cases being instituted each year;[112] resource availability at different benches; insufficient circuit benches; constant rotation and transfer of judges; petitioners buying time; and often the indifferent attitude of governmental authorities to respond within a timeframe by utilising adjournment proceedings. These factors are increasing the backlog of cases.[113] Interestingly, the Chairperson of the NGT, Justice Swatanter Kumar, disposed of 112 cases and large numbers of miscellaneous applications by 11 different judgments in a day.[114]

On a positive note, the growing awareness of the environmental and ecological decision-making of the NGT is promoting a change in societal attitudes towards the environment and related challenges. The transformation sought by the NGT is a metamorphosis of societal environmental interests that encapsulate what is important for the well-being not only of the individual but also the larger public interest. The NGT's legitimacy is grounded in its inclusive participatory mechanisms. The NGT's expansionist approach has injected further rigour into its procedures that recognise that environmental considerations should be given priority in policy formulation and implementation. These powers and procedures promote transparency and attempt to ensure regulatory authorities and private enterprise are fully accountable for the choices or decisions they make.

Notes

1 *Bhopal Gas Peedith Mahila Udyog Sangathan v Union of India* (2012) 8 SCC 326, 347. The Supreme Court Bench comprised Chief Justice of India, S H Kapadia, and Justices A K Patnaik and Swatanter Kumar. Shortly thereafter, Justice Kumar took up his appointment as Chairperson of the NGT. In *Adarsh Cooperative Housing Society Ltd v Union of India* Order 10 March 2014, the Supreme Court stayed its own order by which it transferred all environmental cases from High Courts to the NGT. In *Vellore Citizens Welfare Forum v Union of India* 2016 SCC Online Mad 1881, the Madras High Court stated: 'however, it appears that the application was withdrawn on 11.8.2014' (para 78). Additionally, the Supreme Court of India transferred more than 300 cases to the NGT in 2015. The Green Bench, headed by the then Chief Justice H L Dattu, decided to let go of several cases for swift decisions, thereby also shedding its pendency. See *T N Godavarman Thirumulpad v Union of India* (Order 5 November 2015) for details.
2 *Goa Foundation v Union of India* Judgment 18 July 2013, para 18.
3 Preamble NGT Act 2010.
4 See also *Court on its Own Motion v State of Himachal Pradesh* Judgment 4 February 2014.
5 '13 out of 20 most polluted cities in world are from India' India TV News Desk, 4 December 2015 www.indiatvnews.com/news/india/13-out-of-20-most-polluted-cities-in-world-are-from-india-54104.html.
6 '80% of India's surface water may be polluted, report by international body says' *Times of India*, 28 June 2015 http://timesofindia.indiatimes.com/home/environment/pollution/80-of-Indias-surface-water-may-be-polluted-report-by-international-body-says/articleshow/47848532.cms.
7 'Horrifying fact: almost all India's water is contaminated by sewage' Scroll.in, 1 July 2015 http://scroll.in/article/737981/horrifying-fact-almost-all-indias-water-is-contaminated-by-sewage.
8 For a detailed discussion of the role and interaction of bench members, see Chapter 5.
9 Section 4 NGT Act.
10 Section 6 NGT Act.
11 Ibid.
12 Section 5 NGT Act.
13 Ibid.
14 See Chapter 2.
15 According to Census India, about 72.2 per cent of the population lives in some 638,000 villages and the rest, 27.8 per cent, in about 5480 towns and urban agglomerations. India has the largest illiterate population in the world www.censusindia.gov.in/Census_Data_2001/India_at_Glance/rural.aspx and www.indiaonlinepages.com/population/india-current-population.html.
16 See also *M C Mehta v University Grants Commission* Judgment 17 July 2014; *J P Dabral v MoEF* Judgment 14 December 2011.

17 *K L Gera v State of Haryana* Judgment 25 August 2015.
18 See also *Sudeip Shrivastava v State of Chattisgarh* Judgment 24 March 2014.
19 *V G Bhuganese v G Sugar and Energy Ltd* Judgment 20 December 2013.
20 Section 19 NGT Act. See below for details.
21 'Green Tribunal forms experts' panel to inspect Chemfab unit' *The Hindu*, 6 March 2015 www.thehindu.com/news/cities/puducherry/green-tribunal-forms-experts-panel-to-inspect-chemfab-unit/article6965673.ece.
22 NGT (Practices and Procedure) Rules 2011, rule 12(2).
23 Ibid.: rule 12(1)).
24 See also *Aadi Properties v State Level Environmental Impact Assessment Committee* Judgment 26 September 2013; *Vijay Singh v Balaji Grit Udyog* Judgment 25 April 2014; see the section on 'Costs' below.
25 NGT (Practices and Procedure) Rules 2011, rule 8, prescribes the procedural requirements for filing the petition. An original (application) or appellate (appeal) is presented to the Tribunal in Form I by the applicant or appellant, as the case may be, in person or by an agent or duly authorised legal practitioner, to the registrar or any other officer authorised in writing by the registrar to receive the same. The application for relief and compensation (special) is made in Form II. The application or appeal is presented in triplicate in two compilations: compilation I contains the application or appeal, along with the impugned order, if any; compilation II includes all other documents and annexures referred to in the application or appeal, in a paper book form. An application or appeal is ordinarily filed by an applicant or appellant with the registrar of the Tribunal at his or her ordinary place of sitting falling within the jurisdiction where the cause of action, wholly or in part, has arisen. An application for review can be entertained by the NGT on grounds of merit to be filed within 30 days from the date of receipt of copy of the order sought to be reviewed.
26 Section 14 NGT Act states:

> (1) The Tribunal shall have the jurisdiction over all civil cases where a substantial question relating to environment (including enforcement of any legal right relating to environment), is involved and such question arises out of the implementation of the enactments specified in Schedule I; (2) The Tribunal shall hear the disputes arising from the questions referred to in sub-section (1) and settle such disputes and pass order thereon; (3) No application for adjudication of dispute under this section shall be entertained by the Tribunal unless it is made within a period of six months from the date on which the cause of action for such dispute first arose: Provided that the Tribunal may, if it is satisfied that the applicant was prevented by sufficient cause from filing the application within the said period, allow it to be filed within a further period not exceeding sixty days.

The enactments in Schedule I include: the Water (Prevention and Control of Pollution) Act 1974; the Water (Prevention and Control of Pollution) Cess Act 1977; the Forests (Conservation) Act 1980; the Air (Prevention and Control of Pollution) Act 1981; the Environment (Protection) Act 1986; the Public Liability Insurance Act 1981; and the Biological Diversity Act 2002.
27 See also *Neelam Kalia v Union of India* 2013 SCC Online NGT 196 and *S M Sanghavi v Tree Officer* Judgment 6 May 2014 wherein the NGT refused to entertain the matter covered under Maharashtra (Urban Areas) Protection and Preservation of Trees Act 1975.
28 Section 2(c) NGT Act defines 'environment' to include water, air and land and the inter-relationship which exists among and between water, air and land and human beings, other living creatures, plants, micro-organisms and property.
29 *Goa Foundation v Union of India* Judgment 18 July 2013; *Nasik Fly Ash Bricks Association v MoEF* Judgment 21 March 2014; *Madhya Pradesh Pollution Control Board v Commissioner, Municipal Corporation Bhopal* Judgment 8 August 2013; *Chhattisgarh*

Environment Conservation Board v M/S Mangala Ispat Pvt Ltd 2013 SCC Online NGT 3035.
30 Oxford Dictionary; also see *In re Net Books Agreement* [1962] 1 WLR 1347.
31 'Delhi's waste site story' Toxics Link, 19 November 2014 http://toxicslink. org/?q=article/delhi%E2%80%99s-waste-site-story.
32 www.karmayog.com/cleanliness/bmcstatsdata.htm.
33 'Bengaluru garbage mafia issues threat to residents' *India Today*, 5 December 2015 http://indiatoday.intoday.in/story/bengaluru-garbage-mafia-issues-threat-to-residents/ 1/539362.html.
34 'Garbage mounds: spreading urban eyesores' *Times of India*, 5 June 2014 http://times-ofindia.indiatimes.com/city/ahmedabad/Garbage-mounds-Spreading-urban-eyesores/ articleshow/36074988.cms.
35 http://toxicslink.org/?q=content/national-conference-waste-energy-30th-march-2015-new-delhi.
36 www.gktoday.in/blog/problem-of-municipal-solid-waste-msw-in-india/).
37 SLP(C) No 22111/2003 and CONMT.PET (C) No 8/2009 in WP(C) No 888/1996.
38 'Managing waste, irregularities a tough call for India's metros' Live Mint, 25 December 2008 www.livemint.com/Politics/6c9QI6oD8fZ6ydfXhdVDCM/Managing-waste-irregularities-a-tough-call-for-India8217.html; see also dnaSyndication (2014).
39 See n 34 above.
40 See n 33 above.
41 See also Chapter 2, particularly on Article 21 Constitution of India.
42 See also *Permanand Klanta v State of Himachal Pradesh* Judgment 10 December 2015.
43 'Maharashtra bans emergency vehicle sirens between 10pm and 6am' *Times of India*, 11 June 2014 http://timesofindia.indiatimes.com/city/pune/Maharashtra-bans-emergency-vehicle-sirens-between-10pm-and-6am/articleshow/36364429.cms.
44 'Breathing poison in the world's most polluted city' BBC News, 19 April 2015 www. bbc.co.uk/news/magazine-32352722; 'Delhi is world's most polluted city: WHO' *Times of India*, 2 December 2015 http://timesofindia.indiatimes.com/life-style/ health-fitness/health-news/Delhi-is-worlds-most-polluted-city-WHO/articleshow/ 50010011.cms.
45 'Most polluted city in the world, Delhi suffers from a toxic blend, says UK study' *Indian Express*, 25 December 2015 http://indianexpress.com/article/cities/delhi/the-most-polluted-city-in-the-world-delhi-suffers-from-a-toxic-blend-study/#sthash.Eu Nkc5vf.dpuf.
46 'Air pollution causes 30,000 deaths in Delhi annually' *First Post*, 16 December 2015 www.firstpost.com/india/air-pollution-causes-30000-deaths-annually-in-delhi-fifth-leading-cause-of-death-in-india-254.
47 'Deadly air: 40% children in Delhi have weak lungs, finds survey' *Hindustan Times*, 4 June 2015 www.hindustantimes.com/delhi/deadly-air-40-children-in-delhi-have-weak-lungs-finds-survey/story-aEtYQWzg4Xvqbe8e2a6RCI.html.
48 See Chapter 5 for a discussion.
49 Order dated 28 November 2014.
50 'National Green Tribunal worried over rising pollution in Delhi' *India Today*, 30 October 2014 http://indiatoday.intoday.in/story/ngt-air-pollution-delhi-justice-swatanter-kumar-delhi-government-departments-vardhaman-kaushik/1/398156.html.
51 'NGT flays DTC over report on inspection of buses' *Hindustan Times*, 8 June 2015 www.dnaindia.com/delhi/report-ngt-flays-dtc-over-report-on-inspection-of-buses-2064414; see also 'Green Court takes bold steps to improve city air', *Hindustan Times*, New Delhi, 8 June 2015.
52 'Delhi's odd even rule ends today' *Indian Express*, 15 January 2016 http://indian-express.com/article/cities/delhi/delhis-odd-even-rule-ends-today-a-look-back-at-the-last-15-days/#sthash.0CM0A8jy.dpuf.

53 'Make no mistake, odd even II was a failure' *Huffington Post*, 3 April 2016 www. huffingtonpost.in/2016/04/30/aap-odd-even-ii-delhi_n_9812656.html; 'Impact of odd-even on air blurred by low compliance' *Times of India* 30 April 2016 http:// timesofindia.indiatimes.com/city/delhi/Impact-of-odd-even-on-air-blurred-by-low-compliance/articleshow/52047939.cms?

54 'What would be status of roads after 10,000 new buses: NGT' *Economic Times*, 7 August 2015 http://articles.economictimes.indiatimes.com/2015-08-07/news/65317826_1_ public-service-vehicles-electric-buses-delhi-government.

55 'Act on Delhi's foul air – now' *Times of India*, 6 June 2015: Panel Discussion (Environment Minister P Javadekar discussed the alarming level of air pollution in Delhi with top experts and outlined an action plan) http://timesofindia.indiatimes. com/home/environment/pollution/Act-on-Delhis-foul-air-now/articleshow/475615 41.cms.

56 http://aqicn.org/map/india/.

57 'Government will come up with construction and waste management rules' Assocham, 10 February 2016 www.assocham.org/newsdetail.php?id=5504. Also see Chetan Chauhan, 'Political will needed to clean toxic air', *Hindustan Times*, New Delhi, 8 June 2015.

58 Section 2(m)(2) NGT Act.

59 See also *Dalip v Union of India* Judgment 29 April 2014.

60 See also *Society for Protection of Culture v Union of India* Judgment 10 August 2015; *Pankaj Sharma v MoEF* Judgment 20 September 2013.

61 Section 14(2).

62 Section 20 NGT Act. For a detailed discussion, see Chapter 4.

63 *Collector, Land Acquisition, Anantnag v Katiji* AIR 1987 SC 1335; *Balwant Singh (Dead) v Jagdish Singh* (2010) 8 SCC 685; *Kehar Singh v State of Haryana* Judgment 12 September 2013; *P Mohapatra Union of India* Judgment 8 August 2013; *Nisarga Nature Club v Satyawan* Judgment 21 February 2013; *N H Almeida v M/S Lenzing Modi Fibres* Judgment 28 November 2013; *B K Patel v MoEF* Judgment 13 December 2013.

64 See also *J Mehta v Union of India* Judgment 24 October 2013; *Goa Foundation v Union of India* Judgment 18 July 2013; *Amit Maru v MoEF* Judgment 1 October 2014; *R J Koli v Secretary, MoEF* Judgment 27 May 2014; *Kehar Singh v State of Haryana* Judgment 12 September 2013; *Cavelossim Village Forum v Village Panchayat Cavelossim* Judgment 8 April 2015; *Mohar Singh Yadav v Union of India* Judgment 15 September 2015.

65 Interview 14 April 2015; 'SC stays own decision to transfer environmental cases' *Down To Earth*, 15 April 2014 www.downtoearth.org.in/news/sc-stays-own-decision-to-transfer-environmental-cases-from-high-courts-to-green-Tribunal-44068.

66 Section 16 NGT Act states:

> Any person aggrieved by an order or decision made, on or after the commencement of the National Green Tribunal Act, 2010, by the (a) Appellate Authority under section 28 of the Water (Prevention and Control of Pollution) Act, 1974; (b) State Government under section 29 of the Water (Prevention and Control of Pollution) Act, 1974 (c) a Board, under section 33A of the Water (Prevention and Control of Pollution) Act, 1974 (6 of 1974); (d) Appellate Authority under section 13 of the Water (Prevention and Control of Pollution) Cess Act, 1977; (e) State Government or other authority under section 2 of the Forest (Conservation) Act, 1980; (f) Appellate Authority under section 31 of the Air (Prevention and Control of Pollution) Act, 1981; (g) any direction issued under section 5 of the Environment (Protection) Act, 1986; (h) granting environmental clearance in the area in which any industries, operations or processes or class of industries, operations and processes shall not be carried out or shall be carried out

subject to certain safeguards under the Environment (Protection) Act, 1986 (i) refusing to grant environmental clearance for carrying out any activity or operation or process under the Environment (Protection) Act, 1986; (j) any determination of benefit sharing or order made by the National Biodiversity Authority or a State Biodiversity Board under the provisions of the Biological Diversity Act, 2002, may, within a period of thirty days from the date on which the order or decision or direction or determination is communicated to him, prefer an appeal to the Tribunal: Provided that the Tribunal may, if it is satisfied that the appellant was prevented by sufficient cause from filing the appeal within the said period, allow it to be filed under this section within a further period not exceeding sixty days.

67 *Oxford Dictionary* Vol. 1, 398.
68 *Vijay D Mehra v Collector of Customs (Preventive) Bombay* FN-1988 SCR Suppl (2) 434; *Nand Lal v State of Haryana* AIR 1980 SC 2097.
69 See also *D V Girish v Secretary, Department of Environment Bangalore* Judgment 9 April 2015.
70 Section 16(f) NGT Act; see also *M/S Athiappa Chemical (P) Ltd v Puducherry Pollution Control Committee* Judgment 14 December 2011.
71 'POSCO verdict' *First Post*, 8 April 2012 www.firstpost.com/india/posco-verdict-finally-environmental-justice-in-india-269201.html; see Chapter 4 for further discussion.
72 'India's Green Tribunal suspends environmental clearance to Posco' MAC: Mines and Communities, 30 March 2012 www.minesandcommunities.org/article.php?a=11597).
73 'POSCO verdict' *First Post*, 8 April 2012 www.firstpost.com/india/posco-verdict-finally-environmental-justice-in-india-269201.html.
74 'Green Tribunal suspends environmental nod to Posco' *The Hindu*, 30 March 2012 www.thehindu.com/news/national/other-states/green-tribunal-suspends-environmental-nod-to-posco/article3261507.ece.
75 See *M/S Sterlite Industries (India) Ltd v Tamil Nadu Pollution Control Board* Judgment 8 August 2013; *M/S Sesa Goa Ltd v State of Goa* Judgment 11 April 2013; *Ashish Rajanbhai Shah v Union of India* Judgment 11 July 2013; *M/S Techno Engineering v Maharashtra Pollution Control Board* Judgment 1 January 2015; *Kranti S S Karkhana v Revenue and Forest Department* Judgment 15 January 2015.
76 Section 16(h) NGT Act.
77 *Save Mon Region Federation v Union of India* Judgment 14 March 2013; *Medha Patkar v MoEF* Judgment 11 July 2013; *Nikunj Developers v M/S Veena Developers* Judgment 14 March 2013; *Sudeip Shrivastava v Union of India* Judgment 25 September 2014.
78 Section 19(2) NGT Act.
79 Section 19(1) NGT Act. The CPC consolidates and amends the laws relating to the procedure of the courts of civil judicature.
80 The power to review its own decisions would be guided by the principles underlining Order XLVII, rule 1, CPC.
81 *Nisarga Nature Club v S B Prabhudessai* Order 31 May 2013; *State of West Bengal v Kamalsen Gupta* (2008) 8 SCC 612; *S P Muthuraman v Union of India* Judgment 1 September 2015.
82 For further discussion, see Chapters 5 and 7.
83 *Tribunal on its Own Motion v State of Kerala* 2014 SCC Online NGT 6763.
84 *Tribunal on its Own Motion v Secretary, MoEF* 2013 SCC Online NGT 1083.
85 For further discussion and case illustrations, see Chapter 5.
86 For discussion on *suo moto*, see Chapter 7.
87 See also Chapters 5 and 7.
88 See also Chapter 7.

89 Statement by environmental activists (who happen to be lawyers) Ritwick Dutta and Rahul Choudhary www.firstpost.com/india/national-green-tribunal-asserts-independence-environment-minister-listening-1625527.html.
90 Statement of Rajeev Dhavan, senior advocate www.downtoearth.org.in/coverage/tribunal-on-trial-47400.
91 Ibid.
92 Section 22 NGT Act.
93 *Gadbad v Ramrao* 2013 SCC Online Bombay 82, para 87.
94 Article 226 Constitution of India deals with the power of High Courts to issue certain writs. It states:

> Notwithstanding anything in Article 32 every High Court shall have powers, throughout the territories in relation to which it exercise jurisdiction, to issue to any person or authority, including in appropriate cases, any Government, within those territories directions, orders or writs, including writs in the nature of habeas corpus, mandamus, prohibitions, quo warranto and certiorari, or any of them, for the enforcement of any of the rights conferred by Part III and for any other purpose …

95 See also *Vijaylakshmi Shanmugam v Secretary, MoEF* (2014) SCC Online Mad 256.
96 See also *Anil Hoble v Kashinath Jairam Shetye* (2015) SCC Online Bom 3699.
97 See also *P S Jayachandran v Member Secretary, Tamil Nadu Pollution Control Board* (2015) SCC Online Mad 10336.
98 'Supreme Court swamped with pending cases' *Hans India*, 22 November 2016 www.thehansindia.com/posts/index/Telangana/2015–11–22/Supreme-Court-swamped-with-pending-cases-Judge/188090.
99 www.bloomberg.com/news/articles/2015–01–08/indias-courts-resist-reform-backlog-at-314-million-cases.
100 *NGT International Journal on Environment* (2016) volume 1.
101 Section 23 NGT Act.
102 Section 26 NGT Act.
103 See also *Lokendra Kumar v State of Uttar Pradesh* Judgment 14 January 2015.
104 Section 19(5) NGT Act.
105 'Green Court to hear contempt plea against Sri Sri Ravi Shankar' NDTV, 26 May 2016 www.ndtv.com/india-news/green-court-to-hear-contempt-plea-against-sri-sri-ravi-shankar-1411307. The legitimate exercise of contempt power was challenged in *Manoj Misra v Delhi Development Authority* (Order 25 May 2016) and is posted for hearing.
106 'NGT issues notice to pollution panel over "illegal" sand mining' *Tribune*, 26 September 2016 www.tribuneindia.com/2014/20140927/delhi.htm#3.
107 'NGT admits contempt plea against Madhya Pradesh CM' *Times of India*, 18 May 2015 http://timesofindia.indiatimes.com/city/bhopal/NGT-admits-contempt-plea-against-Madhya-Pradesh-CM/articleshow/473325.
108 'NGT issues contempt notice to government' *The Hindu*, 6 November 2016 www.thehindu.com/todays-paper/ngt-issues-contempt-notice-to-govt/article7848293.ece.
109 Order 20 November 2015 Principal Bench.
110 Section 27 NGT Act.
111 See n 98 above.
112 See Chapter 6, for caseload data.
113 Interviews with advocates between 2014–2015 in all NGT benches.
114 Official Note, NGT, 13 January 2015 www.greentribunal.gov.in/news_detail.aspx.

References

Boyd, D R (2012) *The Environmental Rights Revolution: A Global Study of Constitutions, Human Rights, and the Environment* (UBC Press).

Boyle, A (1996) 'The role of international human rights law in the protection of the environment' in A Boyle and M Anderson (eds), *Human Rights Approaches to Environmental Protection* (OUP).

dnaSyndication (June 2014) 'HC pulls up government over mafia nexus' http://dnasyndication.com/showarticlerss.aspx?nid=641PWB3tuoqPagLpt9dgw1nfZ5P2eOVVKBLkwN7tFgo=.

Central Pollution Control Board (January 2015) 'Status of Compliance by CPCB with MSWs (Management and Handling) Rules 2000' (MoEF).

Centre for Science and Environment (1999–2015) *Annual Reports* www.cseindia.org/node/222.

Chandra, N (June 2013) 'New study warns "dangerous" levels of noise pollution in New Delhi are causing age-related hearing loss 15 years earlier than normal' *Mail Online India* www.dailymail.co.uk/indiahome/indianews/article-2334486/Delhi-uncivilised-city-Dangerous-levels-noisepollution-Capital-causing-onset-age-related-hearing-loss-early-60-new-study-warns.html.

Davis, M and Lemezina, Z (2010) 'Indigenous Australians and the preamble: towards a more inclusive constitution or entrenching marginalisation?' 33(2) *University of New South Wales Law Journal* 239–266.

Fraser, N (2001) 'Recognition without ethics?' 18(2–3) *Theory, Culture and Society* 21–42.

International Human Rights Clinic/ESCR-Net (2013) *The Price of Steel: Human Rights and Forced Evictions in the POSCO-India Project* (NYU School of Law).

Jessup, B (2012) 'The journey of environmental justice through public and international law' in B Jessup and K Rubenstein (eds), *Environmental Discourses in Public and International Law* (CUP).

Kiss, A and Shelton, D (2003) *International Environmental Law* (UNEP).

Korsah-Brown, D (2002) 'Environment, human rights and mining conflicts in Ghana' in L Zarsky (ed.), *Human Rights and the Environment* (Earthscan) 81.

Lalchandani, N (January 2013) 'Rules on paper, Delhi stays noisy' *Times of India* http://timesofindia.indiatimes.com/city/delhi/Rules-on-paper-Delhi-stays-noisy/articleshow/18190784.cms.

Nandi, J (November 2013) 'Most parts of Delhi in grip of noise pollution' *Times of India* http://timesofindia.indiatimes.com/home/environment/pollution/Most-parts-of-Delhi-in-grip-of-noisepollution/articleshow/25717955.cms.

Rajamani, L (2010) 'The increasing currently and relevance of rights-based perspective in the international negotiations on climate change' 22(3) *Journal of Environmental Law* 409.

Rana, R, Ganguly, R and Kumar Gupta, A (2015) 'An assessment of solid waste management in India' 20(6) *E-Journal of Geotechnical Engineering* 1547–1572.

Sahu, G (2008) 'Implications of the Indian Supreme Court's innovations for environmental jurisprudence' 4(1) *Law, Environment and Development Journal* 375–393.

Schlosberg, D (2007) *Defining Environmental Justice* (OUP).

Twomey, A (September 2011) *Constitutional Recognition of Indigenous Australians in a Preamble* (Constitutional Reform Unit Sydney Law School).

4 National Green Tribunal

Normative principles

International treaties and agreements obligate states to take appropriate domestic action to enforce the laws they enact pursuant to international obligations. India's constitutional provisions mandate that its constituent states foster respect for international law and treaty obligations.[1] The scope and ambit of international law in an Indian context has been explained thus:

> International law today is not confined to regulating the relation between the states. Scope continues to extend. Today matters of social concerns, such as health, education and economics apart from human rights fall within the ambit of international regulations. International law is more than ever aimed at individuals. It is almost an accepted proposition of law that the rules of customary international law which are not contrary to the municipal law shall be deemed to be incorporated in the domestic law.
>
> (*People's Union for Civil Liberties v Union of India* (1997) 1 SCC 301, 311)

Recognising the importance of promoting international obligations under environmental conventions and articulating the commitment of being a 'good international citizen' (Cordes-Holland 2012: 288), the Preamble to the National Green Tribunal (NGT) Act 2010 commits India to the implementation of decisions adopted at the Stockholm Conference 1972 and Rio Conference 1992.[2] Significantly, section 20 mandates the Tribunal to apply the sustainable development, precautionary and polluter-pays principles when passing any order, decision or award.[3] These principles are read in conjunction with the domestic right to an environment as recognised in the Preamble, thereby advancing both national and global interests. The Tribunal is obliged to adhere to and apply the above-mentioned principles for effective implementation of environmental rights and duties in India. These principles are the foundation of the determinative process before the Tribunal for dispensation of environmental justice. This chapter examines the application of these principles to cases as spelled out in section 20 NGT Act.

The precautionary principle

The precautionary principle is a fundamental tool for achieving sustainable development and plays an important role at international and national levels. As affirmed in the 1992 Rio Declaration on Environment and Development, it provides for action to avert risks of serious or irreversible harm to the environment or human health in the absence of scientific certainty about that harm[4] and provides the 'philosophical authority to take public policy decisions covering environmental protection in the face of uncertainty' (Cameron 1999: 29; see also Cross 1996; Stone 2001). Where there is no uncertainty in the calculation of risks, there is no justification for the employment of precautionary principle (Birnie *et al.* 2009: 156). Thus, scientific uncertainty is at the core of the precautionary principle.[5]

The precautionary principle rallies actors with ranging interests and expertise – scientists, law and policy-makers, environmentalists, economists, ethicists, public authorities etc. The interaction among these interested actors often produces vague, ambiguous or unwanted results, thereby prompting a re-examination of the issues or debate. This 'fosters a mutual understanding to accommodate differences in the production of knowledge and the reaching of judgments' (Ellis 2012: 128). One ongoing argument is about the 'legal status of the precautionary principle' as a result of its inclusion in international agreements. Some argue it is an *approach* (Hey 1992), others that it has become a *principle* of customary international law (Freestone 1994; Cameron 1999: 30). Yet others suggest that the use of these terms in treaties contradicts any such distinction and reveal that European treaties and European Union (EU) laws generally refer to the precautionary principle, whereas global agreements often refer to a precautionary approach or precautionary measures (Birnie *et al.* 2009: 155). Consequently, the concept of precaution faces the challenge of establishing a consensual interpretation of core meaning and the means for predictable and effective implementation.[6]

Though the precautionary principle's international legal status is an open question, at domestic level it has 'become the "leitmotif" of European and Commonwealth environmental law and policy' (Fisher 2001: 315). Sometimes, it is argued as a 'legal issue in the domestic courts in the commonwealth and applied as a principle of the highest courts' (Birnie *et al.* 2009: 159). National and cultural differences influence its understanding and usage. Harding and Fisher state that factors like 'attitudes to risk management, the role of science and scientists in decision-making processes, openness of decision-making processes, nation's economy including level of "development" and nature of "natural environment" affect the application of the precautionary principle' (1999: 14).

In India, the Supreme Court has recognised the principle as an essential feature of sustainable development and, as such, part of customary international law.[7] In the municipal context, the principle envisages three conditions:[8]

1   state government and statutory authorities must anticipate, prevent and attack the causes of environmental degradation;

2 where there are threats of serious and irreversible damage, lack of scientific certainty should not be used as a reason for postponing measures to prevent environmental degradation; and
3 the 'onus of proof' is on the actor or developer/industrialist to show their actions are environmentally benign.

The NGT interprets and applies the precautionary principle as mandated by section 20 NGT Act. Following and bolstering the rulings of the Supreme Court,[9] the Tribunal declared the precautionary principle an integral part of national environmental law:

> The applicability of [the] precautionary principle is a statutory command to the Tribunal while deciding or settling disputes arising out of the substantial questions relating to environment. Thus, any violation or even an apprehended violation of this principle would be actionable by any person before the Tribunal. Inaction in the facts and circumstances of a given case could itself be a violation of the precautionary principle, and therefore bring it within the ambit of jurisdiction of the Tribunal, as defined under the NGT Act.
>
> (*Goa Foundation v Union of India* Judgment dated 18 July 2013 at para 42)

In the case of *Gram Panchayat Totu (Majthai) v State of Himachel Pradesh* (Judgment 11 October 2011), the NGT examined an application in which the project proponent, the municipal council, had failed to obtain mandatory EC from the authorities concerning the proposed construction of a MSW plant located close to human habitation. It observed that the precautionary principle mandates the necessary preventive and control measures which had to be implemented before the plant could be commissioned. These included obtaining ECs under EIA rules and statutory citing permissions for locating MSW facilities. The preventive measures were aimed at avoiding adverse environmental impacts, especially on groundwater and surface-water bodies.

Durga Dutt v State of Himachel Pradesh (Judgment 6 February 2014) related to environmental degradation and damage to the Rohtang Pass Valley glacier (the 'Crown Jewel of Tourism'). Unregulated, heavy tourism, overcrowding, misuse of natural resources, construction of buildings and infrastructure, litter, deforestation and global warming have resulted in environmental problems in this eco-sensitive area. Such tourist spots are both unique and vulnerable – their ecology and environment can be subject to rapid degradation. Tourism's negative impacts can only be managed effectively if they have been identified, measured and evaluated. Its effects could be direct or indirect. Direct impact is caused by the presence of tourists and indirect impact by the new infrastructure and services. The Tribunal decided there was a need to restore the glacier's degraded environment and prevent further damage by adopting precautionary measures, including: regulating and restricting vehicular traffic; introducing stringent emission norms; using clear natural gas and environmentally friendly fuels;

prohibiting plastic bags and littering; and banning commercial activity at the glacier.

In *Asim Sarode v Maharashtra Pollution Control Board* (Judgment 6 September 2014), the NGT applied the precautionary principle by prohibiting unauthorised, unscientific burning of tyres in open areas and public spaces, as they emit smoke containing toxic gases and pollutants that adversely affect public health and the environment:

> Tyre burning in open atmosphere generates highly toxic, mutagenic and hazardous emissions ... The open tyre burning emissions include 'criteria' pollutants such as particulates, carbon monoxide (CO), sulphur oxides (SO$_2$), oxides of nitrogen (NOx) and volatile organic compounds (VOCs). They also include 'non-criteria' hazardous air pollutants (HAPs), such as polynuclear aromatic hydrocarbons (PAHs), dioxins, furans, hydrogen chloride, benzene, polychlorinated biphenyls (PCBs), and metals such as arsenic, cadmium, nickel, zinc, mercury, chromium, and vanadium. Both criteria and HAP emissions from an open tyre fire can represent significant acute (short-term) and chronic (long-term) health hazards to the public. Depending on the length and degree of exposure, these health impacts could include irritation of the skin, eyes, and mucous membranes, respiratory effects, central nervous system depression, and cancer. The piled used tyres can also be health hazard as they become breeding grounds for diseases causing pests and can even catch fire.
>
> (Paras 5–6)

The matter is ongoing and guidelines are currently not in place.

In *B S Gajendragadkar v Sri Theatre* (Judgment 22 July 2015), the issue was the application of the precautionary principle to monitor noise pollution from the respondent's cinema. The cinema was located in a residential and commercial complex that included a hospital. The decibel level from the cinema exceeded legal noise levels. The applicant and nearby residents faced health problems and noise pollution that made it difficult to converse. The NGT applied the precautionary principle, directing the cinema theatre to install an automatic sound-amplifier control system and erect acoustic 9–10ft rubber cladding to help regulate noise levels.

Jal Biradari v MoEF (Judgment 22 January 2015) is another illustration of the application of the precautionary principle by the NGT to quash coastal zone clearance. The NGO appellant challenged the clearance granted by the statutory authorities – Maharashtra Coastal Zone Management Authority (MCZMA) and MoEF – to the Mumbai Metropolitan Region Development Authority (MMRDA) and state government for failing to follow due process of law. The clearance was granted to widen and deepen the river Mithi to improve its flood-carrying capacity by removal of encroachments on the floodplains and de-silting measures. However, MMRDA undertook concretisation in the river and on its banks – the coastal zone and wetland areas – that would irreversibly damage the river's ecosystem instead of reviving it. Further, the concretisation impacted on groundwater percolation and aggravated the flooding problem. The NGT applied the precautionary principle as MCZMA and the MoEF had not followed the legal procedure required before granting the EC. There was no reference to the project's critical nature, the completion of a large part before grant of clearance, the provision and adequacy of environmental safeguards, the effect of existing structures on the river and mangroves, and the adequacy of stretches of the system for tidal exchange or the river's water-quality status.

In *M/S Sterlite Industries v Tamil Nadu Pollution Control Board* (Judgment 8 August 2013), the appellant challenged the legality of the order issued by the respondent under section 31a Air (Prevention and Control of Pollution) Act 1981, ordering closure of a copper-smelting plant as its excessive sulphur dioxide emissions were affecting public health. The board exercised its power with primary reference to the precautionary principle. The appellant contended that there was no cogent or reliable evidence or reasonable scientific data, even by implication, to link the leakage to the plant. It claimed the closure order was arbitrary and passed in undue haste without proper application of mind. The NGT ruled that the order was not based on the precautionary principle, but was punitive. Shutting down an industry amounts to 'civil death'. A direction of closure in relation to a running unit not only results in stoppage of production, but has far-reaching economic, social and labour consequences. Before directing the civil death of a company, the decision-making authority should have reliable and cogent evidence or reasonable scientific data. There should be a direct nexus between the leakage, its source and its effect/impact on ambient air quality and public health. Accordingly, the NGT concluded that the closure order was not sustainable.

The NGT in *Murugandam v MoEF* (Judgments 23 May 2012 and 11 November 2014)[10] applied the precautionary principle and directed the project proponents, M/S IL and F S Tamil Nadu Power, to undertake a cumulative impact assessment with regard to a proposed coal-based power plant. Cumulative impact assessments were required to identify adequate mitigating measures and environmental safeguards to avoid adverse impacts on the ecologically fragile mangrove ecosystem and the local marine environment.

A review of these cases suggests that the precautionary principle is employed as a guiding and overarching principle within Indian environmental jurisprudence. It has received formal recognition as a statutory norm thereby influencing and permeating the NGT's decision-making process. The principle is a determinative norm rather than rhetoric. The greatest factor in promoting its judicial application has been the availability of merit and judicial review to the NGT. As a merit court, the NGT becomes the primary decision-maker and can undertake in-depth scrutiny which involves not only manifestly unreasonable law but also the technical evaluation underpinning a particular decision. For example, in the *M/S Sterlite Industries* case, it stated:

> The Tribunal, in exercise of its power of merit-review and being an expert body itself has to examine all aspects of such cases whether they are factual,

technical or legal … Furthermore, the scope of 'merit review' by the Tribunal is not confined to the Wednesbury's principle. Besides this, other considerations like no evidence, no specific and scientific data or abuse of authority can be additional grounds that can be considered by the Tribunal while determining such a controversy.

(Para 143)

The power of judicial review is not only concerned with the merits of the decision but also the process. The NGT exercises the limited power of judicial review to examine the procedural or constitutional validity of a notification issued under one of the Acts scheduled to the NGT Act. In *Wilfred J v MoEF* (Judgment 17 July 2014), the NGT stated: '…the language of the various provisions of the NGT Act by necessary implication gives power of judicial review to the Tribunal. There is no specific or even by necessary implication exclusion of such power indicated in any of the provisions' (para 88).[11]

However, the application of the precautionary principle at municipal level appears to have conflated the determinants 'uncertainty' and 'absolute or reasonable certainty' based on scientific information of harm. As a consequence, the threshold of risk and harm involving the precautionary intervention becomes debatable. To clarify the question of threshold, James Cameron notes:

The precautionary extent of standards would depend on the relative certainties embodied in the risk … If both the probability of accidental pollution and the magnitude of the consequences of that pollution are known, the standards would be unprecautionary because the level of uncertainty is low … However, if the probability and magnitude are relatively unknown, because, for instance, it is not known what cause and effect relationships are involved, then the standards would be precautionary because of the relative uncertainties involved.

(1999: 37–38; see also Deville and Harding 1997: 31)

To illustrate, in *Sarang Yadwadkar v Commissioner, Pune Municipal Corporation* (Judgment 11 July 2013), the Tribunal stated:

The precautionary principle can be explained to say that it contemplates that an activity which poses danger and threat to [the] environment is to be prevented. Prevention is better than cure. It means that the state governments and local authorities are supposed to anticipate and then prevent the causes of environmental degradation. The likelihood of danger has to be *based upon scientific information, data available and analysis of risks*. Ecological impact should be given paramount consideration and it is more so when resources are non-renewable or where the end results would be irreversible. The principle of precaution involves the anticipation of environmental harm and taking measures to avoid it or to choose the least environmentally harmful activity. Again it is *based on scientific uncertainty*[12] (emphasis added).

Similarly, in the M/S *Sterlite Industries* case, the Tribunal observed:

> Precautionary principle is one of the most important concepts of sustainable development. This principle essentially has the element of prevention as well as prohibition. In order to protect the environment, it may become necessary to take some preventive measures as well as to prohibit certain activities. These decisions should be based *on best possible scientific information* and analysis of risks. Precautionary measures may still have to be taken where there is *uncertainty* but potential risk exists … Precautionary principle should be invoked when the reasonable scientific data suggests that without taking appropriate preventive measure there is a plausible indication of some environmental injury or health hazard.[13]
>
> (Paras 120 and 148, emphasis added)

These rulings create uncertainty regarding the scope and application of the precautionary principle through the conflation of precaution and prevention. Despite the uncertain rationale of the judgments, the interpretation and application of the precautionary principle reinforces and gives primacy to the most developed form of prevention which remains the general basis for environmental protection measures. The Tribunal invokes the precautionary principle when either there is good reason based on empirical evidence, or plausible causal hypotheses to believe that harmful effects might occur, even if this is remote; and a scientific evaluation of the consequences and likelihoods reveals such uncertainty that it is impossible to assess the risk with sufficient confidence to inform decision-making.[14]

The judgment in *Ajay Kumar Negi v Union of India* (Judgment 7 July 2015) is illustrative of good reason to believe that harmful effects might occur and the extent of scientific uncertainty. The NGT explained:

> Precautionary Principle is a pro-active method of dealing with the environment, based on the idea that if costs of the current activities are uncertain but are potentially both high and irreversible, then society should take action before the uncertainty is resolved. The intent is to avert major environmental problems before the most serious consequences and side effects would become obvious. It works as 'do-no-harm' principle *stricto sensu*. The precautionary principle is a tool for making better health and environmental decisions. It aims to prevent harm from the outset rather than manage it after the fact has occurred. In common language, this means 'better safe than sorry'. The Precautionary Principle denotes a duty to prevent harm, when it is within our power to do so … In the recent times a serious challenge that has appeared before the courts more often than not, is the basis on which the precautionary principle is to be applied. While making such decisions, best possible scientific information, analysis of risk, ecological impacts and indication of costs, are the factors to be considered.
>
> (Paras 20 and 22)

Nevertheless, this principle in India mandates well-judged usage in favour of observing, preventing and mitigating an undetermined potential threat as modern risk factors become more complex and far-reaching.

The polluter-pays principle

The polluter-pays principle plays an important role in national and international environmental policy. It is embedded within legislation in some nations; in others, it is an implicit subtext for both environmental regulation and liability for pollution. This principle supplies the means by which the cost of pollution prevention, control and reduction measures is borne by the polluter (see, generally, Førsund 1975; Baldock 1992; Seymour *et al.* 1992; Birnie *et al.* 2009). It implies that those who caused environmental damage should pay the costs of reversing that damage and controlling further damage. The overarching principle is recognised as an integral component of sustainable development.

Though the principle appears simple, its function has evoked criticism. Nicolas de Sadeleer argued that its main function is to internalise the social costs borne by public authorities for pollution prevention and control. It is seen as an economic rule whereby polluters pay a price for the right to pollute by paying part of their profits to the public authorities responsible for environmental protection. Environmental degradation is taken for granted provided the polluter pays: 'I pay, therefore I pollute' (Sadeleer 2002: 34; see also Coase 1960; Gaines 1991). Thus polluters can decide to pollute if they can afford the fines in situations where it is the only negative sanction. It is a cost-benefit choice. Further, the relevance of the principle in situations where ecological damage has already occurred remains debatable.

Implementing the polluter-pays principle can be difficult and complex. Concerns have been raised, mainly due to the difficulty of identifying polluters, apportioning responsibility and methods of payment. Even the difficulties in restoring the ecological system, once it is contaminated, makes the assessment of payment in – terms of loss of biodiversity, habitat, groundwater and top soil – problematic. Moreover, payment is, in the end, financial and sometimes monetary compensation cannot truly compensate for ecological loss or loss of resources and, therefore, in reality the polluter is not paying the real cost of the pollution, even if restitution is possible (see Moreno-Mateos *et al.* 2012; Mauerhofer *et al.* 2013: chapter 5 n.68).

Kiss and Shelton suggest that the application of the principle is easy and effective in a geographic region subject to uniform environmental law, such as a nation state (2003: 119). The polluter-pays principle is simpler to apply when the impact is local and well defined.

In the Indian context, the polluter-pays principle includes environmental costs, as well as direct costs to people or property. The Supreme Court has expanded the *ratio* by stating that the 'remediation of the damaged environment is a part of the process of sustainable development and as such the polluter is liable to pay the cost to the individual sufferers as well as the cost of reversing the damaged ecology'.[15] The NGT has accepted and strengthened Supreme Court rulings. In *Hindustan Cocacola Beverages Pvt Ltd v West Bengal Pollution Control Board* (Judgment 19 March 2012), it stated:

> it is no more *res integra*, with regard to the legal proposition, that a polluter is bound to pay and eradicate the damage caused by him and restore the environment. He is also responsible to pay for the damages caused due to the pollution caused by him.
>
> (Para 17)

Hereafter Gaines' and Sadeleer's analyses are applied to better appreciate the NGT's interpretation and application of the polluter-pays principle. Gaines' work suggested that the principle in its original formulation applied to allocating costs of pollution prevention and control measures decided by public authorities (Gaines 1991: 473). He argued that polluter claims cover a wide range of costs and can be divided into three categories: first, pollution control at individual facilities; second, collective measures on behalf of a group of polluters; and, third, associated administrative costs.

The first category requires the cost to be borne by the facility without direct or indirect subsidy from the public treasury. The failure on the part of the polluter to comply with environmental standards attracts financial costs. The economic incentive is a good application of the polluter-pays principle as it promotes environmental protection through the polluter, instead of rigid quantitative pollution limits (ibid.). The case of *Vitthal Gopichand Bhungase v Gangakhed Sugar and Energy Ltd* (Judgment 30 July 2014) illustrates this point. The polluter, i.e. the respondent sugar industry, committed gross negligence resulting in the release of untreated industrial waste, spillage of molasses and chemical-mixed water that caused environmental damage to the surrounding area and Mannat lake. The Tribunal stated:

> In the instant case where the damages are related to change in water quality of Mannat lake, change in the characteristics of agricultural fields and also loss of means of livelihood due to not taking crop in the agricultural fields, the respondent sugar factory is liable to pay Rs.500,000 (£5,000) towards the environment restitution costs.[16]

In *Himanshu R Borat v State of Gujarat* (Judgment 22 April 2014) the NGT invoked the polluter-pays principle by imposing a pollution cost of Rupees 1,000,000 (£10,000) on account of smells and pollutants from the applicant's starch factory. The industry generated dust and particulate concentrations exceeding prescribed limits.

In *Forward Foundation v State of Karnataka* (Judgment 7 May 2015), the Tribunal applied the polluter-pays principle and directed the respondents to pay Rupees 139.85 crores (£14,126,164) at the first instance for environmental and ecological restoration, restitution and other measures to rectify damage resulting from unauthorised and illegal construction in the wetland and catchment areas of Agara and Bellandur Lakes. The default and non-compliance of ignoring and exceeding constructional threshold limits for the purpose of EC and ground-water extraction beyond permissible limits rendered the project proponents liable to pay compensation at the rate of 5 per cent of the cost of the project.[17]

In *Hazira Macchimar Samiti v Union of India* (Judgment 8 January 2016), the NGT imposed a penalty of Rupees 25 crores (£2,500,000) for carrying out development of port activities at Hajira by exceeding threshold standards and limits for environmental and CRZ clearances. It also stated that non-payment would result in the demolition of the 25 hectares of reclamation work carried out.

In *Gurpreet Singh Bagga v MoEF* (2016) SCC Online NGT 92, the NGT entertained applications from environmentalists who complained of illegal mining in the Saharanpur area and, more particularly, on the Yamuna river-banks and riverbed. While imposing a complete prohibition on further mining of minor minerals in Yamuna's floodplain, the NGT applied the polluter-pays principle and directed the five leaseholders to pay 'environmental compensa-tion' of Rupees 50 crores (£5,000,000) for and on behalf of 13 mine-lease firms for carrying out excessive unauthorised mining resulting in environmental damage and degradation. Additionally, a Rupees 2.5 crores (£250,000) fine was imposed on each of the stone-crusher firms for illegally operating stone-crushing units without consent from the state pollution control board.

A second category of environmental costs, according to Gaines, encompassed situations where control of pollution required collective measures. Where there is one group of collective users, each polluter pays its fair share of the facility's capital and operating costs based on established rate structures (1991: 474). The use of a sewage treatment plant (STP) or common effluent treatment plant (CETP) illustrates one such group. The pollution control boards (federal and state-level) in India are regulatory agencies, as well as scientific and technical organisations. The Water (Prevention and Control of Pollution) Act 1974 is legislation that aims to maintain the integrity of water-courses. Section 25 places restrictions on new outlets and new discharges lacking previous consent of state boards, or regarding existing discharge of sewage or trade effluent under section 26. The concept of CETP evolved in the 1980s to support small-scale industries to address effectively the problem of water pollution control by pro-viding common facilities to treat cost-effectively their composite effluent thereby adhering to specified norms. This concept was expanded to include large and medium-scale industries which would have their own effluent treat-ment facility and discharge treated effluent as a hydraulic load. CETPs not only help industries to control pollution, but also act as a step towards a cleaner environment and as a service to society. CETPs have the advantage of a single point of control and compatibility of effluents by homogenisation and neutrali-sation. They also facilitate better enforcement of water pollution regulations vis-à-vis impact on the environment (receiving water bodies) by having a single or fixed number of outlets. Thus, CETPs over the years have become an essential part of the environmental infrastructure in industrial areas (see Guha and Harendranath 2013: 7).[18]

The NGT has applied the polluter-pays principle in situations where industries operate as collective users on a commercial basis. In order to identify and apportion the costs between such industries, the NGT relies on state pollution control boards having sufficient data about the industries' operations over time, their effluent generation capacity, effluent quality and compliance levels. Even though CETPs are provided, they may not operate efficiently thereby wilfully releasing untreated effluent. For example, there have been major environmental impacts in terms of deteriorated water quality and disturbance to estuarine ecologies. In *Vanashakti Public Trust v Maharashtra Pollution Control Board* (Judgment 2 July 2015), the indiscriminate discharge of toxic, coloured, untreated/treated industrial effluent from six inefficiently operating and improperly maintained CETPs caused environmental pollution to several water bodies including the rivers Ulhas and Waldhuni, and badly polluting the area's groundwater. Relying on data provided by the state pollution control board, the Tribunal applied the polluter-pays principle and directed the units to lodge Rupees 76 crores (£7,600,000) with the Divisional Commissioner (Revenue) within four weeks. Failure to comply with the order attracted penal consequences.

In *R K Patel v Union of India* (Judgment 18 February 2014), the NGT imposed a charge of Rupees 1,000,000 (£10,000) towards environmental damage due to unscientific disposal and spillage of about 7,320.4 tonnes of toxic hazardous waste resulting from improper handling at the Common Hazardous Waste Treatment Storage and Disposal Facility at Vapi, Gujarat. The applicants, village farmers and residents, were aggrieved by damage caused to agricultural fields and surrounding lands, groundwater and the adjoining river by the industrial association and waste and effluent management company.

Again, the 'one group of collective users', as the polluter, was directed to pay the cost of causing pollution in *Ravindra Bhusari v MoEF* (Judgment 6 November 2015). On the basis of the polluter-pays principle, the firecracker sale agencies and shops were directed to pay Rupees 3000 (£30) each to the municipal authority as 'environmental cleanliness charges', to be used for cleaning up the solid waste generated by the firecrackers. In case of non-payment, the municipal authority was directed to take stringent action against defaulters, including black-listing or not renewing their licences. The NGT expressed concern about the ill-effects of the firecrackers in terms of noise pollution, toxic air pollution and hazardous solid waste generated, thus posing a serious threat to human health and the environment.

However, the polluter-pays principle, according to Gaines, becomes ineffective when a large and diverse group of sources cause pollution, such as motor-vehicles or urban waste discharges. They make the apportionment of costs payment (who and how) more challenging. Local authorities often do not pursue a strictly based pollution cost formula, thereby making the polluter-pays principle ineffective (Gaines 1991: 474).

In order to reach a practical solution, the NGT has introduced general 'environmental compensation' on the basis of the polluter-pays principle. In

Manoj Misra v Union of India (Order 8 May 2015), the Tribunal directed civic authorities to charge every household in Delhi, irrespective of whether they have a sewerage connection, a monthly 'environmental compensation', directly proportionate to their property tax or water bill, whichever is higher. The fund created will be utilised to provide new STPs and other technology to clean the river Yamuna. For unauthorised colonies, Rupees 100 (£1) or 500 (£5) per month will be added to electricity bills, water bills or property taxes by the respective departments which will then transfer the money to the Delhi government. The NGT's order was a consequence of the continuing river Yamuna litigation.[19] In *Vardhman Kaushik v Union of India* (Order 7 October 2015),[20] the NGT ordered diesel trucks and heavy vehicles entering NCT Delhi to pay 'environmental compensation' of Rupees 700 (£7) for two-axle, 500 (£5) for four-axle and 1000 for three-axle (£10), on the basis of the polluter-pays principle, to be utilised by the Delhi pollution control board to improve air quality.

The third category of cost, according to Gaines, includes administrative and ancillary expenses for environmental protection. This cost includes development and administration of the permit programme, including review of applications, monitoring, preparation of regulations and air quality modelling studies.

In *R K Patel v Union of India*, the NGT ordered the Vapi industries' association and waste and effluent management company to deposit with the state board Rupees 15 lakhs (£15,000) towards the cost of evolving the remediation programme by undertaking the study of contamination of affected areas, including agricultural lands and water bodies. The expenditure of monitoring, sampling/analysis, investigations and supervision was also included as a cost on the basis of the polluter-pays principle.

The work of Sadeleer introduces a final determinant which emphasises the contribution of the polluter-pays to the reduction of pollution through its preventive function and allowing victims of ecological damage to receive curative compensation. According to Sadeleer, the polluter-pays principle should be identified as a preventive norm. The rule is capable of persuading polluters from polluting if the costs, as allocated by the principle, are considered too high. However, such a preventive role seems somewhat limited in practice. According to Sadeleer:

> ...put at the service of prevention, the polluter-pays principle should no longer be interpreted as allowing a polluter who pays to continue polluting with impunity. The true aim of the principle would henceforth be to institute a policy of pollution abatement by encouraging polluters to reduce their emissions instead of being content to pay charges. The polluter pays and preventive principles would constitute two complementary aspects of a single reality.
>
> (Sadeleer 2002: 36)

The case of *Krishan Kant Singh v National Ganga River Basin Authority* (Judgment 16 October 2014) is illustrative of the preventive function of the polluter-pays principle. An application was filed jointly by an environmentalist and an NGO, SAFE, alleging the Simbhaoli Sugar Mills and Distillery discharged untreated, highly toxic and harmful effluents into the Phuldera drain which joins the holy River Ganges. The contamination was so high that it not only polluted the Syana Escape canal and the River Ganges but also threatened endangered aquatic species, such as dolphins and turtles. Allegations included the pollution of the groundwater of villages adjacent to the river. The NGT held that the sugar unit was a serious polluter, observing:

> ...this unit has continuously failed to comply with the requirements of law and discharge its statutory obligations on the one hand while on the other it has also failed to fulfil its corporate social responsibilities. Therefore, the unit is liable to make good and to restore damage, degradation and the pollution of environment caused by its activity particularly, the water bodies and with greater emphasis on the River Ganga.
>
> (Para 59)

Accordingly, the NGT applied the polluter-pays principle and imposed a penalty of Rupees 5 Crores (£500,000). Additionally, it imposed on the sugar mill the installation cost of an incinerator for its spent wash and concentrate effluents to achieve zero discharge. The financial difficulties – Rupees 20 crores (£2,500,000) – of installation were not considered a tenable plea against preventing and controlling excessive pollution caused by the sugar mill. The mill was also directed to remove sludge and clean the Puldhera drain within three months, failing which a further sum of Rupees 1 Crore (£100,000) was to be paid to the regulatory authorities.

The curative function of the polluter-pays principle 'represents a further step forward. Instead of simply obliging the polluter to pay for restoration carried out by the public authorities, it would also ensure that victims could obtain compensation from polluters' (Sadeleer 2002: 37). The curative function is in consonance with section 15 NGT Act. The special NGT's jurisdiction empowers it to order relief and compensation to victims of pollution and other environmental damage arising out of the enactments in Schedule 1, including restitution of property damaged and the environment.[21] In *Ramdas Janardan Koli v Secretary, MoEF* (Judgment 27 February 2015), the affected 1630 fishermen's families were awarded Rupees 951,920,000 (£9,519,200) for loss of livelihood, as well as implementation of rehabilitation of those unsettled on account of the developmental projects in question. In *R K Patel v Union of India*, the NGT awarded Rupees 326,225 (£3300) each to 21 farmers as compensation towards actual loss, probable future loss, non-pecuniary damages (mental harassment) and loss due to lower soil fertility. Failure to pay on the part of industries would lead to attachment of their properties.

A review of the above judgments demonstrates that the NGT has applied the polluter-pays principle where the rights of the parties are clearly defined and information is complete. However, the polluter-pays principle on occasion has been used controversially, especially when powerful interests and politically influential parties are involved. The much publicised case of *Manoj Misra v Delhi Development Authority* (Orders 9 and 10 March 2016),[22] where a cultural festival organised by Art of Living (AOL) Foundation was directed to pay Rupees 5 crores (£500,000) as an interim environmental fine for allegedly damaging the Yamuna floodplains. It is suggested that the NGT backed down and allowed the festival to take place via an initial deposit of Rupees 25 lakhs (£25,000). The festival was attended by Prime Minister Modi and his cabinet. Sri Sri Ravi Shankar, the spiritual leader, stated: 'we have not done anything wrong. We have been taintless and will remain so. We will go to jail but not pay a penny'.[23]

Permission to allow the event was a consequence of delay on the part of the applicant to approach the NGT – a case of fait accompli – as AOL had substantially completed the construction work on the floodplain.[24] The NGT failed to enforce its orders against AOL. Ironically, on 13 January 2015, the NGT in the Yamuna case (*Manoj Misra v Union of India*) had prohibited constructional activity or celebrations on the floodplain and it was severely criticised for violating its earlier order. Ritwick Dutta, an environmental lawyer, stated:

> NGT's order has set a bad precedent. This order communicates the message of 'Pay & Pollute' and that's what has happened in this case. Here the message that has gone to public is very clear – those who have big pockets and right connections can flout the law and escape – be it Sri Sri Ravi Shankar or others.[25]

Shehzad Poonawala, a legal and social activist, agrees:

> I'm thoroughly disappointed by the lack of spine and conviction by the NGT in upholding its own order. It has allowed the 'Polluter pays' principle to be inverted into a 'Pay and Pollute' principle (very little of course). Moreover, relaxing the amount of fine and payment period!, what's worse is the convenient concessions granted to a law breaker, who happens to be a good friend of our PM! What message does it send to others? Break environmental guidelines, challenge the courts, be brazen and the tribunal/court will back off?[26]

Public interest lawyer and activist, Prashant Bhushan, tweeted: 'NGT's expert panel said 120 crores. Yet NGT levied 5 crores fine. Even that deferred! Clearly Sri Sri enjoys impunity!'[27] Former Environment Minister, Jairam Ramesh, wondered whether some 'higher-ups' had made phone calls to the NGT which had resulted in the event going ahead.[28]

The AOL episode exposes a weakness in India's environmental regulatory system, demonstrating the willingness of authorities to bend rules at the dictate of the affluent and influential. The NGT's fait accompli argument is disconcerting and turns back the clock. The effectiveness of imposing environmental costs depends upon monitoring and enforcement by regulatory agencies. More generally, pressure or corruption and ineptitude pose immense threats to the environment and the public at large. The environmental compensation cost only works if payment is enforced and is sufficiently punitive to act as a deterrent. The NGT, normally a pillar of strength, within this national controversy should have been bold enough to set an exemplar by demonstrating its independence and freedom from external, high-level pressure.

The principle of sustainable development

Sustainable development has become the hegemonic key obligation and aspiration in various national and international legal instruments. Over time, the mainstream understanding of sustainable development has been presented in terms of 'vision expression, value change, moral development, social reorganisation or transformational process' (Gladwin *et al.* 1995: 876; see also Clark 1989; Lee 1993). It is a challenging concept, essentially an 'anthropocentric concept of sustained intra-generational and intergenerational justice, claiming for humans the right to a dignified life … to include a decent standard of living, social cohesion, full participation, and healthy environment' (Hak *et al.* 2009: 2). Although the core appreciation of sustainable development appears clear, its definition and practical interpretation has produced strong discussion from different academic perspectives, thereby turning it into a complex and multi-dimensional issue.[29]

Sachs' work (2015) argues that sustainable development is both a science of complex systems and a normative concept. Sustainable development can be seen as a *science of complex systems* that 'gives rise to behaviours and patterns that are not easily discernible from the underlying components themselves … to produce something that is "more than the sum of its parts"' (ibid.: 7). The use of sustainable development expertise is essential to provide appropriate solutions to technical or complicated environmental problems.[30]

In its *normative outlook*, sustainable development 'recommends a set of goals to which the world should aspire … sustainable development recommends a holistic framework, in which society aims for economic, social, and environmental goals' (Sachs 2015: 3).[31] The normative concept reconciles economic development, social development and environmental protection by adopting a path that 'meets the need of the present without compromising the ability of future generations to meet their own needs' (Brundtland Commission 1987: 41). The fundamental concepts of integration and equity are interwoven in an explicitly normative principle which represents a formalisation of the intuitively attractive idea of a balanced synthesis of economic and social development compatible with environmental protection. The three-part vision was emphasised in the Rio+20 Summit[32] and reinvigorated in the universally applicable SDGs.[33]

Further, in its normative form, the principle of good governance underpins sustainable development. According to Sachs, 'from a normative perspective then, we could say that a good society is not only an economically prosperous society (with high per capita income) but also one that is also socially inclusive, environmentally sustainable, and well governed' (Sachs 2015: 12; see also Choudhury and Skarstedt 2005: 21; Grant and Das 2015: 303–304). Accountability, transparency, participation, the application of polluter-pays and the commitment to sustainable development are the principles of good governance that need to transcend key institutions and organisations to achieve this goal (Sachs 2015: 502–505; see also Santiso 2013: 166).

Applying Sachs' interpretation to the NGT suggests that the Tribunal operates as a fulcrum of sustainable development. The NGT's invocation of principles of good governance to achieve sustainable development is a consequence of the regulatory failure to create substantive, effective prohibitions on environmental destruction. The slack performance of inadequately funded statutory bodies and enforcement agencies, political interference and a lack of will to tackle ensconced industrial and commercial interests contribute to poor environmental administration (Divan and Rosencranz 2001: 2–3; South Asian Human Rights Documentation Centre 2008: 423). The committee appointed by the Ministry of Environment of Forest and Climate Change (MoEF) known as the TSR Subramanian Committee[34] submitted a damning report[35] highlighting the failure of environmental governance:

> A knee-jerk attitude in governance, flabby decision-making processes, ad hoc and piecemeal environmental governance practices have become the order of the day ... legal instruments have really served only the purpose of a venal administration, at the Centre and the States, to meet rent-seeking propensity at all levels. This impression has been further strengthened by waves of large scale 'clearances', coupled with major delays in approvals in individual cases. It should also be added that our business-men and entrepreneurs are not all imbued in the principles of rectitude – most are not reluctant, indeed actively seek short-cuts, and are happy to collaboratively pay a 'price' to get their projects going; in many instances, arbitrariness means that those who don't fall in line have to stay out. The state – arbitrary, opaque, suspiciously tardy or in-express-mode at different times, along with insensitivity – has failed to perform, inviting the intervention of the judiciary. The administrative machineries in the Government in the domain of Environment & Forests at all the levels, authorised to administer by Parliament's statutory mandate, appear to have abdicated their responsibilities.[36]

The failure and incapacity of the regulatory agencies to act in good faith has perversely resulted in side-lining environmental interests. The race for economic growth has resulted in the fast-tracking of ECs by failing to comply with the statutory norms. For example, between June 2014 and April 2015, 103 mining projects and 54 infrastructure projects were granted ECs.[37] The worst affected are the poor tribal and backward classes.[38] As tribal-inhabited regions are rich in minerals, forests and natural resources, large-scale development projects, such as construction of dams, power projects, mining and industrial operations, are often located in such areas. For example, the disappearance of forest cover due to mining and industrial operations over the years, coupled with weak enforcement of compensatory afforestation programmes, has resulted in environmental degradation and displacement of the marginalised. As a part of the nation-building process through a state-sponsored development agenda corresponding with economic liberalisation and corporate entry, there is minimal regard for the rights of affected people (see Ministry of Tribal Affairs: 2014).

The operationalisation of the principle of sustainable development for projects of strategic and national importance and the larger interests of the people (particularly, but often detrimentally, affecting the poor and backward classes) raises important challenges that involve complex synergies and trade-offs. The word 'development' (Sarkar 2009: xvi)[39] is interpreted as 'economic betterment', but this may be a misnomer. The dichotomy appears when economic development, linked with environmental protection and the human rights of tribal and backward classes, conflicts with state development plans and multinational operations. In many cases there is involvement by powerful local elites capable and willing to manipulate political, legal and judicial systems.

In the light of the above discussion, the current and contentious debate in India involves either giving 'greater weight to economic benefits [which], because of their tangibility and quantifiability, tend to be given greater weight in these balancing exercises than the often less tangible or immediate benefits for society of environmental protection' (Woolley 2014: 25; see also Owens 1997), or acknowledging that 'acceptability of economic growth should be determined and limited by reference to [the] carrying capacity of the natural system' (Garver 2012: 322–334; see also Bosselmann 2011: 204–213).

The NGT recognises that 'development' is the essence of any pragmatic and progressive society based upon a 'balancing act' that includes the full spectrum of civil, political, cultural, economic and social process to conserve ecology and improve the well-being of citizens. In a series of cases, the Tribunal succinctly expressed sustainable development as:

> …development that can take place and which can be sustained by nature/ ecology with or without mitigation. While applying the concept of sustainable development, one has to keep in mind the 'Principle of Proportionality' based on the concept of balance and there is a need to have trade-off between the development & environment. As such, the Tribunal has to balance the priorities of development on the one hand and environmental problems on the other. So sustainable development should address the requirement of development that can be allowed and which can be sustained by environment with or without any significant adverse impacts, keeping in view the public interests rather than the interests of handful of persons or group of persons, according to a 'reasonable person's test'.[40]

The following judgments are illustrative of trade-offs exercised in pursuing economic, social and environmental goals. *Leo Saldhana v Union of India* (Judgment 27 August 2014) is an example of change of use, namely the diversion of a grassland ecosystem known as Amrit Mahal Kaval for non-forest purposes involving proposed urban and industrial infrastructure development and research and defence-related projects. In an application before the NGT, Leo F Saldanha, an environmental activist, prayed the NGT to direct state and central government authorities to maintain Amrit Mahal Kaval free from diversion or encroachment and sought to remove civil constructions illegally erected there and restore it to its earlier condition. Amrit Mahal Kaval are grassland ecosystems with rich biodiversity and distinctive ecological attributes. They have traditionally supported local communities for multiple purposes, such as collection of firewood, green-leaf vegetables and fruits. They are an important source of survival for livestock and rural people, protecting soil, water and rare wildlife, and crucial to biodiversity conservation. The grasslands are unique semi-arid ecosystems supporting a variety of floral and faunal species, many of which are endangered and endemic to the region. They are also known to be the abode of endangered fauna including black bucks, great Indian bustards and lesser floricans.

The respondents (Bhabha Atomic Research Centre (BARC), Defence Research and Development Organisation (DRDO), Indian Institute of Science (IISc) and Indian Space Research Organisation (ISRO)) refuted the allegations and defended their position that the land was lawfully allotted to establish projects of strategic and national importance concerning national security and development. BARC, a constituent of the Department of Atomic Energy, is engaged in nuclear science and technology activities concerning atomic energy development – a policy requirement for energy security, including social needs covering healthcare, food, agriculture, drinking water etc. DRDO, a national organisation under the Ministry of Defence, specialises in researching unmanned aerial vehicles for effective security monitoring and reducing human casualties. IISc is the premier research institute in India. It intends to expand its climate research laboratory, for which foreign funding has been approved. ISRO is a central government-owned premier organisation undertaking space research and development. Its communication satellites have improved systems for mobile phones, telecommunication, satellite television and internet communication, and are also used for nationwide satellite distance education programmes.

The NGT, relying on Supreme Court *dicta*,[41] applied the sustainable development principle to balance competing interests using the 'larger public interest' rule. For the Tribunal, if a project is beneficial for the larger public, inconvenience to a smaller number is acceptable. The balancing of equities entails policy choices and involves applying the 'margin of appreciation' doctrine. Making these choices necessitates decisions, not only about risk regulation, but also how much protection is sufficient and whether ends served by environmental protection could be pursued more effectively by diverting resources to other uses. There was cause to preserve Amrit Mahal Kaval land and maintain the grassland ecosystems. However, allotments were made to contesting respondents for their respective projects of national importance and useful from the larger public interest viewpoint. Hence, the Tribunal decided not to interfere with their proposed activities in the lands allotted.

In *Prafulla Samantray v Union of India* (Judgment 30 March 2012) (the POSCO case),[42] the Tribunal sought to reconcile environmental considerations to ensure sustainability, social equity and an inclusive interpretation of 'development', particularly for tribal and poor people. For years, the affected people, physically and culturally dependent on their environment, faced violation of their human rights as a result of having to live under siege – a price paid for voicing their opposition to POSCO, a South Korean multinational steel company, and the state of Orissa. An independent NGO report in 2013 tells the story of a human rights and sustainability crisis induced by a mega-development project, specifically the proposed construction of an integrated steel plant with a service sea-port, that would result in the forced migration of thousands of poor people. It states:

> India's attempts to forcibly evict these communities stand in violation of international and domestic law. The Government of India must end human rights abuses tied to its project with the South Korean steel giant POSCO, and must immediately cease illegal seizure of land which threatens to forcibly displace as many as 22,000 people in the state of Odisha. Should the project move forward, entire villages will be decimated, livelihoods will be destroyed, and families will be rendered homeless, all in the name of 'development'. Entire communities in the project-affected area have been living under siege and have suffered clear violations of their rights to security of person and freedom of movement; their rights to be free from arbitrary arrest and detention; and their right to be free from discrimination – particularly on the basis of political or other opinions. Living under siege has also resulted in significant disruptions to many villagers' ability to access health care, schools, markets, and crops, undermining their rights to health, education, work, and food. On the environmental front, the construction of the proposed plant and port threatens the area's unique biodiversity. Many species of animals live and breed in the area's waters, lush estuaries, and dense forest. Among them is the endangered olive ridley turtle, which is protected under Indian law. The site of the proposed captive port includes beaches which serve as a nesting site for over 100,000 olive ridley turtles every year, one of only three such sites worldwide and the only site in the Eastern Hemisphere. Ecologically important horse shoe crabs also depend on the sediment along the coast in the port area, and fish and shrimps use the estuaries and coastal waters as breeding grounds. There also exist well-founded concerns regarding air pollution and the diversion of water resources.
>
> (International Human Rights Clinic/ESCR-Net 2013: 1–4, 15)

The NGT suspended the EC thereby supporting and vindicating the claims of the affected tribal people. It found that approval was granted improperly to POSCO and it directed the MoEF to conduct a fresh review in accordance with the law.

There are often competing interests concerning the construction of dams. The state is responsible for the appropriate and equitable collection, storage, availability and usage of water. India is monsoon-dependent for water and its irregular supply is under increasing competitive pressure from industrialisation, new farming processes and a growing population. There is continuing debate concerning the effectiveness and environmental impact of large as opposed to multiple small dams. Large dams involve submergence or destruction of forests and have significant social consequences, including large-scale rehabilitation and resettlement, family and community disruption and employment issues for relocated tribal people. This debate is well illustrated by the Sardar Sarovar dam in Maharashtra (Cullet 2010).[43] The importance of the caretaker role of the state and of relevant government agencies in approving appropriate development projects after assessing technical data, social and environmental impact studies and compliance with environmental legal requirements is crucial.

The NGT adjudicated a mega-dam dispute when required legal procedures prior to construction of the Mapithel dam were ignored by the MoEF and state of Manipur. The completed dam would submerge 778 hectares of agricultural land and 595 hectares of forest, resulting in the displacement of thousands of mainly tribal people. Under the Forest Rights Act 2006, certain procedures must be followed before permission can be granted to use forest land for non-forest purposes. The Act requires that affected people must be consulted and must approve the change of use. Since almost 80 per cent of the affected villagers are dependent on agriculture and forest produce, it is perhaps unsurprising that state officials attempted to circumvent the legislation and ignore the rights of locals. The villagers took their grievances to the NGT (*Themrei Tuithung v State of Manipur* (Original Application 167/2013 5 August 2013)), arguing that the project did not have the necessary MoEF clearance. More generally, it was stated that Manipur's neoliberal policies, which had attracted significant inward infrastructure investment, were exploiting natural resources at the expense of residents. The result was growing land alienation, community displacement and human rights violations. In November 2013, the NGT suspended construction of the dam on grounds of non-compliance with the relevant environmental protection regulations and in the public interest (Order 12 November 2013).

In *Lower Painganga Dharan Virodhi v State of Maharashtra* (Judgment 10 March 2014), the NGT was faced with the issue of deciding on dam construction approval in the light of its social, economic and environmental consequences. The applicants approached the NGT to quash the EC issued for the construction of an irrigation project (dam) in order to protect the ecology and interests of tribal farmers and villagers. According to the applicants, the proposed project would adversely affect 90,000 hectares of land, including forest land, and displace 7102 families, consisting of 35,388 tribal people whose families have lived in the area for generations. It was alleged that the EC was obtained illegally by the respondents as the procedural requirement of a public hearing was not followed.

The respondents contended that the EC was lawfully obtained. They submitted a special study conducted by an expert agency that had evaluated the feasibility of the irrigation project. The respondents provided a plan for the rehabilitation and resettlement of the affected tribal people to the Ministry of Tribal Affairs, Government of India, in order to ensure that the affected people were compensated and relocated. The NGT, after going through the voluminous records and documents, decided the irrigation project satisfied the principle of sustainable development and that the environmental safeguards proposed by the project proponent and stipulated by the regulatory authorities were adequately incorporated. The Tribunal observed:

> availability of irrigation facilities in the area will help cultivators to minimize or curtail dependency on annual rainfall, which is many times unpredictable. The right to development includes, of course, protection of fundamental human rights. Thus, if the irrigation project is required for [the] larger benefit of the society, then it must be ensured that the Project Affected Families are given [a] justifiable rehabilitation package. Rehabilitation is not only about providing basic amenities, food and shelter. It encompasses support to restore means of livelihood.
>
> (Para 44)

Despite the recognition by the NGT of the rights of poor people and the need to allow development subject to environmental regulations, a shocking report by the Comptroller and Auditor General (CAG) on the Management of Irrigation Projects in Maharashtra, in June 2014, condemns the state government's repeated failure to undertake its statutory environmental protection duties and social responsibilities in regard to water management. The CAG report stated that as many as 249 projects of the Vidharbha Irrigation Development Corporation (VIDC) commenced without receiving the necessary EC from the central MoEF or the State Environment Department.[44]

In summary, the NGT has become the cynosure of the application of sustainable development. Its direction favours pragmatically embracing development for the maximisation of human welfare without causing irreversible damage to the environment. The principle, despite challenges and difficult choices, has been swiftly and powerfully infused in its decision-making process to achieve and maintain ecologically sustainable human development. The integration of environmental protection with economic and social development maintains and improves human well-being for current and future generations.

Conclusion

The chapter has examined the international treaties and obligations relating to the environment that have been accepted in India and are now embedded in the NGT Act. Established global principles underpinning environmental jurisprudence include the precautionary, polluter-pays and sustainable development principles. Yet each recognised principle carries within it the possibility of challenge and interpretation. Academic discourse continues to dissect these principles to examine their strengths, weaknesses and effectiveness in terms of providing equitable relief and environmental protection. Academic competition and debate has been reviewed alongside the practical application of these principles in NGT cases. The challenges and choices facing the Tribunal are significant and meaningful. An adequate water supply from a mega-dam has to be contrasted with the consequential human impact on the lives of forest-dwellers whose very livelihood may be drowned in much needed water. Such stark choices are made daily by the NGT. Within this institutional framework, the principles laid out above provide decision-making guidance for bench members.

Notes

1 Article 51 Constitution of India states:

> The State shall endeavour to: (a) promote international peace and security; (b) maintain just and honourable relations between nations; (c) foster respect for international law and treaty obligations in the dealings of organised peoples with one another; and (d) encourage settlement of international disputes by arbitration.

Further, it confers plenary powers on Parliament to enter into treaties and agreements and enact necessary legislation. Article 253 states:

> Notwithstanding anything in the foregoing provisions of this Chapter, Parliament has power to make any law for the whole or any part of the territory of India for implementing any treaty, agreement or convention with any other country or countries or any decision made at any international conference, association or other body.

2 UN Conferences on the Human Environment, Stockholm, and Environment and Development, Rio de Janeiro. The use of general environmental protection and conservation legal principles also appear in basic law and judicial construction. The NGT has explained the principle of environmental protection by interpreting its enabling Act in a manner that achieves better results for the environment and ecology by insisting on the adoption of robust environmentally friendly measures. For example, see *S C Pandey v Union of India* (Judgment 20 August 2014), *Deshpande J N Samiti v State of Maharashtra* (Judgment 22 April 2014) and *Bhausaheb v State of Maharashtra* (Judgment 5 November 2014). Its approach includes: 'the classic elements of protection and preservation, including restoration and the safeguarding of ecological processes and genetic diversity besides management of natural resources in order to sustain their maintenance by sustainable utilization' (Birnie *et al.* 2009: 590). The broadened perception and treatment of conservation has given effect to the doctrine of public trust (Sax 1970: 471) as an affirmation of state power to conserve natural resources for public use and enjoyment within a rights and justice discourse. The principle of inter-generational equity (Weiss 1984) underpinning international environmental law has also been absorbed into this doctrine. State responsibility to safeguard natural resources must benefit present and future generations through careful and objective planning and management. In *Goa Foundation v Union of India* (Judgment 18 July 2013), para 17, the NGT observed:

the Preamble of the NGT Act is a sufficient indicator of the jurisdiction that is vested in the Tribunal. This is the first indicator of the legislative intent which provides that a case could relate to environmental protection, conservation of forests and other natural resources or even enforcement of legal rights relating to environment and other matters mentioned thereto. Environmental protection and conservation is not only the obligation of the state but in fact all concerned.

For a detailed discussion, see Gill (2014: 190–194).

3 *Manoj Misra v Union of India* (Judgment 13 January 2015); *Ajay Kumar Negi v Union of India* (Judgment 7 July 2015); *R Lohakare v Maharashtra Prevention of Water Pollution Board* (Judgment 24 September 2014); *J K Pharande v MoEF* (Judgment 16 May 2014); *M P Patil v Union of India* (Judgment 13 March 2014); *Durga Dutt v State of Himachal Pradesh* (Judgment 6 February 2014); *Jeet Singh Kanwar v Union of India* (Judgment 16 April 2013); *Rana Sengupta v Union of India* (Judgment 22 March 2013).

4 See also European Commission (2000: 4): 'recourse to the precautionary principle presupposes that potentially dangerous effects deriving from a phenomenon, product or process have been identified, and that scientific evaluation does not allow the risk to be determined with sufficient certainty'; Beck 1992; Breyer 1993; Fisher 2002; 2006.

5 Descriptors such as 'risk', 'ignorance', 'indeterminacy' and 'uncertainty' have made the concept of scientific uncertainty complex. The threshold of scientific evidence of harm which warrants precautionary action is debatable. For a detailed discussion, see Wynne 1992; Harding and Fisher 1999.

6 Bodansky (1991) remarks: 'it is difficult to speak of a single precautionary principle at all'; whereas Dovers and Handmer (1991: 174) state: 'the precautionary principle is a composite of several value-laden notions and loose, qualitative descriptors'. For a detailed discussion, see Harding and Fisher 1999.

7 *Vellore Citizen's Welfare Forum v Union of India* (1995) 5 SCC 647; *Narmada Bachao Andolan v Union of India* (2000) 10 SCC 664; *N D Jayal v Union of India* (2004) 9 SCC 362.

8 *M C Mehta v Union of India* (2004) 12 SCC 118; *Research Foundation for Science v Union of India* (2005) 13 SCC 186; *Karnataka Industrial Area Development Board v C Kenchappa* (2006) 6 SCC 371; *AP Pollution Control Board v Professor M V Nayadu I* (1999) 2 SCC 718; *AP Pollution Control Board v Professor M V Nayadu II* (2001) 2 SCC 62; *T N Godavarman Thirumalpad v Union of India* (2002) 10 SCC 606; *Tirupur Dyeing Factory Association v Noyal River Ayacutdars Protection* (2009) 9 SCC 737; *M C Mehta v Union of India* (2009) 6 SCC 142; *In re Delhi Transport Department* (1998) 9 SCC 250.

9 Ibid.

10 See Chapter 6.

11 See also *S P Muthuraman v Union of India* (Judgment 7 July 2015).

12 *Sarang Yadwadkar v Commissioner*, para 30.

13 See also *Gurpreet Singh Bagga v MoEF* (2016) SCC Online NGT 92.

14 Good reason to believe that harmful effects may occur are demonstrated by empirical evidence; by analogy with another activity, product or situation shown to carry a substantial adverse risk; or by showing a sound theoretical explanation (tested by peer review) as to how harm might be caused. This interpretation is directly borrowed from the UK Interdepartmental Liaison Group on Risk Assessment www.hse.gov.uk/aboutus/meetings/committees/ilgra/pppa.htm.

15 *Indian Council for Enviro-Legal Action v Union of India* (1996) 3 SCC 212; *Karnataka Industrial Area Development Board v C Kenchappa* (n 8); *M C Mehta v Union of India* (2006) 3 SCC 399.

16 See also, *Sandip Kayastha v Alandi Municipality* (Judgment 1 October 2015).

17 See Chapter 3.
18 See also Maharashtra Pollution Control Board, 'Concept of CETP' mpcb.gov.in/ images/pdf/Concept_of_CETP.pdf; *MoEF&CC*, *'Common effluent treatment'* www. envfor.nic.in/divisions/cpoll/cept.htm; *Central Pollution Control Board Industry Specific Standards* www.cpcb.nic.in/Industry_Specific_Standards.php.
19 The Yamuna is Delhi's lifeline, providing a constant water supply. It is undisputed that the Yamuna is critically threatened by unrelenting encroachments on its flood-plain and increasing population load, with pollutants emanating as much from domestic refuse, as agricultural practices in the floodplain and industrial effluents from the catchment area. The floodplains and riverbed are under increasing pressure of alternative land use, driven primarily by economic growth economy at the cost of the river's integrity as an ecosystem. The state and citizens have failed to discharge their fundamental duty of protecting and preserving the Yamuna. It is polluted by large and diverse polluters. The only way to rejuvenate and maintain its wholesome-ness of the river is by introducing an 'environmental compensation' cost.
20 See Chapter 3.
21 Ibid.
22 The NGT on 9 March 2016 stated:

> the flood plains have been drastically tampered with while destroying the natural flow of the river, reeds, grasses, natural vegetation on the river bed. It has further disturbed the aquatic life of the river and destroyed water bodies. Furthermore, they have constructed ramps, roads, compaction of earth, pontoon bridges and other semi-permanent or temporary structures etc. even without the permission of the concerned authorities including Ministry of Water Resources. For the damage caused to the environment, ecology, biodiversity and aquatic life of the river, the Foundation should be held liable for its restoration in all respects...
>
> (Paras 6–7)

23 'Everything's fine, says Sri Sri Ravi Shankar, except the fine' *Indian Express*, 11 March 2016 indianexpress.com/article/india/india-news-inda/pay-fine-by-tomorrow-or-face-action-ngt-tells-aol-sri-sri-ravi-shankar.
24 A different note was struck by the NGT in other cases. For example, in *Forward Foundation v State of Karnataka* (Judgment 7 May 2015), it rejected the plea that the projects' construction is nearing completion and huge amounts of the respondents' money is at stake. The respondents cannot be permitted to take advantage of their own wrong.
25 'NGT vs AOL: how the green Tribunal flouted its own order against Sri Sri's organisation' *First Post India*, 11 March 2016 www.firstpost.com/india/ngt-vs-aol-how-the-green-tribunal-flouted-its-own-order-against-sri-sris-organisation-2670494.html.
26 Ibid.
27 'How Art of Living managed to circumvent the NGT ruling' Legally India, 12 March 2016 www.legallyindia.com/bar-bench-litigation/how-art-of-living-managed-to-circumvent-the-ngt-ruling-and-get-away-paying-only-rs-2–5-cr-despite-its-open-defiance.
28 'Maybe someone called up NGT to clear Sri Sri event' *Indian Express*, 18 March 2016 http://indianexpress.com/article/india/india-news-india/wcf-ngt-aol-sri-sri-jairam-ramesh/.
29 For a literature review, see Dernbach 1998; Bosselmann 2008; Ciegis *et al.* 2009; Cordonier-Segger and Khalfan 2004; Bándi *et al.* 2014; Dernbach and Cheever 2015; Grant and Das 2015.
30 For a discussion of scientific expertise and sustainable development, see Chapter 6.
31 According to Sachs, the definition of sustainable development has developed into a more practical approach, focusing less on intergenerational needs.
32 'The Future We Want' A/RES/66/228 GA Resolution 27 July 2012:

> We recognize that poverty eradication, changing unsustainable and promoting sustainable patterns of consumption and production and protecting and managing the natural resource base of economic and social development are the overarching objectives of and essential requirements for sustainable development. We also reaffirm the need to achieve sustainable development by promoting sustained, inclusive and equitable economic growth, creating greater opportunities for all, reducing inequalities, raising basic standards of living, fostering equitable social development and inclusion, and promoting integrated and sustainable management of natural resources and ecosystems that supports, inter alia, economic, social and human development while facilitating ecosystem conservation, regeneration and restoration and resilience in the face of new and emerging challenges
>
> (Para 4)

https://sustainabledevelopment.un.org/futurewewant.html.

33 'Transforming our World: the 2030 Agenda for Sustainable Development' A/RES/70/1 GA Resolution 25 September 2015:

> We envisage a world in which every country enjoys sustained, inclusive and sustainable economic growth and decent work for all. A world in which consumption and production patterns and use of all natural resources – from air to land, from rivers, lakes and aquifers to oceans and seas – are sustainable. One in which democracy, good governance and the rule of law as well as an enabling environment at national and international levels, are essential for sustainable development, including sustained and inclusive economic growth, social development, environmental protection and the eradication of poverty and hunger...
>
> (Para 9)

https://sustainabledevelopment.un.org/post2015/transformingourworld.

34 MoEF&CC, Government of India OM No 22–15/2014-IA.III 29 August 2014. The MoEF was renamed as MOEFCC in 2014.

35 Report of the High Level Committee on Forest and Environment Related Laws, November 2014. See also Chapter 7.

36 High Level Committee Report (n 35), 8 and 22.

37 See Introduction.

38 Note: 'backward class' is collective term used by the government of India to classify castes that are educationally and socially disadvantaged. It is one of several official classifications of the population of India other than the Scheduled Castes and Scheduled Tribes in the lists prepared by the government of India. See http://socialjustice.nic.in/aboutdivision4.php.

39 Sarkar writes: 'For most practitioners and theorists ... the overall objectives of alleviating poverty and human suffering and of improving the human condition more generally are the desired end product of the development process.'

40 *Shobha Phadanvis v State of Maharashtra* (Judgment 13 January 2014); *Sarang Yadwadkar v Commissioner* (Judgment 11 July 2013); *Devender Kumar v Union of India* (Judgment 14 March 2013); *Pathankot Welfare Association v State of Punjab* (Judgment 25 November 2014); *K L Dagale v Maharshtra Pollution Control Board* (Judgment 18 February 2015); *A Gothandaraman v Commissioner* (Judgment 17 March 2015); *K G Mohanaram v Tamil Nadu Pollution Control Board* (Judgment 22 April 2015); *T V N Sangam v Secretary, MoEF* (Judgment 7 August 2015); *Paryawaran Sanrakshan Sangarsh Samiti Lippa v Union of India* (Judgment 4 May 2016); *M/S Riverside Resorts Ltd v Pimpri Chinchwad Municipal Corporation* Judgment 29 January 2014.

41 *Narmada Bachao Andolan v Union of India* (n 7); *Lafarge Uranium Mining Private Ltd v Union of India* (2011) 7 SCC 338; *T N Godavarman Thirumapad v Union of India* (n 8); *N D Jayal v Union of India* (2004) 9 SCC 362.

42 See Chapter 3.
43 'The Ups and Downs of Dams' *Economist,* 20 May 2010 www.economist.com/node/16136280.
44 'Rampant environmental violation of Maharashtra Water Resource Department' South Asia Network on Dams, Rivers and People, 21 June 2014 https://sandrp.wordpress.com/2014/06/20/press-release21–06–14-rampant-environmental-violations-of-maharashtra-water-resource-department/.

References

Baldock, D (1992) 'The polluter pays principle and its relevance to agricultural policy in European countries' 32(1) *Sociologia Ruralis* 49–65.

Bándi, G, Szabo, M and Szalai, A (2014) *Sustainability, Law and Public Choice* (Europa Law).

Beck, U (1992) *Risk Society* (Sage).

Birnie, P, Boyle, A and Redgwell, C (2009) *International Law and the Environment* (OUP).

Bodansky, D 'Scientific uncertainty and the precautionary principle' 33(7) *Environment* 4–44.

Bosselmann, K (2008) *The Principle of Sustainability* (Ashgate).

Bosselmann, K (2011) 'From reductionist environmental law to sustainability law' in P Burdon (ed.), *Exploring Wild Law: The Philosophy of Earth Jurisprudence* (Wakefield Press).

Breyer, S (1993) *Breaking the Vicious Circle: Toward Effective Risk Regulation* (Harvard UP).

Brundtland Commission (1987) *Report of the World Commission on Environment and Development: Our Common Future* www.un-documents.net/our-common-future.pdf.

Cameron, J (1999) 'The precautionary principle: core meaning, constitutional framework and procedures for implementation' in R Harding and E Fisher (eds), *Perspectives on the Precautionary Principle* (Federation Press).

Choudhury, N and Skarstedt, C E (2005) 'The principle of good governance' CISDL Draft Legal Working Paper (CISDL).

Ciegis, R, Ramanauskiene, J and Martinkus, B (2009) 'The concept of sustainable development and its use for sustainability scenario' 2 *Inzinerine Ekonomika-Engineering Economics* 28–37.

Clark, W C (1989) 'Managing planet earth' 261(3) *Scientific American* 47–54.

Coase, R H (1960) 'The problem of social cost' 3 *Journal of Law and Economics* 1–44.

Comptroller and Auditor General (2014) *Performance Audit on the Management of Irrigation Projects of Government of Maharashtra* (CAG: New Delhi).

Cordes-Holland, R (2012) 'The national interest or good international citizenship? Australia and its approach to international and public climate law' in B Jessup and K Rubenstein (eds), *Environmental Discourses in Public and International Law* (CUP).

Cordonier-Segger, M and Khalfan, A (2004) *Sustainable Development Law* (OUP).

Cross, Frank B (1996) 'Paradoxical perils of the precautionary principle' 53 *Washington and Lee LR* 859.

Cullet, P (May 2010) *The Sardar Sarovar Dam Project* (Ashgate 2007).

Dernbach, J (1998) 'Sustainable development as a framework for national governance' 49(1) *Case Western Reserve LR* 1–103.

Dernbach, J C and Cheever, F (2015) 'Sustainable development and its discontents' 4 *Transnational Environmental Law* 247–287.

Deville, A and Harding, R (1997) *Applying the Precautionary Principle* (Federation Press).

Divan, S and Rosencranz, A (2001) *Environmental Law and Policy in India* (OUP).

Dovers, Stephen R and Handmer, John W (1999) 'Ignorance, sustainability, and the precautionary principle: towards an analytical framework' in R Harding and E Fisher (eds), *Perspectives on the Precautionary Principle* (Federation Press).

Ellis, J (2012) 'Perspective on discourses in international environmental law: expert knowledge and challenges to deliberative democracy' in B Jessup and K Rubenstein (eds), *Environmental Discourses in Public and International Law* (CUP).

European Commission (2000) *Communication on the Precautionary Principle* COM 1 (Brussels: EU).

Fisher, E (2001) 'Is the precautionary principle justiciable?' 13(3) *Journal of International Environmental Law* 315.

Fisher, E (2002) 'Precaution, precaution everywhere: developing a "common understanding" of the precautionary principle in the European Community' 9(1) *Maastricht Journal of European and Comparative Law* 7.

Fisher, E (2006) 'Risk and environmental law: a beginner's guide' in B Richardson and S Wood (eds), *Environmental Law and Sustainability* (Hart).

Førsund, F R (1975) 'The polluter pays principle and transitional period measures in a dynamic setting' 77(1) *Swedish Journal of Economics* 56–68.

Freestone, D (1994) 'The road from Rio: international environmental law after the Earth Summit' 6(2) *Journal of International Environmental Law* 193.

Gaines, S E (1991) 'The polluter-pays principle: from economic equity to environmental ethos' 26 *Texas International Law Journal* 463.

Garver, G (2012) 'Introducing the rule of ecological law' in L Westra, C Soskolne and D W Spady (eds), *Human Health and Ecological Integrity* (Routledge).

Gill, G N (2014) 'The National Green Tribunal of India: a sustainable future through the principles of international environmental law' 16(3) *Environmental LR* 183–202.

Gladwin, T N, Kennelly, J J and Krause, T S (1995) 'Shifting paradigms for sustainable development: implications for management theory and research' 20(4) *Academy of Management Review* 847–907.

Grant, E and Das, O (2015) 'Land grabbing, sustainable development and human rights' 4(2) *Transnational Environmental Law* 289–317.

Guha, S and Harendranath, C S (2013) 'Common effluent treatment plants (CETPS): the concept, problems and case study' *Directions* 7–15.

Hak, T, Moldan, B and Dahl, A (2009) *Sustainability Indicators* SCOPE 67 Series (Island Press).

Harding, R and Fisher, E (eds) (1999) *Perspectives on the Precautionary Principle* (Federation Press).

Hey, E (1992) 'The precautionary concept in environmental policy and law: institutionalizing caution' 4 *Georgetown International Environmental LR* 303.

International Human Rights Clinic/ESCR-Net (2013) *The Price of Steel: Human Rights and Forced Evictions in the POSCO-India Project* (NYU School of Law).

Kiss, A and Shelton, D (2003) *International Environmental Law* (UNEP).

Lee, K N (1993) 'Greed, scale mismatch and learning' 3(4) *Ecological Applications* 560–564.

Mauerhofer, V, Hubacek, K and Coleby, A (2013) 'From polluter pays to provider gets: distribution of rights and costs under payments for ecosystem services' 18(4) *Ecology and Society* 41.

Ministry of Tribal Affairs (2014) *Report of the High-Level Committee on Socio-Economic, Health and Educational Status of the Tribals of India* (Ministry of Tribal Affairs).

Moreno-Mateos, D, Power, M, Comín, F and Yockteng, R (2012) 'Structural and functional loss in restored wetland ecosystems' 10(1) *PLOS Biology* e1001247.

Owens, S (1997) 'Negotiated environments: needs, demands and values in the age of sustainability' 29(5) *Environment and Planning A* 571–580.

Sabharwal, Y K (2006) 'Role of judiciary in good governance' keynote address, B M Patnaik Memorial Lecture, 18 November.

Sachs, J (2015) *The Age of Sustainable Development* (Columbia UP).

Sadeleer, Nicolas de (2002) *Environmental Principles: From Political Slogans to Legal Rules* (OUP).

Santiso, C (2013) 'Towards democratic governance: the contribution of multilateral development banks in Latin America' in P Burnell (ed.), *Democracy Assistance* (Routledge) 150–190.

Sarkar, R (2009) *International Development Law: Rule of Law, Human Rights, and Global Finance* (OUP).

Sax, J L (1970) 'The public trust doctrine in natural resource law: effective judicial intervention' 68(3) *Michigan LR* 471–566.

Seymour, S, Cox, G and Lowe, P (1992) 'Nitrates in water: the politics of the "polluter pays principle"' 32(1) *Sociologia Ruralis* 82–103.

South Asian Human Rights Documentation Centre (2008) *Human Rights and Humanitarian Law: Developments in Indian and International Law* (OUP).

Stone, C (2001) 'Is there a precautionary principle?' 31(7) *Environmental Law Reporter* 10790.

Weiss, E B (1984) 'The planetary trust: conservation and intergenerational equity' 11(4) *Ecology Law Quarterly* 495–582.

Woolley, S (2014) *Ecological Governance Reappraising Law's Role in Protecting Ecosystem Functionality* (CUP).

Wynne, B (1992) 'Uncertainty and environmental learning: reconceiving science and policy in the preventive paradigm' 2(2) *Global Environmental Change* 111.

5 National Green Tribunal

Science and law

This chapter argues, on the basis of fieldwork data gathered in India, that the involvement of technical experts at the heart of courtroom decision-making promotes better environmental results (Gill 2016). The importance of experts is recognised because:

> ... experts define the regime of truth; they tell us what the world looks like, identify and quantify relevant variables, provide statistical measurements and risk analyses, and solve the equations that indicate the path towards increasing the aggregate level of well-being ... Experts define the system.
>
> (Lawrence 2014: 186)

There is an impressive array of academic literature that defends the involvement of experts on the ground of their contribution to decision-making (Buchanan and Keohane 2003; Steffek 2003; Ericsson *et al.* 2006; Kronsell and Backstrand 2010: 38–39; Ambrus *et al.* 2014). Environmental decision-making may involve science.[1] Consequently, scientific expertise may provide appropriate solutions to technical or complicated environmental problems. Effective environmental governance calls for procedural values such as transparency, inclusion, deliberation and participation involving experts while at the same time offering collective and effective problem-solving solutions. These procedural values are perceived as integral to legitimating the processes and institutions seeking to impart environmental justice.

The prototypal expert decision-maker plays a fundamental role in advancing the values and goals of institutions, organisations and legislation by inputting expertise. This function is widely supported, though remains debated and unsettled. For instance, the gap between production and use of expert knowledge poses concerns about the extent of expert involvement and accountability in environmental decision-making processes (see Weiss 1979; Lindquist 1988). Issues, including identification and selection of experts, homogeneous or heterogeneous groups of experts, collegial and collaborative decision-making, knowledge application and input to policy decisions, challenge the legitimisation of science-driven environmental decision-making through the employment of experts.

This chapter focuses on the role of experts and their expertise within NGT where they act as decision-makers in environmental disputes. Experts are 'central', not 'marginal', to the NGT's normative structure. For the current purpose, the terms 'expert' and 'expertise' do not include judicial members, but refer to technical members exercising specialised scientific knowledge, including environmental sciences, environmental studies, environmental engineering, technology, ecology, forestry, plant sciences, soil sciences, zoology and related categories. Experienced scientists, practising ecologists and natural resource managers are considered experts (Drescher et al. 2013: 2). Thus, scientific expertise and its input into decision-making are vital to the character, decisions and working practices of the NGT.

The chapter is divided into three sections. The first briefly reviews science and its reliability, along with the value of expert testimony. The second offers the theoretical framework encompassing epistemic communities and knowledge utilisation. Section three tests this framework by applying it to the NGT in light of fieldwork data. Relevant, illustrative case law is also considered.

Questionable science and expert testimony

The involvement of experts and expert knowledge in policy and decision-making commands an important place in academic discourse. Nevertheless, the relationship between science and politics is problematic and subject to widespread debate (see Limoges 1993; Oreskes and Conway 2010; Sprujit et al. 2014). Scientific evidence can be massaged into supporting particular vested interests including government, industry and commercial capital. Such power-houses may underwrite or promote research to serve their particular interests.[2] For example, in 2015 the Harvard School of Public Health cited 22 peer-reviewed articles in leading medical journals supporting the claim that rising consumption of sugary drinks is a major contributor to the obesity epidemic.[3] On the other hand, it is little known that the European Hydration Institute, a not-for-profit body, is funded by Coca Cola to the tune of £6.6 million. Worldwide Coca Cola has pumped huge sums into scientific research and not-for-profit organisations – more than $120 million since 2010 in the USA alone. Carrie Ruxton, a board member of Food Standards for Scotland, co-wrote a 2010 UK Sugar Bureau-sponsored report which concluded that 'there didn't appear to be any relationship' between sugar consumption and obesity. This study and 17 others were reviewed by Spanish researchers who found that those sponsored by or with links to the food and drink industry were five times more likely to find no link between sugar and obesity. This suggests how scientific evidence can be represented to favour a particular view. Indeed, the UK government in 2015 demonstrated reluctance to respond to evidence that excess sugar intake is deleterious to human health.[4]

Misuse of science by pressure groups is further illustrated by published research that blamed pesticides for the decline of honeybees. A leaked note suggested that a group of scientists decided, in advance, to support evidence for a ban on certain chemicals to persuade EU regulators to suspend the use of neoni-cotinoids, thus reversing evidence-based policy-making into policy-based evidence-picking.[5]

Scientific cherry-picking and suppression of inconvenient evidence is commonplace at governmental level, as shown by the findings of the USA-based Union of Concerned Scientists (2004) regarding distortion and suppression of scientific findings that failed to support or contradicted Bush administration policies. It found a serious pattern of the undermining of science by the administration, crossing disciplines, including climate change, reproductive health, mercury in the food chain and forestry.

A simple reliance on science for explanations or progressive development has had its own pitfalls as illustrated by the fatal technical design flaws of Comet passenger planes, the technically debated responses to BSE/mad-cow disease or Cumbrian sheep farmers' challenges to government scientific advisers' responses to Chernobyl's contamination of their land (see Collins 2014). Additionally, science may be overtly captured by politicians, as in the USSR by Stalin's catastrophic farming policy, or government responses to the AIDS crisis in South Africa (ibid.). Consequently, the objectivity of science is questionable as policy issues are discussed and resolved. Objection to the neutrality of science is reflected in the view that it is rooted in wider social, political and economic contexts. What is clear is that research on expert roles is mostly theoretical. While theories are well developed, there is only limited empirical evidence supporting these changes and procedures.[6]

However, the introduction of scientific determinants, as presented by experts, into legal rationality, as exercised by the judiciary, raises the question of the role and limits of judicial creativity. Should the judiciary be acknowledged as authorised to exercise such expansive powers? If yes, are judges fit for purpose? Judges are seldom scientifically trained, therefore may be ill-informed assessors of the claims of paid or retained scientific experts who offer fact-based evidence on behalf of parties to the case (Twining 1992: 1, 14; Faigmann 1999).[7] It has been suggested that inadequately trained judicial 'gatekeepers' lay themselves open to being overwhelmed by junk science. The common law courtroom is the forum for adversarial advocacy that sometimes involves the participation of numerous expert witnesses advancing competitive scientific evidence. An outcome can be a battle of scientific opinions, where strongly held positions are debated, tested, deconstructed and challenged (Bocking 2006). The court may be particularly vulnerable where one financially strong party is able to employ a parade of experts (Huber 1991). Courts are aware of the dangers of unproven science, as laid out by Lord Phillips in *Sienkiewicz v Greif UK Ltd* (2011) 2 AC 229 where the court recognised that scientific evidence may have limitations: 'epidemiological data may not be reliable' as 'science is still ignorant of how causation in fact occurs ... There is a real danger that so-called "epidemiological evidence"' 'will carry a false air of authority' (261, 290). A potential consequence is that courtroom truth and legal rationality can be affected or replaced by questionable, biased or 'purchased' scientific knowledge (Jasanoff 1995; 2006; Cooper 2013).

This chapter does not address the challenging issues within the sociology of knowledge that include the multiple roles of experts vis-à-vis policy creation and its promotion. The relationship of science and policy has generated a body of lively and disparate opinion and literature beyond the scope of this book. Nor does this chapter consider the relationship or functionality of expert witnesses introduced to the courtroom to promote the cases of litigants. The author accepts that there may be several, alternative or competing scientifically-based solutions to a problem, rather than a solitary solution: 'the solution'. These may be advanced to the court by retained expert witnesses or scientifically-based evidence may be generated within the court by 'in-house' scientific experts. Thus there is both 'flexibility' and 'uncertainty' in science.

The chapter traces and evaluates the way in which by an Act of the Indian Parliament a symbiotic relationship has been created between legal and scientific experts operating as joint decision-makers and adjudicators of environmental conflicts within the context of the NGT. The courtroom is a place of dispute resolution. It is not a 'maybe-discussion' forum where policy is debated or negotiated among sometimes powerful interest groups. The consequence of the NGT's statutory establishment and function is that there are decisions declaring winners and losers.

Any potential discord within the courtroom between science and law has been addressed by the NGT through its appointment procedures, choice of scientific experts and public and private decision-making processes. This chapter considers the NGT's efforts to reach decisions that involve and reflect 'good science' by centralising scientific experts, as full court members, within the decision-making process thereby promoting a collective, symbiotic, interdisciplinary bench that seeks to harmonise legal norms with scientific knowledge.

Theoretical framework: epistemic communities and knowledge utilisation

Political science scholarship offers an analytical tool that can be applied to the NGT to unwrap and review the data presented hereafter. Thus, here there is a transmigration of theory and its application from one social science discipline to another: political science to law.

The concept of 'epistemic communities' is usually applied by political scientists for a 'clearer theory of state' and for 'formulating interest and reconciling differences of interest' (Haas 2014: 30). Peter Haas describes distinctive features of 'epistemic communities' as:

> Networks ... often transnational – of knowledge-based experts with an authoritative claim to policy relevant knowledge within their domain of expertise. Their members share knowledge about the causation of ... phenomena ... and a common set of normative beliefs about what actions will benefit human welfare in such a domain. Members are experts with

professional training who enjoy social authority based on their reputation for impartial expertise.

(Haas 2007: 793)

The validation of epistemic communities' claims to expertise and impartiality are judged by external social standards such as 'peer review, non-political appointment based on merits to authoritative panels, track record, publications and training' (Haas 2014: 30).

The engagement of the NGT's scientific experts in the decision-making process is akin to Haas' epistemic communities operating within an environmental regime. It is suggested that the involvement of experts as 'constructive science scholars' in environmental decision-making is subject to similar analysis.

Further, Schrefler, another political scientist, contends that interactive scientific expert involvement increases structural output in an institution, governance or political order (Schrefler 2010: 2014). She argues that expert knowledge and expertise play key roles in the successful functioning and credibility of independent regulatory agencies (IRAs) based on the premise of 'technical policy makers operating in isolation from political factors'. Schrefler states: 'IRAs are considered as central producers and users of policy relevant knowledge. Inhouse expertise is often a core feature of their independence' (Schrefler 2014: 65). The use of scientific knowledge provides legitimacy in output via this expertise, coupled with the requirement to publish reasons justifying IRA regulatory decisions.

Upon reviewing the literature on the importance and use of expertise by policy-makers, Schrefler constructs three principal approaches to knowledge utilisation: *instrumental, strategic* and *symbolic*. The rationale underpinning these is based on the use of expertise provided the 'experts are the fabric from which the organization is cut' (Lawrence 2014: 193). These approaches are hereafter applied and tested through the data on the NGT and its expert members.

Symbolic usage, often referred to as the 'logic of appropriateness' and decoupled from policy decisions, aims to gain legitimacy and strengthen the agency's reputation as a credible player in the policy arena, conforming to external expectations and pressures.

The *instrumental* use of knowledge is associated with the agency identifying the best solution for the issue at stake. The problem-solving approach lies in an agency's need to perform its mandate and deliver outputs in line with the goals it assigned itself or received from the political principals. The problem-solving abilities can be chosen to tackle 'specific policy issues in short term, but also to cope with future problems by accumulating relevant expertise' (Schrefler 2014: 69).

The third type of knowledge utilisation is *strategic* and is subdivided into two categories: political and substantiating. *Strategic political usage*, that Weiss (1979) defines as 'tactical use of knowledge' (429), expands the powers and resources of the regulatory agency in order to convince the 'political principals to review/

extend the agency's mandate' (Schrefler 2014: 70). The *strategic substantiating approach* involves well-crafted scientific knowledge that justifies and supports a predetermined or preferred policy solution. It can also serve as 'ammunition in an adversarial context' (Schrefler 2010: 315).

Expert knowledge can be employed in different ways. Nor need each IRA routinely adopt an identical approach to scientific knowledge. Schrefler recognises that empirical testing of different approaches to knowledge utilisation is limited as 'it is relatively difficult to operationalise and measure expert knowledge utilization variables and, more broadly, to distinguish the influence of expertise from other factors affecting policy decisions' (Schrefler 2014: 71). Variables, such as availability of adequate human and financial resources, degree of disagreement between actors over policy values and goals involved in the policy environment, power distribution between the agency and its principal(s), and pressures from different categories of stakeholders are likely to affect IRAs' production and use of scientific knowledge. To overcome this, Schrefler suggests 'employing qualitative methods as process tracing and case studies' in order to better understand the conditions leading to different uses of knowledge utilisation in policy-making that could be relevant for experts inside and outside regulatory agencies (ibid.).

The creation of IRAs offers the opportunity to allow utilisation of expert knowledge and thereby IRAs can perform their functions impartially and neutrally. However, this assumption, according to Schrefler, is difficult to defend as a simple use of technical power inevitably results in political consequences: 'regulatory policy making is better depicted as a continuum ranging from "government of experts" to "government by politicians". We have to accept that a portion of regulatory policy making is political' (Schrefler 2014: 76). To ensure that the use and production of expertise is legitimate, Schrefler concurs with Vibert's (2007) claim for 'an independent but accountable locus for policy making' embedded in 'an effective procedural and organizational set up' (ibid.).

Although Schrefler's work focuses on IRAs, the superimposition of her theoretical analysis of experts onto the NGT produces credible evidence that supports her analytical framework. Like IRAs, the NGT is a statutory creation and its constitution and powers are laid out in the NGT Act 2010, which also guarantees its independence from political interference or control. Accountability is achieved by a series of established procedures and appeals, operational both in courts of law and in the NGT. NGT decisions are not subject to judicial review, unlike IRAs, but they are subject to review by appeal to the Supreme Court. Further, the proceedings of the NGT occur in open court, reflecting commonly accepted established rules and procedures. Judgments and associated reasons are also given in open court. Thereafter the decisions and their rationales are available for public scrutiny, as they are published online as case reports.[8] As in Schrefler's work, the presence of the expert, fully integrated, accepted and operational within the institution, is recognised as a key and unique factor contributing to the ultimate decision; now legal rather than the creation of policy. Schrefler's analysis is applied to the NGT fieldwork with special reference to the scientific experts sitting alongside judges, allowing them to input their scientific knowledge and contribute as equal partners to the decision-making process.

The legitimacy of the NGT's environmental decision-making rests in part upon its inclusive and participatory in-house scientific expertise – an important feature within the decision-making process. The interface between science and law is particularly visible in the NGT where the scientific experts work alongside legally qualified judges as collective environmental decision-makers of homologous standing.

In this context, I advance my empirical Indian fieldwork to analyse the NGT's scientific 'epistemic community' and its practical application.

Applying the theory to the NGT

This section deals with the important theoretical work developed by two political scientists, Haas (2007; 2014) and Schrefler (2010; 2014), although neither has applied their work within an adjudicatory institution, such as the NGT. Haas characterised epistemic communities as comprising experts with professional training enjoying social authority based upon the reputation for impartial activities. Schrefler's contribution concerns the application of her theory of knowledge utilisation as embedded in a specific procedural decision-making tribunal: the NGT. This section commences with the application of Haas' work and is followed by relating Schrefler's knowledge utilisation to the NGT.

Expert value

A scientific consensus that applies regulations and promotes scientific input focusing upon environmental sustainability and human welfare creates the 'epistemic community'. The 'community' is comprised of neutral scientific experts as active contributors within a decision-making legal forum: the NGT.

The diverse scientific expertise lends further credence to the NGT's environmental legitimacy. The 'epistemic qualities' of the experts as competent individuals recognised as national and international experts in different environmental areas promotes independence from any party line, organisational bias or corporate association. The NGT benches include scientists with expertise in environmental sciences, environmental engineering, environmental governance, environmental safeguards, industrial and urban environmental management, urban environmental pollution, environmental law and policy, and forestry. The status of NGT experts as 'nationally and internationally recognised specialists' can be judged by external indicators, including previous appointments to high-level committees, representing India in environmental issues, drafting and negotiating multilateral environmental agreements, peer-reviewed publications and recognition through professional awards.[9]

The value of expert bench members is acknowledged and appreciated by the judicial members. Judge 1 stated: 'the expert members come with wide knowledge. Professors, technocrats and administrators with wide environmental knowledge are a part of the NGT decision making process. Their contribution is substantial'.[10] Judges 2 and 5 added: 'the real solution comes from the expert members. The input of expert members is much more valuable for environmental matters'.[11] Judges 3 and 4 commented: 'this is the speciality of the Tribunal which has not only judicial talent but also expert talent. This is a peculiarity of the Tribunal. It is a balanced way of doing work'.[12]

The scientific input of the experts in the five benches is appreciated by those appearing before them as lawyers or litigants. For instance, Senior Lawyer 1 stated:

> the presence of expert members on the NGT bench is a step in the right direction. The expert members better understand and deliberate the complex environmental issues. Expert members have specialist knowledge on environmental matters which many a time the lawyers do not have.[13]

Senior Lawyer 2, with 25 years' standing and appointed as an *amicus* by Bench 2, said:

> ...this is a bench having an expert member with relevant expertise and is a body predisposed to environmental issues. You do not have to argue why you are here but you have to argue your case. Judges in the High Courts of India are not necessarily acquainted with environmental law and the lawyer has to start from scratch. However, in the NGT, the expert member knows and understands the problem. I have seen expert members asking questions which both parties have not thought of.[14]

Young Lawyers in Benches 2 and 3 felt that expert members introduce ecological awareness and try to solve problems, rather than simply deciding cases. This creates a steep learning curve for many lawyers:

> ...the composition of the NGT bench with its expert member is an effective way to deal with environmental matters. The High Court or the Supreme Court judges fail to understand the environmental issues. A bench of this kind with an expert member is creating new environmental jurisprudence. The expert members help young lawyers understand environmental issues.[15]

Similarly, litigants praise bench composition. Litigants 1, 2 and 3 stated:

> ...the NGT is our only hope because there are experts sitting who understand the problem. We are ordinary citizens who daily see the environmental destruction and its impact on us and future generations. Honestly, the environment is a sensitive issue which should only be handled by experts. Our experience has been tremendous in the NGT benches. We are attending the case in person and have come three to five times to the NGT.

Judges are very sensitive and understand what we have placed before them and are able to take our cause without us knowing the law. For us this is a heartening experience. This NGT is a life saver. NGT has given us justice and in future we will get justice because the judges are experts who are concerned about the environment and understand what they are saying. Most importantly, this we do not find in other courts, such as the High Court.[16]

Expert neutrality

At present there are eight NGT professionally qualified, expert members, although there is a strong case to increase the number on regional benches.[17] However, they must have a minimum of 15 years' experience in the relevant field or administrative experience, including five years' practical experience in environmental matters in a reputed national institution or central or state government.[18] The expert members, working alongside legally qualified judges, constitute an interdisciplinary decision-making body.

The selection process laid out in the National Green Tribunal Appointment Rules is structured to minimise executive influence, promoting transparency, accountability, neutrality and independence[19] In *Wilfred J v MoEF* (Judgment 17 July 2014), the NGT observed:

> There is nothing in the provision of the NGT Act that directly or even by necessary implication is indicative of any external control over the National Green Tribunal … [MoEF] is merely an administrative ministry for the National Green Tribunal to provide for means and finances. Once the budget is provided, the Ministry cannot have any interference in the functioning of the National Green Tribunal. The entire process of appointment and even removal is under the effective control of the Supreme Court of India, as neither appointments nor removal can be effected without the participation and approval of a sitting judge of the Supreme Court of India. The administration is merely an executing agency within the framework of the Act.
>
> (Para 34)

NGT Judge 1 said he identified himself as the leader of a team that he was involved in selecting. He sought experience, expertise, character and awareness that would make appointees effective judges of environmental matters throughout India. He stated:

> I am really very happy with the experts. All the experts have been picked by me. I was a judge of the Supreme Court and the Chairman of the Selection Committee. So I have made some contribution in this regard. I find these people extremely good in their field.[20]

India's patronage culture of providing sinecure, post-retirement assignments to former judges, senior administrators and technocrats in judicial and quasi-judicial bodies at national and state levels has been questioned and accusations of 'give and take' made.[21] Suggestions, such as a transparent selection process or 'cooling-off period' of three or four years before accepting any such positions, have been made to dissuade the 'senior and most respected people' on the verge of retirement from entering into improper or questionable associations with corporations, institutions or influential individuals. For instance, in *Kalpavriksh v Union of India* (Judgment 17 July 2014), the NGT addressed the issue of relevant qualifications for MoEF appointments to committees dealing with environmental issues, specifically the Expert Appraisal Committee (EAC) or State Expert Appraisal Committees (SEACs). The Tribunal asked the ministry to provide revised eligibility criteria and specific requirements regarding EAC and SEAC chairperson and member appointees under provisions of the Environment Impact Assessment Notification 2006. A note of caution was added:

> ... if people who are not strictly qualified and eligible in the field of environment are selected ... The obvious result would be improper application of mind ... It would lead to improper consideration and disposal of application for clearance filed by the project proponent.
>
> (Para 33)

A US environmental judge visiting India commented: 'the tribunal is a proven model for my state as its bench is comprised of independent, carefully appointed judges who are unafraid of making difficult decisions. NGT is an example of informed judicial courage'.[22] For the NGT, the statutory provisions act as a benchmark for a rigorous appointment process subject to public scrutiny. This reduces the possibility of cronyism and encourages independent and impartial decisions leading to transparent, effective environmental decision-making which, in turn, promotes awareness and trust among citizens. Interview data from court lawyers and litigants demonstrates that they appreciate a selection procedure that has appointed qualified scientists who apply expertise to make informed decisions promoting environmental justice.[23]

Schrefler's variables

Schrefler's work suggests that undertaking effective, empirical institutional research is limited by the presence of variables such as multiple external stakeholders seeking to pursue claims to participate in environmental regulation. Schrefler states: 'the higher the number of stakeholders, the greater the degree of conflict, as each player is likely to generate conflicting pressures and demands on the agency' (2010: 316). Fortunately, the NGT, as a judicial body, enjoys a high but not absolute degree of jurisdictional immunity from the advances of the stakeholders and, indeed, acknowledges them largely on its own terms, such as through the 'stakeholder consultative adjudicatory process'.[24] These consultations take place within NGT premises and stakeholders are invited to participate under the jurisdiction, procedures and chairing of the NGT.

Further, the NGT has been shielded from potentially challenging agendas of external stakeholders by the well-established Indian doctrine of an independent judiciary.[25] While NGT decisions are subject to appeal to the Supreme Court,[26] what is not open to appeal is the internal, confidential, decision-making process itself. This process is not public, although this chapter, through detailed field-work, identifies and explains the process, which is founded on the 'principle of collegiality'. Thus, in the absence of effective pressure from external stake-holders, NGT benches exercise judicial independence[27] which has allowed the NGT to develop its own internal decision-making process. The small number of bench members, exercising a jointly constructed, decision-making procedure in a private setting, produces a sense of collegiality and reduces the importance and influence of external stakeholders.

Scientific expert involvement through collegiality offers an effective way to generate enhanced legitimacy and public approval. Harry Edwards notes that collegiality results in a 'process' that creates conditions that ultimately produce a principled agreement: the judgment. He does not accept that collegiality is founded simply upon friendship, homogeneity or conformity. Instead, it is a matter of common concern to get the law right: 'collegiality plays an important role in mitigating the role of partisan politics and personal ideology by allowing judges of different perspectives and philosophies to communicate with, listen to, and ultimately influence one another in constructive and law-abiding ways' (2003: 1656).[28]

This is not to deny that individuals have personal, social or political positions that might influence their decisions, but rather the overriding process of collegiality helps ensure that decisions are not pre-ordained as a consequence of extraneous relationships, thoughts and influences. This process is not uni-structural. It is a sophisticated combination of rules, customs, routines, legal obligations, leadership skills, mutual trust, personal confidence and the shared belief in common goals. Together, they create collegiality.

Strong, positive collegial relationships allow and promote judicial independence of mind and discussion resulting in an interdependent and interdisciplinary decision-making process. This ensures that each person's intellectual and judicial strengths are recognised and introduced to the collective decision-making process. It allows judges to check their personal positions against an alternative view from a possibly better-informed or experienced colleague. Edwards welcomes this diversity: 'differences in professional and personal background, areas of expertise ... diversity among the judges makes for a better informed discussion' (2003: 1668).

Deliberation is one of the most valued components of collegiality. The rules that structure it bring judges together as a group. Collegiality has a function in institutionalising judges into shared understanding and action, particularly on small benches. The NGT's collegiality is illustrated by its deliberative process of drafting a judgment. Conformity and cohesion is reflected in teamwork and collective practice exercised throughout the five benches. The lead provided by Judge 1 to teamwork practice is based upon a collaborative approach:

...what we do is to have a pre-hearing conference and a post hearing conference. Normally even while passing a small order, I like to interact with the
judicial and expert members so that there is complete coherence and unan-
imity because sometimes what you think may be wrong and what the other
person may suggest is right. I give full margin to that possibility. Secondly,
whosoever authors the judgment, we have a pre-writing session where we
discuss the facts and I and other judicial members state what is the law and
the legal position. Then the experts tell us the technical aspects. I ask the
technical members to give me a short note. Then we consider it. Then I or
another judicial member or expert member prepares a draft. Next, we deliberate the draft. Then we get in writing an agreement by each expert and judicial member. Ultimately, the judgment is finalized. It is a process so far we are
handling well. I hope that things will go even better with time.[29]

Experts 1, 2 and 6 (Bench 1) find this drafting process extremely valuable:

...we always have a discussion before we go to the court on the important
issues in the morning at 10.00am in the Conference Room. We sit together
and talk. This is one platform. But also before writing every judgment a
technical note is required by the judicial member who is writing the judgment. Many a time the entire technical note is reproduced and forms part
of the judgment. We have never had a dispute as we always discuss and
have an agreement before we pronounce the judgment. The final judgment
is always written in a draft form circulated to all the members who will sign
the judgment. Every member reads it and has a right to correct or delete or
modify even if it is a major part of the judgment. This is allowed at this
point. Finally the judgment is signed and pronounced. This is a practice followed in NGT and is a procedural requirement as stated by our Chairperson. Though there are no written rules it is a practice we follow. The
Chairperson always says that you have the full right to make any correction
or addition or deletion or suggestion. Everything is allowed.[30]

Bench 5 follows a similar procedure. According to Judge 2 and Expert 7:

...before the matter is taken up, the papers are circulated to us. Individually we go through the papers. Both of us come prepared. We sit in the
court with an open mind. We hear the parties. In a case where technical
issues are raised, we discuss the matter in the court. After the hearing is
concluded we sit together in the chamber and discuss the way the judgment
is to be delivered and environmental material is given by the expert
member. Based on that the judicial member drafts a judgment and that is
circulated to the expert member. Sometimes the judicial member also
invites the expert member to draft the judgment. Additions, deletions and
modifications or suggestions are permissible in the draft judgment. Then
the final judgment is formulated and delivered.[31]

Teamwork is also acknowledged by Judge 3 and Expert 4 (Bench 4):

> ...before the matter is heard, we do not engage in any type of discussion. We hear the matter. Before hearing the matter, we go through the records and prepare ourselves. After the matter is heard, we enter into discussion. In the NGT, we are helped by the advocates. There is no original trial but being a Tribunal, we have to hasten the process and not leisurely decide any case where we can call witness. First assistance is by way of advocates. Many advocates are not familiar with environmental issues. There may be gaps. These gaps are understood and recognized by the Expert Member. Merely reading an affidavit would not make complete sense. The expert member provides the technical know-how. A technical note is submitted by the expert member. Thus, with this assistance, we come to our conclusion and then we discuss and come to our answer so that we can arrive at a decision. This is reflected in the judgment. The judgments are drafted and circulated. As we understand each other, it becomes easier to reach a conclusion and dispose of the case.[32]

According to Judge 4 and Expert 5 (Bench 3), consensus and clarity lead to an amalgam of views that seek to deliver environmental justice:

> ...most of the cases involve a technical point of view and technical expertise is required. Prior to the time of decision making both the judicial and technical members must necessarily have an in depth discussion on the matter. A clear mind and consensus is needed for a judgment. It must not only be unimpeachable but also stand and answer the question. We must work before writing a judgment. A clear discussion, consensus and the same frame of mind brings a good judgment.[33]

The combination of opinions and expertise is the essence of good drafting, according to Judge 5 and Expert 8 (Bench 2):

> The matter is taken to a logical end and it is only possible with the blend of judicial and technical minds. We are two in number. We meet regularly – morning, afternoon and evening. Communication is not an issue. Formally as well as informally we discuss the issue before going to the hearing as well as before settling any judgment or theme of a judgment. We discuss and all the time we are on the same track. The judicial and technical inputs are given by the respective members. This happens because there is a regular communication. The thought process is the same. A common blend amounts to qualitative judgment and delivers justice from such a combination.[34]

Further, the experience of shared customs, procedures, rules, courtrooms and working and dining-rooms – along with regular formal meetings conducted either through personal contact or video-conferencing and common bench hearings – produces, according to Edwards, a cross-fertilisation effect between collegiality and internal rules (2003: 1664).

The cross-fertilisation has been good for collegial relations and collaboration among NGT judges. A formal full court meeting on a regular basis is one way of maintaining collegiality. Judge 1 explained: 'we hold full court meetings. We not only discuss the administrative matters but also judicial matters with respect to improving the justice delivery system'.[35]

New technology (video-conferencing, email, NGT website) connects the benches in real time, despite significant geographical distances. Judge 1, who introduced video-conferencing, stated: '...even if there is a smallest problem, I put them on video conferencing and have all the members deliberate on it and thereafter take the decision. This leads to a uniform and consistent approach'.[36] The benches appreciate this facility. It not only provides a confidential, secure connection, but also offers instant communication across India thereby encouraging fruitful discussion between benches.

Informal discussions and consultations through exchange of emails and reference to the website[37] also promote collegiality. This is helpful in sharing new information or broadening the knowledge base with respect to national and international developments. Staying frequently connected helps promote objectivity, as Edwards, quoting Traweek, describes 'as employed in physical sciences ... pure objectivity is tacitly recognized as impossible; but error can be estimated and minimized. The means is peer review, or collective surveillance; the final degree of order comes from human institutions' (Traweek 1992: 125; Edwards 2003: 1685). This applies equally to environmental studies, environmental management and environmental law.

The nature of judge-craft is that ultimately the court is obliged to arrive at a decision and thereby establish the law. Over time, individual judges become more confident in their roles and colleagues. They may become more flexible, open to persuasion and less entrenched and more ambitious in their thinking and thereby in their decisions. Initially, the NGT commenced with narrow statutory interpretations and strict rule application. However, over time, such thinking has been joined by purposive interpretations of statutes, policy-based decisions and even policy development suggestions or requirements. Edwards' assessment is that an experienced court, led by a strong leader, with a small diverse bench that has worked together over time, enjoying a clear understanding of purpose and internal court rules, will, through collegiality, find common ground and arrive at better decisions.

My fieldwork suggests there is a close personal and working relationship between Tribunal members which in part reflects the small numbers on each bench. There appears to be no hierarchy, disciplinary priority or external pressures that determine a scientific or legal bias in decision-making. Members' accounts of their internal operating processes and interpersonal relationships reflect the recognition of seeking the common goal of environmental justice.

The application of expert knowledge

Schrefler identifies three possible uses of expert knowledge by regulators: *instrumental* (identifying the best solution to a problem); *strategic* (advocating a predefined policy position or providing arguments to expand the agency's power); and *symbolic* (strengthening the agency's reputation and legitimacy, decoupled from policy decisions) (Schrefler 2010; 2014).

My fieldwork highlights the judge–scientists' contribution to the NGT's environmental decision-making through the independent application of science free from political considerations. It shows how scientific expert participation, in cases and interviews, demonstrates the different typologies of the use of expert knowledge and provides an opportunity for the empirical application of Schrefler's categories.

Symbolic

The *symbolic* use of expertise is reflected in the NGT as it is a specialised body equipped with the necessary expertise to handle environmental disputes involving multidisciplinary issues. A five-bench judgment in *Wilfred v MoEF* stated:

> the tribunal must inspire confidence and public esteem. It should be manned by expert minds and persons of judicial acumen and experts from the relevant field with capacity to decide cases with the judicial members. The tribunal should have effective and efficacious mechanisms.

The NGT is a forum for testing the idea that economic advancement is tightly wired to public safety and to the security of water, air and land (Schneider 2014).

In *Ramdas Janardan Koli v Secretary, MoEF* (Judgment 27 February 2015), the Tribunal observed:

> …we cannot and must not overlook the fact that a substantial environmental dispute or question relating to environment, under the enactments under Schedule-I, of the NGT Act, 2010, need determination by taking pragmatic view. This kind of litigation is not adversarial in nature. The *lis* is not between the parties. The jurisdiction available to NGT, is, therefore inquisitive, investigative and if so required research oriented. The purpose of having Hon'ble Expert as Member of the Bench, is to render expert's conception to the judicial decision making process. Otherwise, for mere adversarial litigation perhaps, the Legislature might not have made such arrangement to establish the national level Green Tribunal.
>
> (Para 48)

In *Braj Foundation v Government of Uttar Pradesh* (Judgment 5 August 2014), the Tribunal stated:

... it is clear that the NGT is distinct from other tribunals either created as per the provisions of the Constitution of India or otherwise. It is a constitutional creature with a specific purpose on the basis of certain principles like sustainable development, precautionary principle and polluter pay principle. The NGT which proceeds to adjudicate the disputes which involves substantial questions relating to environment consists of expert members apart from judicial members ... there is nothing to presume that the NGT is either subordinate to any High Court or under the powers of superintendence of any High Court.

(Paras 23 and 25)

Instrumental

Instrumentally, NGT experts believe in a scientific problem-solving approach to the decision-making process which subsequently filters through to improve environmental management. This innovative development moves traditional, single issue, legal dispute 'adjudication' between disputing parties beyond the 'courtroom door' in its implicit and sometimes explicit creation of scientifically justified policy that seeks to ensure minimal damage to the environment and protect society's wider interests. For instance, Expert 4 illustrates this approach and its wider impact by reference to tree-cutting:

Where there are gaps or limitations in the policy, the NGT interferes and gives directions to the government to incorporate the same. For example, cases were filed against the cutting of fully grown trees in Delhi due to various developmental activities. There were no policy guidelines by the [MoEF] to state governments or urban bodies. I asked the authorities about exploring the possibility of trans-locating the tree elsewhere depending upon the season, soil, species, age and other factors. Accordingly, guidelines were issued to the MoEF to incorporate translocation of trees as a mandatory policy prescription before permitting the cutting of trees.[38]

In *K D Kodwani v District Collector* (Judgment 25 August 2014), the Tribunal emphasised the need to consider the translocation of trees as an alternative to felling. No doubt, it is an expensive proposition, but it must be given due weight and consideration. On the importance of trees, the Tribunal stated:

... it must always be kept in mind as the trees, the open spaces and the green areas not only protect the environment but are also helpful in purifying the air in the cities which are getting congested and polluted as a result of various factors and more particularly because of ever increasing vehicular traffic. The trees, the green areas and open spaces therefore become the lungs of the cities and are of utmost importance not only for beautification but more particularly for the health of the residents. The rise in the cases of respiratory and asthma related diseases is also the cause and concern and therefore all possible measures for maintaining sufficient green cover and planting of trees and allowing them to survive must be taken into account.

(Para 8)

Tulsi Advani v State of Rajasthan (Judgment 19 February 2015) also recognised translocation as following the principle of sustainable development.

J R Chincham v State of Madhya Pradesh (Judgment 8 May 2014) also illustrates the use of scientific expertise to help affected communities regenerate degraded forests. The government of India via its National Forest Policy 1988 and subsequent notifications envisages people's involvement in the development and protection of forests. A participatory approach to forest management and constitution of joint forest management (JFM) committees at state level involving forest communities is essential. JFM is a policy wherein all forest-dependent villagers of a given village organise themselves into a cohesive group with the objective of protecting, regenerating and managing the forests in the vicinity. In this case, the applicant, president of the regional group, took up the cause of tribal inhabitants, contending that local communities were not taken into confidence concerning forestry operations. Accepting the contention, the Tribunal stated that forest communities should be motivated to identify themselves with the development and protection of forests from which they derive benefits. Access to forest and usufructuary benefits should only be for beneficiaries who are organised into a village institution, specifically for forest regeneration and protection. Additionally and importantly, it observed that no updated or revised guidelines regarding JFM have been issued by the Madhya Pradesh state government, despite national developments. Therefore, urgent revision of the aforesaid guidelines was required. Further, local community involvement and adoption of a participatory approach was central to forest regeneration and protection.

Asim Sarode v Maharashtra Pollution Control Board (Judgment 6 September 2014) identifies the use of Expert 8's expertise in a judgment that develops a scientifically-based approach to used-tyre disposal. Expert 8 considered the urgent need to develop regulations to deal systematically with the issue, based on the 'lifecycle approach' – considering the pollution potential, tyre-generation data, technology options, techno-economic viability and social implications on the sustainable development and precautionary principles (paras 8, 17). The judgment reflects the Expert 8's scientific input wherein approaches, including extended producers' responsibility, advanced recycling charges, common facilities, use of bar-coding etc., were suggested to ensure effective collection and disposal of used tyres.

Similarly, in *Sonyabapu v State of Maharashtra* (Judgment 24 February 2014), Expert 8 identified the absence of notified emission standards for clamp-type traditional brick kilns by regulatory authorities. The air and water legislation requires 'consent to operate' as mandatory for brick kilns. In appraisal of the consent application, the regulatory authority – the state pollution control board – needs to consider emission standards and stipulation of necessary pollution control arrangements. In Sonyabapu's case, the expert member found it difficult to understand how the state board had approved the clamp-type traditional brick kilns when it had not set emission standards. Accordingly, the Tribunal directed the state board to formulate and notify emissions standards for the kilns under the provisions of the air legislation within four months, following due process of law.

The *instrumental* element is further evidenced by the NGT intervening and expanding the scope of environmental legislation through an expansive interpretation of the law. An example is bio-medical waste treatment plants. Bio-medical waste by its very nature is hazardous. A medical waste incinerator may release into the air a wide variety of pollutants including dioxins, furans, metals – e.g. lead, mercury, cadmium – particulate matter, acid gases, etc. These have serious adverse consequences for safety, public health and the environment. The Bio-Medical Waste (Management and Handling) Rules 1998 only contemplate issuance of authorisation to a person or occupier for storing, dealing with, handling and disposal of bio-medical wastes. The rules are silent about whether the establishment and operation of a treatment plant requires EC. However, according to experts, such treatment plants are required to obtain EC which would help in ensuring an appropriate analysis of the suitability of the location and its surroundings and a more stringent observation of parameters and standards by the project proponent and the impact on public health.

According to Expert 2:

> …environmental issues are complex. We are dealing with natural systems and future events based upon impacts. While framing the rules or regulations no one had visualized the scenario that activities such as bio-medical waste treatment facility would come up in the near future. However, in today's world bio-medical waste and associated activities need serious consideration based upon the likely impacts and magnitude. So, if we feel that the activity is injurious to public health and environment, we pass appropriate orders of expanding the scope of rules and regulations by adopting the principle of constructive intuition to give it a wider meaning to attain the primary object and purpose of the Act in question. Such an interpretation would serve the public interest in contrast to the private or individual interest. Thus, the project proponents are required to obtain environment clearance for bio-medical waste treatment plants in terms of site location, potential environmental impacts and proposed environmental safeguards from MoEF in accordance with law. In *Haat Supreme Wastech Ltd v State of Haryana*, we had ordered that environmental clearance be a mandatory requirement.[39]

In a similar vein, the Tribunal in *M/S Ardent Steel Ltd v MoEF* (Judgment 27 May 2014) directed the inclusion of pelletisation – a steel-making process – as a primary metallurgical industrial process requiring mandatory EC in terms of the EC Regulations 2006. This is a notification of wide spectrum, making EC mandatory for the specified project and industries. The iron and steel industry requires the preparation of raw materials, agglomeration of fines in sinter plants, feeding of burden to blast furnaces, manufacturing of coke in ovens, conversion of pig iron to steel, making and shaping of steel, granulation of slag, recovery of chemicals in by-product plants, etc. All these processes add to air, water, solid waste and noise pollution. Steel industry growth and depleting high-grade ore resources have led to a strong demand for pelletising and sintering. Pellets have the benefit of lower gangue on account of beneficiated ore. However, pelletising is a direct source of environmental pollution. With the rapid and extensive industrialisation and urbanisation in much of India, there is growing realisation that the ultimate prerequisite for humankind's survival is environmental preservation. Thus, greater restrictions on pelletisation are needed. Expert 2 stated:

> ...environmental impacts of pellet plants whether they are stand alone or part of an integrated steel plant are severe in terms of air and water pollution and solid wastes generated. The sector specific EIA manual on metallurgical industry indicates that pellet plants, whether they are stand alone or are part of an integrated steel plant fall within the purview of the metallurgical industry requiring prior environmental clearance under the EIA Notification, 2006.[40]

The NGT in its commitment to resolve environmental issues may adopt an investigative procedure, thereby suggesting the *instrumental* use of knowledge. This procedure, upheld by the Supreme Court in *MoEF v Nirma Ltd*,[41] involves expert members inspecting affected sites[42] to compare and contrast contradictory claims, positions and reports filed by the parties.[43] The use of the Expert 1 in a MSW case illustrates this point:

> Normally we go into the details of technical and scientific aspects of the issue and its impact. We also conduct local inspections at the site and examine the prevailing conditions. We discuss the situation with the people inhabiting in the area.
>
> We go into the entire submission of parties and look into the feasible options to solve the problem. For example, in the state of Punjab, MSW is a big problem and litigation is pending before us. Punjab generates 4250 tons of MSW every day. We asked the secretary to the local bodies to present the case before us. The secretary informed us that the department of local government has divided all the urban centres of Punjab into eight clusters comprising of 8 to 26 urban local bodies in each cluster. For each sector there is a plan prepared by the authorities to handle MSW. However, we found that the plans are more theoretical rather than practical.
>
> The chairperson NGT asked me to prepare a technical note on MSW due to my experience as I was reporting to the Supreme Court of India on MSW related matters. I drafted a model action plan for the handling of the MSW based upon important principles, namely, effective segregation,

collection and transportation; maximum resources recovery; effective treatment; and safe disposal. This technical note i.e. model action plan was circulated to the Punjab government and all engineers were asked to study and look into its feasibility aspects. The engineers studied the plan and modified wherever required and resubmitted with their comments for NGT's reconsideration. The NGT is now deliberating on the plan and looking into its detail in order to formulate it as a policy and implement at the earliest. The copy of the model action plan was circulated to the Bhopal Bench on their request so that the same could be replicated in the state of Madhya Pradesh. This is a democratic way of dealing with the government. Eighty percent of pollution in India is because of sewage due to rapid urbanization. There is no proper way to treat sewage as the government has no money. Sewage is increasing at a steep rate in India and there is not even a single city that has the capacity to provide total scientific methods for the collection and disposal of MSW. Such a facility if fully established and made optimally operative, would not only help the public at large but would largely serve the purpose of environmental protection. To solve the waste management problem, the NGT favoured the application of the polluter pays principle as the citizens are the ultimate beneficiaries. The Punjab government should charge every household, shop, hotel, or any industrial building to pay a specific amount along with the property tax payable for the property, or on monthly basis, whichever is permitted by the concerned authorities. The amount collected should only be used for effective collection and disposal of MSW in accordance with the rules and for educating people in relation to the need for helping bodies and authorities concerned to collect the MSW in an appropriate manner. It appears that the Punjab government will be implementing the plan. It is the only way to solve the problem.[44]

The NGT, in *Pathankot Welfare Association v State of Punjab* (Judgment 25 November 2014), gave effect to this model MSW action plan by pronouncing it as general law. NGT directions were issued that, in relation to the establishment and operationalisation of MSW projects, it should be completed by all authorities concerned, including state government, in a time-bound manner and no variation to the plan shall be permitted. Encapsulating such wide-ranging policy within the judgment promotes the larger public interest and dramatically expands traditional judicial functions associated with case-management and disposal of individual cases.

The stakeholder consultative adjudicatory process is the most recent NGT problem-solving procedure. It demonstrates the *instrumental* usage within the NGT's formal structure of both internal and external experts alongside stakeholders in order to understand and seek solutions to issues of national importance. Judge 1 stated:

> ...for protection and preservation of the environment, all stakeholders involved in the consultative adjudicatory process for enforcement of

environmental law have to come together and act. It is not applicable to a day to day case or a party to party case. This process is applicable to cases of wider ramification involving major issues like river cleaning or air pollution. Major issues having a public impact either on public health, environment or ecology can be better handled and resolved when stakeholders are brought together with the tribunal's scientific judges for eliciting the views of all concerned – government, scientists, NGOs, public and the NGT. Stakeholder process will provide a greater element of consent rather than opposition to a judgment.[45]

Expert 2 echoed this by identifying the ongoing Ganga river,[46] Yamuna river[47] and air pollution[48] cases as illustrations of the new stakeholder consultative adjudicatory process involving open dialogue with interested parties.[49] In this way, efforts are being made to ensure scientifically-driven judgments reflect the interests, expectations and plans of stakeholders to produce decisions which support sustainable development and recognise the wider public interest. According to Expert 2:

> …initially there was indifference or reluctance on the part of the stakeholders, particularly the governmental agencies, to take these meetings seriously. However, the determination and willingness of the NGT to solve the environmental issues have made the governmental authorities respond in an appropriate manner. The blame game attitude and buying more time to solve the issues has been replaced by the submission of clear cut proposals and suggestions and a time frame for making changes. This is indeed a very helpful exercise for not only understanding the problems and challenges but also finding the best possible solution.[50]

Schrefler also states that *instrumental* usage can be adopted by agencies 'to develop and strengthen [their] ability to cope with thorny policy problems in the future' (Schrefler 2014: 315, see also 69). India's environmental issues, reflecting its economic development policies, are an ongoing challenge regularly addressed by the NGT. It is in this context of current and future challenges that the use of Expert 4's expertise became central in the matter relating to Biosphere Reserves (BR), particularly the sensitive Achanakmar-Amarkantak (AA) BR, in *Narmada Khand Swabhiman Sewa v State of Madhya Pradesh* (Judgment 1 October 2014). An application was filed by a social-activist organisation against mining activities in the AABR. It contended that mining would cause irreparable damage to the ecology, flora and fauna, besides polluting the river Narmada which originates there.

BR is a UNESCO international designation for representative parts of natural and cultural landscapes extending over large areas of terrestrial or coastal/marine ecosystems or a combination thereof.[51] These are internationally recognised within the framework of UNESCO's Man and the Biosphere Programme, after receiving consent from the participating country. BRs are designated to deal with the question of reconciling the conservation of bio-diversity with the quest for economic and social development and maintenance of associated cultural values. BRs are divided into three zones – core (dedicated to conservation); buffer (sustainable use); and transition (equitable sharing of benefits). The AABR is included in the UNESCO BR World Network. MoEF guidelines were issued in 2007 to manage BRs efficiently by focusing on environmental stability, biodiversity monitoring and management, restoration of ecological balance of disturbed areas and improvement of livelihood oppor-tunities and standards of residents in consonance with local practices. However, BRs are not declared or notified under any MoEF law and thus no legal issues are involved. A BR does not create new regulations nor restrict the rights of citizens.

In *Narmada Khand Swabhiman Sewa v Madhya Pradesh*, the NGT recognised:

> BRs are thus special environments for both people and nature and are living examples of how human beings and nature can co-exist while respecting each other's needs. The world's major ecosystem types and landscapes are represented in this network. Here there is no bar on utilization of natural resources, provided they do not have any adverse effect on the ecological diversity. However, these economic uses should be characteristic of the region in the buffer and transition zones and should be in consonance with the site conditions giving more emphasis on rehabilitation of the area and restoring the ecology in a way that it turns to sustainable productivity and must involve the local communities besides utilizing the natural resources in a rational and responsible manner and for the well-being of the local people besides contributing to economic development of the nation.
>
> (Para 27)

Partially accepting the contention of the activists regarding BRs' importance, the Tribunal allowed mining activities only in the buffer and transition zone, provided a broad planning approach is adopted by the regulatory agencies. This is aimed at the conservation and wise use of the BR's natural resources without compromising the local biodiversity and lifestyles.

It was in this context that Expert 4's knowledge became central. He sug-gested the introduction of policy change to integrate aspects of biodiversity pro-tection and commercial activities in the BRs, critically assessing sustainability, accompanied by a set of related quantitative, qualitative or descriptive attributes by preparing a landscape plan on the principle of sustainable development, taking the following factors into account:

- conservation and maintenance of biological diversity, sustainable utilisa-tion of natural resources, and stabilisation of terrain;
- improvement and regulation of the hydrological regime;
- people's involvement in planning and management of natural resources; and
- fulfilling people's socio-economic and livelihood.

Although mining and other related industries negatively impact, directly and indirectly, on biodiversity and communities, they can make a significant contribution to sustainable development when environmental, social and corporate governance issues are effectively managed. Preparation of a detailed landscape plan was required, followed by a detailed EIA study to ensure ecological integrity is maintained.

According to the Tribunal:

> … preparation of a landscape plan is a highly technical job and now-a-days technological advancements like remote sensing, GIS, GPS, computational and analytical systems are available for preparation and for real time monitoring of dynamics of BRs which can be taken into account while preparing the plan and assessing the resources and their sound management. Quality economies require quality environments and that conservation is important for both.
>
> (*Narmada Khand Swabhiman Sewa v Madhya Pradesh*, para 45)

The matter of environmental damage assessment costing is another evolving subject, considering the increasing incidences of groundwater contamination in India.[52] It can involve both non-market valuation as well as market valuation. In *Ashok Gabaji Kajale v M/S Godhavari Bio-Refineries Ltd* (Judgment 19 May 2015), the Tribunal observed:

> … the immediate corrective and remedial measures are necessarily to be initiated to improve the ground water quality and also, the degradation of the land … the corrective and remedial measures as far as the ground water quality require highly skilled and analytical expertise; and the process itself is highly expensive and time consuming besides it requires co-ordinated efforts from all stake-holders. The Tribunal is not expected to go into the details of such methodology or techniques of the remediation of the ground water but it is suffice to say that enough literature is available on this topic. The Tribunal is also aware that the ground water remediation has been practiced in India at very limited places and no significant material or literature is available on the actual implementation of ground water remediation … However, with the knowledge of such background and also the experience, the Tribunal is conscious of the fact that at some stage an initiative needs to be taken to remediate the ground water in a time bound manner in a scientific way and we therefore are of the opinion that the regulatory authorities will have to utilise their powers conferred by the environmental regulation to ensure that the ground water remediation is done in a time bound manner.
>
> (Paras 44 and 45)

In *Shri Sant Dasganu Maharaj Shetkari Sangh Akolner v Indian Oil Corporation Ltd* (Judgment 10 November 2014), an application was filed by 24 families at

Akolner village, Taluka, Ahmednagar District, alleging groundwater pollution caused by leakage from petroleum storage tanks and pipelines installed by the Indian government. The applicants submitted that, since 2008, the applicants were subject to noisome smells from petrol, diesel and kerosene. The situation was aggravated in 2012 when the well-water was mixed with about 50 per cent of petroleum products and they were unable to use it either for drinking or agricultural purposes. The lack of safe water affected their livelihoods, resulting in a decline in agricultural yield, depletion of livestock and adverse health effects. The Tribunal decided that the well-water was contaminated with a high concentration of oil and grease similar to products handled at the oil companies' storage facilities. There was a strong co-relation between type of contamination of the well-waters and the activities of the oil companies.

The Tribunal observed:

> In the instant case where the damages are related to contamination of ground water quality of Akolner village, change in the characteristics of agricultural fields and also loss of means of livelihood due to not making crops in the agricultural fields or cattle growing, a multi-pronged approach based on methodologies (direct market method, surrogate market based method, constructed market based method and experimental method) needs to be taken by this Tribunal. The identification and scoping of pollution sources plays an important rate in remediation and containment of contaminant plume. The reliable and accurate estimation of ground water pollution sources remains a challenge because of uncertainties involved and the lack of adequate observation data in most cases. Ground water clean-ups are never easy, especially in fractured geological formations. With petroleum contamination, however, these are a few physical and chemical characteristics which allow it to be cleaned up more easily than a soluble, dense non-aqueous-phase liquid or metal or salt contamination. Petroleum products accumulate and float at the first saturated zone with the resulting dissolved-phase contamination, rarely migrating for a very long distance. We are of the opinion that close co-ordination among various stake holders, and use of highly scientific and analytical tools and techniques is required for proper assessment and required remediation. Accordingly, the Maharashtra Pollution Control Board ... and the Directorate of Groundwater Survey and Development Agency ... are specialised agencies of highly technical and scientific human resources and as per the relevant legal framework, both these agencies are expected to identify such source of pollution and also, take effective control and remedial measures.
>
> (Paras 27 and 28)

Accepting the contention of the applicants, the Tribunal ordered the appropriate authorities to ensure the polluted well-water be subjected to necessary treatment and disposal; conduct an assessment of groundwater quality and status of pollution at the disputed wells; suggest restoration and remediation measures within two months; and pay compensation of Rupees 500,000 (£5000) to affected residents.

Additionally, Experts 2, 5 and 8 believed that the internalisation of environmental issues at the project-planning stage of development projects is the way forward to reduce adverse environmental impacts to the minimum. Internalisation would be addressed quickly by policy interventions and financial commitments at the initial stage. In *Ranjana Jetley v Union of India* (Judgment 1 April 2014), the Tribunal affirmed this by directing the regulatory authorities to recognise that the environmental and forestry issues should be addressed early and become an integral part of the proposed developmental project.

Strategic

Schrefler's framework recognises the exercise of expert knowledge for political and substantiating purposes. *Strategic political usage* can be employed 'to expand its (agency) power and strengthen its prestige and reputation'. The *strategic political use* of knowledge is illustrated in the NGT through the expansion of its power by its decision to initiate *suo motu* proceedings (on its own motion) in environmental cases. Normally, the NGT is triggered by an aggrieved person filing a motion. In *suo motu* the court acts on its own volition in the absence of parties. Interestingly, the NGT Act does not expressly provide the authority to initiate *suo motu* proceedings. Further, in 2012, the NGT, in *Baijnath Prajapati v MoEF* (Judgment 20 January 2012), stated 'at the same time it is mentionable that we are not conferred with *suo motu* powers' (para 9) Nevertheless, within a couple of years the NGT's position changed so as to strengthen its position and power by claiming *suo motu* jurisdiction.

It did this by taking *suo motu* cognisance of stories published in the media. Cases such as increased vehicular traffic in Himachal Pradesh,[53] dolomite mining in Kanha National Park tiger reserve,[54] groundwater contamination in water-supply lines and bore-wells in Delhi,[55] high levels of pollution near the Adyar estuary,[56] setting up a petrol bunk in Sathyamanglam tiger reserve[57] are illustrative NGT-initiated *suo motu* proceedings. These cases reflect the self-proclaimed, expansionist power to review environmental issues, *ab initio*, simply on the grounds of environmental protection and human welfare. According to Judge 1 '... *suo motu* jurisdiction has to be an integral part of the NGT for better and effective functioning of the institution. There are some inherent powers which are vital for effective functioning and *suo motu* jurisdiction is one such power'.[58] While this proactive decision to adopt the practice of *suo motu* falls squarely within the Schrefler's *political strategic* categorisation, it also simultaneously attracted the negative attention of external stakeholders.[59]

Schrefler's *strategic substantiating* use of knowledge involves well-crafted scientific knowledge that justifies and supports a predetermined or preferred policy solution. In this context, the NGT's statutory mandate is to apply the sustainable development, precautionary and polluter-pays principles.[60] According to Experts 1, 2 and 8:

...the concept of sustainable development is well documented but to practice it in the field is a challenge. The application of sustainable development is only possible if the judge is technically sound. The balancing act is a ticklish issue. It is based upon facts and circumstances of the case. If the larger interest of the society is to be considered with minimal damage to the environment then perhaps it can be balanced. Economic interest of the society cannot proceed over the environmental interests. For instance, residential and commercial infrastructure development is one such area. On one side the population of India is growing and we need housing for the people. Agricultural land is being diverted for the residential development. However, there are coastal zone regulations, forests laws that need to be taken into account before such development is permitted. The [EIA] regulations ... need to be strictly complied with. That is one of the first yardsticks for any evaluation of the sustainable development process. However, in cases before us, the EIA process is often eye-wash. Limited involvement of affected people in the hearing, publication, scoping and screening issues, no provision in place to cover landscape and visual impacts in the Indian EIA regulations are some of the steps not followed properly. We go into the details to examine the project and make the project proponent accountable for his activities.[61]

The NGT scientific experts played a crucial role in the application of cumulative environmental impact assessments (CEIAs) to strike the balance between developmental interest and environmental protection. The ability to incorporate cumulative effects analysis into the development of alternatives for an EIA can minimise negative cumulative effects, promote resource sustainability and make room for future development.[62] In India, there have been serious failures regarding CEIA studies often rendering this crucial process meaningless, resulting in the violation of September 2006 EIA Notification, wherein Form 1 section 9 asks for a CEIA.[63] On occasions, the MoEF EAC has taken a 'casual approach' and granted EC for projects without performing due diligence.[64]

According to Expert 2, who specialises in environmental and social impact assessment:

Cumulative impact consists of an impact that is created as a result of the combination of the project evaluated in the EIA together with other projects in the same vicinity causing related impacts. These impacts occur when the incremental impact of the project is combined with the cumulative effects of other past, present and reasonably foreseeable future projects. Cumulative impact may be same or different and those arising out of individual activities and tend to be larger, long lasting and spread over a greater area within the individual impact. Such studies are therefore commonly expected to:

1   assess effects over a larger area that may cross jurisdiction boundaries;
2   assess effects during a longer period of time into the past and future;

3   consider effects on other eco-system components due to interactions with other actions, and not just the effect of the single action under review;

4   include other past, existing and future (reasonably foreseeable) action; and

5   evaluate significant effect in consideration of other than just local and direct effects.

The importance of material data in the CEIA process cannot be underestimated. One is expected to make studies regarding cumulative impacts of all the existing as well as proposed industries. It is expected to collect actual field data regarding each of the existing industry and together with information on proposed industry interpret its impacts on land, water, noise, terrestrial ecology and socio-economic environment. Deliberate concealment or submission of false or misleading information for the purposes of screening, scoping or appraisal can lead to either stipulating any other environmental conditions or rejection of application for environmental clearance for the proposed project.[65]

The case of *T Muruganandam v MoEF* illustrates the above NGT's scientific concerns and expectations in relation to acceptable CEIA reports. Against this background, the Tribunal held that the project proponent considered the data available for only eight industries, whereas the appellant contended that there were at least 45 industries in 25 km radius of the project and no reasons were given as to why these were excluded from the CEIA study. As regards the primary baseline data for 10 km radius, the CEIA report does not mention the date and location of sampling as required for EIA reports. Furthermore, no study on impact on air quality as a result of emissions was carried out and no modelling was undertaken for future projects. For prospective industries in the stage of planning, requisite information such as nature of the industrial process, product therefrom, likely effluents or emissions and systems to regulate them and other relevant information could have been collected from the pollution control board and their probable impact on the environment studied accordingly. The NGT quashed the EC given to a 3600 MW thermal power plant in Tamil Nadu on the ground that an appropriate CEIA of the project was not conducted. The CEIA was carried out on the basis of incomplete information and non-existent standards and the MoEF granted EC without application of mind. The NGT ordered a review on the basis of a fresh CEIA study.

In *Krishi Vigyan Arogya Sanstha v MoEF* (Judgment 20 September 2011), the Tribunal expressed concern relating to the grant of EC for a coal-based thermal power project in the absence of a proper CEIA:

No assessment has been done of the expected excess cardio-vascular and respiratory mortality, children's asthma and respiratory dysfunction that is attributable to the exposure to the air pollutants from the plant. No assessment of crop yield loss of net primary production attributable to the plant and air pollutant has been done. Ozone a secondary pollutant which causes immense injury to human health and vegetation including crops, has not been studied and considered in the EIA report. No assessment of the impact on the water bodies has been conducted. Sulphur dioxide and Nitrogen dioxide are acidic and known to decrease pH of water bodies. Such a decrease has immense impact on aquatic life. These things were not properly studied. The effect of nuclear radiation in and around the plant was neither studied nor considered. It is given to understand, no national prescribed standards are available with regard to nuclear radiation for various types of eco-system. Looking from any angle, the grant of Environment Clearance was made without making any scientific study.

(Para 8)

Accordingly, the Tribunal issued directions that recognised the principle of sustainable development. These included instituting a scientific study dealing with nuclear radiation with reference to coal ash generated by thermal power projects; direction to the MoEF to prescribe national standards as to permissible levels of nuclear radiation in residential, industrial and ecologically sensitive areas of India; and synchronising the commissioning of the thermal power project with that of a sewage waste-water treatment plant. The treated water was proposed to be used for the operation of the project, failing which no consent to operate was to be issued by the pollution control boards. Further, all future projects required the project proponent to furnish details of possible nuclear radioactivity and the levels of coal proposed to be used for the thermal power plant. Thus, the decision demonstrates that any procedural lapses, such as collection and evaluation of basic scientific data for the grant of EC, that may lead to threats to the environment, ecology and conservation of natural resources will be taken seriously by the NGT's expert.

Schrefler's *strategic* knowledge utilisation is further justified by the application of polluter-pays and precautionary principles as fundamental tools in achieving sustainable development.[66] The precautionary principle acts as an environmental safeguard to achieve sustainable development. For the NGT, the precautionary principle requires the authority to examine the probability of environmental degradation that may occur and result in damage. It involves taking preventive measures which would ensure no irretrievable damage to the environment is caused. The principle encapsulates the elements of prevention and prohibition.

In *NAB Lions Home for Aging Blind v Kumar Resorts* (Judgment 26 May 2015), the bench examined an application in which the project proponent construction company for the development of resorts and amusement parks illegally carried out the work and removed soil from the top of the hill and cut trees, rendering the site subject to landslides during heavy monsoons. Deep ravine formations indicated that landslides and mudflows were inevitable, thereby jeopardising the safety of buildings and their inhabitants at the foot of the hill, in particular the NAB Home for Aging Blind (a welfare centre for blind people). The Tribunal observed that for the precautionary principle to apply one is not required to prove that the nature of any activity would actually cause environmental degradation or amount to potent danger to the environment. What is required is whether the precautionary principle is necessarily required to be applied, having regard to the particular circumstances of the case, in order to avert the possibility or probability of environmental degradation. Accordingly, the NGT decided to protect the hilly terrain by applying the principle. The bench concluded that, if the soil running with natural water flowed swiftly after rain accompanied by particles, then it is likely to hit and damage the lower-side buildings and constructions. Prevention is better than cure. The existence of probability of environmental degradation called for the application of the precautionary principle.

In *Jeet Singh Kanwar v Union of India* (Judgment 16 April 2013), the issue before the NGT was the application of the precautionary principle and sustainable development to the grant of EC to the proposal for the installation and operation of a coal-based thermal power plant in the state of Chattisgarh. Explaining the scope of sustainable development, the Tribunal observed:

> …the concept is an exercise of balancing the industrial activity with environment protection. The balancing act requires proper evaluation of both the aspects, namely, degree of environmental degradation which may occur due to the industrial activity and degree of economic growth to be achieved. It is well settled that the person who wants to change the status quo has to discharge burden of proof to establish that the proposed development is of sustainable nature.
>
> (Para 25)

Applying the facts of Kanwar's case, the Tribunal decided it was necessary to examine the validity of the project as the installation of the proposed thermal plant based on consumption of coal as fuel would cause additional pollution to the surrounding areas. Such a possibility called for caution and the application of the precautionary principle. Thus, the Tribunal decided that the EC was improperly granted as there was failure to apply the principles of sustainable development and precaution in order to avoid future disaster or irreversible environmental degradation.

The principle was again applied in *Janajagrithi Samiti v Union of India* (Judgment 7 March 2012). The NGT directed the Karanataka Power Transmission Corporation not to fell trees nor destroy the biodiversity in the 8.3 km stretch belonging to Baller reserve forest of Western Ghats in Chikmagalur District in order to erect 400KV double-circuit transmission lines. The Tribunal considered irreparable loss would occur within the rich and rare biodiversity of the Western Ghats and cause restrictions in habitat connectivity and the corridor values of the forest.

The polluter-pays principle is commonly interpreted as that the polluter must pay for the costs of pollution abatement, environment recovery, incident management and compensation for victims of damages, if any, as a consequence of pollution. The overarching principle is recognised as an integral component of sustainable development.

In *Raghunath v Maharashtra Prevention of Water Pollution Board* (Judgment 24 March 2014), the NGT applied the polluter-pays principle against chemical industries not treating their industrial effluents adequately in CETPs and discharging in open areas thereby causing groundwater pollution.

> It is a matter of record that the ground water remedial measures involve significant costs and necessarily such costs need to be paid by concerned industries. This is a fit case where the principle of polluter pay can be applied There is no escape from conclusion that the industries in the industrial area are liable to pay damages caused due to the water pollution, restore the environment and ensure that there shall be no further pollution in the river wells due to discharging of industrial effluent of the units run by the industries.
>
> (Paras 20 and 25)

Accordingly, the NGT directed the state pollution control board to recover the cost of remedial measures on equitable distribution and polluter-pays principle from the industries at an initial amount of Rupees 5 lakhs (£5000) each.[67]

In *Manoj Misra v Union of India* (Judgment 22 July 2013), the Tribunal passed an order for the application of the polluter-pays principle after a petition was filed by Manoj Misra, a leading environmental activist, who opposed the dumping of debris and construction waste on the banks of the river Yamuna. The Yamuna is the lifeline of Delhi, India's capital, providing a constant supply of water (Gill 2014a). The NGT held that any person found dumping debris on the river bank at any site is liable to pay a sum of Rupees 5 lakhs (£5000) for causing pollution. The recovery of the fine was from the person responsible for dumping the debris as well as the person to whom the debris belonged.

The consequence of the NGT order witnessed the removal of debris by government agencies, as major parties responsible for dumping thousands of tonnes of constructional and demolition waste on the banks of the Yamuna. However, there was no plan for an alternative waste site! Delhi generates 5000 tonnes of debris every day but only has a single processing plant handling 500 tonnes per day. Evidence showed that governmental authorities, such as the Delhi Metro Road Corporation, dumped 50,400 tonnes of debris in the river, equivalent to around 8000–9000 truckloads (Singh 2013).

India's environmental jurisprudence considers the polluter-pays principle as a fundamental norm of internalising pollution-related costs within the context of the economic rationality of the enterprise. It should be simple, practical and suited to the conditions obtaining in the country. However, there appears a predicament in its implementation. Judge 5 and Expert 8 highlighted the difficulties in implementing the polluter-pays principle:

...though the principle is very simple, its implementation is rather difficult and complex mainly due to the difficulty in identification of the polluters and apportioning their responsibilities. Another concern in implementation of this principle is to how the polluter should pay. Even the difficulties in restoring the ecological system, once it is disrupted or contaminated makes the assessment of payment in the terms of loss (loss of bio-diversity, loss of habitat, loss of top soil, so on and so forth) difficult. Moreover the payment is at[,] the end of the day, probably a monetary one. It is well documented that the monetary compensation do[es] not essentially fully make up for ecological loss or loss of resource such as ground water, top soil, biodiversity and therefore, in reality to some degree, at least, the polluter never pays the real cost of the pollution, even if, some restitution or compensation is possible. The environmentalist, therefore, advocate[s] the importance of precautionary principle over the polluter pays principle in the enforcement policies.[68]

This section of the chapter applies Schrefler's theoretical framework to the NGT's institutional form and activities. It demonstrates the use of expertise as a continuum process by generating hypotheses about ecological events and their impacts, synthesising information to identify knowledge and policy gaps and providing science-based ecological insights to adjudicate on domain-specific case-based problems.

The availability of a spectrum of scientific knowledge that reflects the wide range of cases heard by the NGT remains an issue yet to be addressed. A balanced bench is a *sine quo non* for decision-making processes. On the one hand, having too many experts can lead to slowing down or even the paralysis of the process but, at the same time, too few can affect the quality of decisions (Gruszczynski 2014: 228). The regional benches of the NGT face the problem of having only one expert and one judicial member. The expert may not have the expertise to handle a particular environmental issue and this could result in a limited decision. This shortfall was echoed by Senior Lawyer 2 at Bench 2 in a case relating to forest matters:

All of my eighteen cases that were transferred from the Bombay High Court were related to forest matters and law. I am afraid that the expert member is not acquainted with the forest law. So in that sense one had to rely only on the judicial member. I feel that the NGT should have taken recourse to an expert in forest matters. I feel that the expert member was not able to make a contribution because that is not his expertise. If the NGT continues in the same fashion and does not keep a panel of experts on the different environmental aspects that they are going to deal with then what you are having is essentially an opinion of one judge. You are not having the opinion of two persons. So to that extent I feel it is a failing of the NGT who have appointed an expert on only one aspect but is expected to be an expert on all matters. In Pune, the expert is able to provide his expertise on pollution related matters, such as industrial pollution, garbage, waste matters and others as he was formally associated with the pollution control board. On forests related matters the expert member certainly did not know the issues and the judicial member had to figure this out on his own. This is a problem of regional benches where there is only one expert member, unlike the principal bench in Delhi where there are six members.[69]

This opinion is shared by regional bench members, Judges 2 and 5,[70] who felt a broader scientific perspective generates hypotheses about environmental events and processes and provides an evaluative statement of comparing possible options in support of decision-making. They agreed that addressing this concern by consulting universities or scientific institutions would contribute to the quality of decision-making and ensure effective use of expert knowledge. For example, in *Ashok Gabaji Kajale v M/s Godhavari Bio-Refineries Ltd* (Judgment 19 May 2015), the Tribunal appointed MS University, Baroda, to provide expertise and report on matters associated with groundwater pollution and improper industrial effluent management systems.[71] In *Charudutt P Koli v M/s Sea Lord Containers* (Judgment 3 February 2015), the NGT appointed the Institute of Chemical Technology, Matunga, to submit a report on the air pollution caused by emissions from volatile organic compounds due to loading, storage and unloading of them by companies engaged in the business of logistic services to the oil, gas and chemical industry. In *Paramjeet S Kalsi v MoEF* (Judgment 15 May 2015), the NGT bench appointed the Directorate of Geology of Mining to visit sites and submit a report where illegal and unauthorised sand-mining adversely affected river banks, riverbeds and ground water circulation and caused pollution of river water.

However, Judges 2 and 5 felt that it is not viable to appoint an expert panel to assist the NGT in judicial decision-making.

> …a bench of regular expert appointees is not viable for the NGT for two reasons. First, it is not expressly spelled out in the Act. Second, in the executive decision making there are experts and agencies appointed for the consultation of the project. They act as consultants and are interested parties. Conflict of interest may arise from the bias that such consultants may have, as a result of their interests in private or other sectors. The credentials of such persons are not sure. We are not sure that these panellists can act independently and assist the NGT in decision making.[72]

This chapter has reviewed the NGT's usage of *symbolic*, *instrumental* and *strategic* scientific knowledge. Being a recent adjudicatory institution, none of the three usages is currently prioritised in the NGT. They enjoy a symbiotic relationship that collectively builds and consolidates public trust in the effectiveness of the NGT decision-making capability as well as formulating scientifically justified policies for environmental sustainability.

Conclusion

This chapter adds to the limited empirical studies on scientific knowledge utilisation at the institutional level. It has employed the theory developed by Hass (epistemic communities) and, in particular, that of Schrefler and her categories that explain knowledge utilisation. While their work does not address courts of law, it is argued that it can be successfully applied and thereby provides an established platform on which to present and test some of the data arising out of the Indian fieldwork and case reports. By offering ecological, technological and scientific resource knowledge, NGT experts either formulate policies or assist states with the implementation of these policies, thereby adopting both a problem-solving and policy-creation approach. The legitimacy not only includes the decision-making process (i.e. accountability and transparency), but also refers to the process through which the 'environment and public interest', as opposed to 'economic development interest', have an influence. The usage of investigative and stakeholder consultative procedures promotes active participation of all parties to resolve the environmental disputes. Nevertheless, the NGT's scientific experts and the use of their knowledge within a judicially controlled forum offers an internalised, accountability-focused approach whereby a diverse set of actors, such as governmental and local authorities, companies and multinational corporations, are restrained from compromising human welfare and the ecology.

Notes

1 In environmental regimes, the use of science and scientific expertise as problem-identifiers and problem-solvers is well documented. See Kuhn 1970; Andresen *et al.* 2000; Green and Epps 2007: 302–307; Feldman 2009; Shaffer 2010: 19; Gupta *et al.* 2012.

2 See Council for Tobacco Research, USA, funded by Philip Morris (McGarity 2004; Collins and Evans 2007; Lesser *et al.* 2007; Jasanoff 2011; Maclean 2015).

3 'Clear as Coke' *Times*, 9 October 2015 www.thetimes.co.uk/tto/opinion/leaders/article4580514.ece.

4 Ibid.

5 'Scientists accused of plotting to get pesticides banned' *Times*, 4 December 2014 www.thetimes.co.uk/tto/environment/article4286838.ece.

6 As early as 1945 this was highlighted by Merton (1945); see also Sprujt *et al.* (2014).

7 See *Case Concerning Pulp Mills on the River Uruguay (Argentina v Uruguay)* (ICJ Judgment 20 April 2010), in particular the dissenting and separate opinions of Judges Al-Khasawneh, Simma, Cançado Trindade, Yusuf, and Vinuesa regarding the role of experts:

> … the Court has had before it a case on international environmental law of an exemplary nature a 'textbook example', so to speak, of alleged trans-frontier pollution yet, the Court has approached it in a way that will increase doubts in the international legal community whether it, as an institution, is well-placed to tackle complex scientific questions.
>
> (Para 3)

8 www.greentribunal.gov.in.

9 Ibid.

10 Interview 16 July 2014.

11 Interviews 4 August 2014 and 8 April 2015.

12 Interviews 25 and 30 July 2014.

13 Interview 17 July 2014.

14 Interview 31 July 2014.

15 Interviews 30 July and 1 August 2014.

16 Interview 1 August 2014.

17 See n 8. The figure taken from the NGT website is accurate as of May 2016.

18 Section 4(1) NGT Act provides that the NGT consists of a full-time chairperson and no fewer than 10 (maximum 20) full-time judicial and expert members. Section 5(2) NGT Act spells out that judicial members must have the requisite legal expertise and experience and expert members will include technical experts from life sciences, physical science, engineering or technology.

19 The NGT (Manner of Appointment of Judicial and Expert Members, Salaries, Allowances and other Terms and Conditions of Service of Chairperson and other Members and Procedure for Enquiry) Rules 2010 and 2012.

20 Interview 16 July 2014.

21 'Stormy sinecures: should former judges get post-retirement jobs in the government?' *Telegraph India*, 24 September 2014 www.telegraphindia.com/1140924/jsp/opinion/ story_18866574.jsp#.VIx04nuHjtU.

22 Interview 14 March 2015.

23 Interview 15 March 2015; see nn 15 and 16 above.

24 See text accompanying n 41 below.

25 *Namit Sharma v Union of India* (2013) 1 SCC 745; *C Ravichandran Iyer v Justice A M Bhattacharjee* (1995) 5 SCC 457.

26 Section 22 NGT Act. The appeal under section 22 NGT Act 2010 can be filed only on grounds provided under section 100, Civil Procedure Code 1908, that includes a substantial question of law (a debatable question, not previously settled by the law of the land or having binding precedent not involving pure question of fact). See *Amol v State of Maharashtra* (Judgment 17 February 2015).

27 This is not to say that this independence is total and absolute, see section below on *suo motu* powers and this chapter's conclusion.

28 For a criticism on 'collegiality', see Paterson (1982; 2013: 142–143). Also see Annison (2014).

29 Interview 16 July 2014. For a detailed discussion on 'Collegiality and the NGT', see Gill (2014b).

30 Interviews 14, 15 and 16 July 2014.

31 Interview 4 August 2014.

32 Interview 25 July 2014.

33 Interview 22 July 2014.

34 Interview 30 July 2014.

35 Interview 16 July 2014.

36 Ibid.

37 www.greentribunal.gov.in/.

38 Interview 25 July 2014.

39 Interview 15 July 2014. Judgment of *Haat Supreme Wastech Ltd v State of Haryana* was pronounced on 28 November 2013.

40 In the interview 15 July 2014, the expert member referred me to the judgment *M/S Ardent Steel Ltd v MoEF* dated 27 May 2014.

41 Civil Appeal No 8781–83/2013, decided 4 August 2014.

42 *K K Singh v National Ganga River Basin Authority* (Judgment 16 October 2014).

43 See Chapter 3.

44 Interview 14 July 2014. I was also supplied with a copy of the Model Action Plan – Municipal Solid Waste Management in Punjab – by Expert Member 1 detailing the technical aspects of MSW.

45 Interview 14 April 2015.
46 *K K Singh v National Ganga River Basin Authority* (Judgment 16 October 2014). In *Indian Council for Enviro-Legal Action v National Ganga River Basin Authority* Judgment 10 December 2015, the NGT observed:

> …the Tribunal adopted the mechanism of 'Stakeholder Consultative Process in Adjudication' in order to achieve fast and implementable resolution to this serious and challenging environmental issue facing the country. Secretaries from Government of India, Chief Secretaries of the respective States, concerned Member Secretaries of Pollution Control Boards, Uttarakhand Jal Nigam, Uttar Pradesh Jal Nigam, Urban Development Secretaries from the States, representatives from various Associations of Industries (Big or Small) and even the persons having least stakes were required to participate in the consultative meetings. Various mechanism and remedial steps for preventing and controlling pollution of river Ganga were discussed at length. The purpose of these meetings was primarily to know the intent of the executives and political will of the representative States who were required to take steps in that direction.
>
> (Para 3)

47 *Manoj Misra v Union of India* (Judgment 13 January 2015) (now called Maily se Nirmal Yamuna Revitalization Plan 2017).
48 *Vardhaman Kaushik v Union of India* and *Sanjay Kulshrestha v Union of India* (Order 7 April 2015).
49 Interview 12 April 2015.
50 Ibid.
51 www.unesco.org/new/en/natural-sciences/environment/ecological-sciences/man-and-biosphere-programme/.
52 Interviews 6 and 8 April 2015. Judge 5 and Expert 8 observed that groundwater remediation and assessment has been practised in India at very limited places and no significant literature is available on actual groundwater remediation. The process is highly expensive and requires skilled and analytical expertise.
53 *Court on its Own Motion v State of Himachal Pradesh* (Judgment 6 February 2014).
54 *Tribunal on its Own Motion v Secretary, MoEF* (Judgment 4 April 2014).
55 *Tribunal on its Own Motion v Government of NCT, Delhi* Order, 19 June 2015.
56 'Adyar rivers turns dump yard' *Hindu*, 11 September 2013 www.thehindu.com/news/cities/chennai/adyar-river-turns-dump-yard/article5113580.ece.
57 *Tribunal on its Own Motion v Union of India* 2013 SCC Online 1095; 'Ecologists question right of way for petrol pump' *Hindu*, 1 August 2013 www.thehindu.com/news/national/tamil-nadu/ecologists-question-right-of-way-for-petrol-pump/article4974675.ece.
58 Interview 16 July 2014; Judges 2, 4 and 6 agreed with Judge 1 in interviews 6 and 8 April 2015; see also www.downtoearth.org.in/interviews/ngt-must-have-suo-motu-powers-47542.
59 The contentious issue of *suo moto* is discussed in detail in Chapter 7.
60 Section 20 NGT Act. For a detailed discussion on the above-mentioned principles, see Chapter 4.
61 Interviews 15 and 22 July and 4 August 2014.
62 See MoEF (2011: chapter 11); also see S Woolley (2014: 184–185). Alternatives in cumulative effect assessment include but are not limited to valuing ecosystem components and strategic environmental analysis.
63 http://envfor.nic.in/legis/eia/eia-2006.htm; see also https://sandrp.wordpress.com/2014/02/18/cumulative-impact-assessment-study-of-siang-basin-in-arunachal-needs-urgent-improvement/.
64 *T Muruganandam v MoEF* (Judgment 11 November 2014); *Samata v Union of India* (Judgment 13 December 2013).

65 Interview 15 July 2014.
66 See Chapter 4.
67 See also *M/S NGT Bar Association v Chief Secretary, Tamil Nadu* (Judgment 3 February 2015), popularly known as the *Ranipet Effluent* case. The NGT ordered the company operating the CETP to pay Rupees 7,500,000 (£75,000) based on the polluter-pays principle. The compensation was to be deposited with the Department of Environment and Forests, Government of Tamil Nadu. INR 2,500,000 (£25,000) would go towards relief for the 10 victims' families while the department would retain the balance of INR 5,000,000 (£50,000).
68 In the interview of 6 April 2015, the judges referred me to their judgment *V G Bhungase v G Sugar and Energy* dated 20 July 2014, para 21.
69 Interview 31 July 2014.
70 Interviews 29 March and 6 April 2015.
71 See also *Sreeranganathan KP v Union of India* (Judgment 28 May 2014); *Goa Paryavaran Savrakshan Sangharsh Samitee v Sesa Goa* (Order 20 October 2014); *Subhas Datta v State of West Bengal* (Order 28 July 2015).
72 Interviews 30 March 2015 and 8 April 2015.

References

Ambrus, M, Arts, K, Hey, E and Raulus, H (eds) (2014) *The Role of 'Experts' in International and European Decision-Making Processes* (CUP).

Andresen, S, Skodvin, T, Wettestad, J and Underdal A (eds) (2000) *Science and Politics in International Environmental Regimes* (Manchester UP).

Annison, H (2014) 'Interpreting the politics of the judiciary: the British senior judicial tradition and the pre-emptive turn in criminal law' 41(3) *JLS* 339–366.

Bocking, S (2006) 'Scientific expertise and environmental politics: cross-border contrasts' conference paper presented at the Canadian Political Science Association, York University, Toronto.

Buchanan, A and Keohane, R O (2003) 'The legitimacy of global governance institutions' 20(4) *Ethics and International Affairs* 405–438.

Collins, H (2014) *Are We All Scientific Experts Now?* (Polity Press).

Collins, H and Evans, R (2007) *Rethinking Expertise* (University of Chicago Press).

Cooper, S L (2013) 'The collision of law and science: American court responses to developments in forensic science' 33(1) *Pace LR* 234–301.

Drescher, M, Perera, A H, Johnson, C J, Buse, L J, Drew, C A and Burgman, M A (2013) 'Towards rigorous use of expert knowledge in ecological research' 4(7) *ECOSPHERE* 1–26.

Edwards, H T (2003) 'The effects of collegiality on judicial decision making' 151(5) *University of Pennsylvania LR* 1639–1690.

Ericsson, K A, Charness, N, Feltovitch, P J and Hoffman, R R (eds) (2006) *Cambridge Handbook of Expertise and Expert Performance* (CUP).

Faigman, D L (1999) *Legal Alchemy* (WH Freeman).

Feldman, R (2009) *The Role of Science in Law* (OUP).

Gill, G N (2014a) 'Environmental protection and development interests: a case study of the River Yamuna and the Commonwealth Games, Delhi 2010' 6(1)(2) *International Journal of Law in Built Environment* Special Issue on Environmental Law 69–90.

Gill, G N (2014b) 'National Green Tribunal: judge craft, decision making and collegiality' 2 *NGT International Journal of Environment* 43–53.

Gill, G N (2016) 'Environmental justice in India: the National Green Tribunal and expert members' 5(1) *Transnational Environmental Law* 175–205.

Green, A and Epps, T (2007) 'The WTO, science and the environment: moving towards consistency' 10(2) *Journal of International Economic Law* 285–316.

Gruszczynski, L (2014) 'The role of experts in environmental and health-related trade disputes in the WTO: deconstructing decision-making processes' in M Ambrus, K Arts, E Hey and H Raulus (eds), *The Role of 'Experts' in International and European Decision-Making Processes* (CUP) 216–237.

Gupta, A, Andresen, S, Siebenhuner, B and Biermann, F (2012) 'Science networks' in F Biermann and P Pattberg (eds), *Global Environmental Governance Reconsidered* (MIT Press) 69–95.

Haas, P M (2007) 'Epistemic communities' in D Bodansky, J Brunee and E Hey (eds), *Oxford Handbook of International Environmental Law* (OUP) 791–806.

Haas, P M (2014) 'Ideas, experts and governance' in M Ambrus, K Arts, E Hey and H Raulus (eds), *The Role of 'Experts' in International and European Decision-Making Processes* (CUP) 19–43.

Huber, P W (1991) *Galileo's Revenge: Junk Science in the Court Room* (Basic Books).

Jasanoff, S (1995) *Science at the Bar* (Harvard UP).

Jasanoff, S (2006) 'Just evidence: the limits of science in the legal process' 34(2) *Journal of Law, Medicine and Ethics* 328–341.

Jasanoff, S (2011) 'Quality control and peer review in advisory science' in J Lentsch and P Weingart (eds), *The Politics of Scientific Advice* (CUP) 19–35.

Kronsell, A and Backstrand, K (2010) 'Rationalities and forms of governance: a framework for analysing the legitimacy of new modes of governance' in K Backstrand, J Khan, A Kronsell and E Lovbrand (eds), *Environmental Politics and Deliberative Democracy* (Edward Elgar) 28–43.

Kuhn, T S (1970) *The Structure of Scientific Revolution* (University of Chicago Press).

Lawrence, J (2014) 'The structural logic of expert participation in WTO decision-making processes' in M Ambrus, K Arts, E Hey and H Raulus (eds), *The Role of 'Experts' in International and European Decision-Making Processes* (CUP) 173–193.

Lesser, L I, Ebbeling, C B, Goozner, M, Wypij, D and Ludwig, D S (2007) 'Relationship between funding source and conclusion among nutrition-related scientific articles' 4(1) *Public Library of Science Medicine* 41–46.

Limoges, C (1993) 'Expert knowledge and decision-making in controversy contexts' 2(4) *Public Understanding in Science* 417–426.

Lindquist, E A (1998) 'What do decision models tell us about information use?' 1(2) *Knowledge, Technology and Policy* 86–111.

Maclean, M (2015) 'The impact of socio legal studies on family justice: from Oxford to Whitehall' 42(4) *JLS* 637–648.

McGarity, T O (2004) 'Our science is sound science and their science is junk science: science based strategies for avoiding accountability and responsibility for risk-producing products and activities' 52(4) *Kansas LR* 897–937.

Merton, R K (1945) 'Role of the Intellectual in public bureaucracy' 23(4) *Social Forces* 405–415.

MoEF (2011) *AHEC/2011: Assessment of Cumulative Impact of Hydropower Projects in Alaknanda and Bhagirathi Basins* www.moef.nic.in/downloads/public-information/CH-1.pdf.

Oreskes, N and Conway, E (2010) *Merchants of Doubt: How a Handful of Scientists Obscured the Truth on Issues from Tobacco Smoke to Global Warming* (Bloomsbury).

Paterson, A (1982) *The Law Lords* (Palgrave Macmillan).

Paterson, A (2013) *Final Judgment* (Hart).

Schneider, K (2014) 'India's National Green Tribunal challenges government and industry to follow the law' Circle of Blue www.circleofblue.org/2014/world/indias-national-green-tribunal-challenges-government-industry-follow-law/.

Schrefler, L (2010) 'The usage of scientific knowledge by independent regulatory agencies' 23(2) *Governance* 309–330.

Schrefler, L (2014) 'Reflections on the different roles of expertise in regulatory policy making' in M Ambrus, K Arts, E Hey and H Raulus (eds), *The Role of 'Experts' in International and European Decision-Making Processes* (CUP) 63–81.

Shaffer, G (2010) 'Risk, science and law in the WTO: the centrality of institutional choice' American Society of International Law 104th Annual Meeting, 24–27 March.

Singh, D (2013) 'Metro chokes Yamuna with Debris' *Hindustan Times* www.hindustan times.com/delhi/metro-chokes-yamuna-with-debris/story-aWuMQaATNAAMWqPOXr30dM.html.

Sprujit, P, Knol, A B, Vasileiadou, E, Devilee, J, Lebret, E and Petersen, A C (2014) 'Roles of scientists as policy advisers on complex issues: a literature review' 40 *Environmental Science and Policy* 16–25.

Steffek, J (2003) 'The legitimation of international environmental governance' 9(2) *European Journal of International Relations* 249–276.

Traweek, S (1992) *Beamtimes and Lifetimes* (Harvard UP).

Twining, W (1992) '"In my experience most lawyers are innumerate and most law students are terrified of figures": preparing lawyers for the twenty-first century' 3(1) *Legal Education Review* 1–32.

Union of Concerned Scientists (2004) 'Scientific integrity' www.ucsusa.org/our-work/center-science-and-democracy/promoting-scientific-integrity/reports-scientific-integrity.html#.VwuaB_krKUk.

Vibert, F (2007) *The Rise of the Unelected Democracy and the New Separation of Powers* (CUP).

Weiss, C H (1979) 'The many meanings of research utilization' (1979) 39 *Public Administration Review* 426–431.

Woolley, S (2014) *Ecological Governance Reappraising Law's Role in Protecting Ecosystem Functionality* (CUP).

6 National Green Tribunal

Judgments and analysis

This chapter interogates and analyses data collected by the author. It consists of 1130 judgments of the NGT taken from the offical website of the Tribunal.[1] The data is solely comprised of reported judgments and excludes daily orders. The data collection is based upon the name of the first named party, plaintiff and defendant, mentioned in the judgment. The period under scrutiny commenced with the first reported judgment, *Deepak Kumar Rai v M/S Prabhu Nath Rai Udyog Ltd* (Judgment 7 July 2011), and concludes on 30 September 2015. Each case was read, analysed and classified according to the year, parties involved, nature of dispute, benches (principal and regional) and dispute outcome. The data was entered into SPSS software for investigation of frequencies and cross-tabulation. The data in this chapter reflects a proportion of the SPSS files – the database being too voluminous to be attached as an appendix and too detailed to fit within this chapter.[2]

The intention of the analysis is to focus on a number of key issues. These include the growth and nature of the NGT's caseload over a period of five years and the expansion of the caseload of the principal and regional benches. Questions asked include: who are the plaintiffs in terms of access to environmental justice and who are the defendants? What are the environmental issues that bring plaintiffs to the NGT? Are there parties who commonly appear as either plaintiffs or defendants? Who are the winners and losers and in what sort of dispute?

In order to investigate and address these questions, key variables were created and coded for the SPSS software. The selected key variables were constructed by studying every case and drawing details from the judgments to include:

1 year (2011–2015);
2 benches (Delhi, Pune, Chennai, Bhopal and Kolkata);
3 plaintiffs (affected individuals/communities/residents; NGOs/social activists/public-spirited citizens; industry; builders/developers; governmental authorities; public sector undertakings; and *suo motu* cases);
4 defendants (MoEF; state government; local authorities; pollution control boards; industry; builder/developers; public sector undertakings; and private individuals/companies);

5   disputes (EC); administrative governance; pollution; condonation of delay; constructional/infrastructure permission and activities; no objection certificate/consent order/closure order; forest clearances (including cutting of trees); coastal zone management/ecologically sensitive area/no development area; and not within the mandate of the NGT);

6   outcome (allowed; not allowed/dismissed; partly allowed/dismissed; not to interfere/decide (including matters pending in the higher courts); dissent; and application/appeal withdrawn).

The following figures and text seek to answer the above questions.

Caseload 2011–2015

Figure 6.1 illustrates the growth, year on year, of reported judgments. In its first year 2011, the NGT decided 18 cases, mostly transferred from the dissolved National Environment Appellate Authority.[3] The slow start of the NGT was exacerbated by initial teething problems concerning the provision of appropriate infrastructure.[4] In 2012, there were 87 reported judgments followed by 166 in 2013 and 398 in 2014. Finally, in this analysis that finished on 30 September

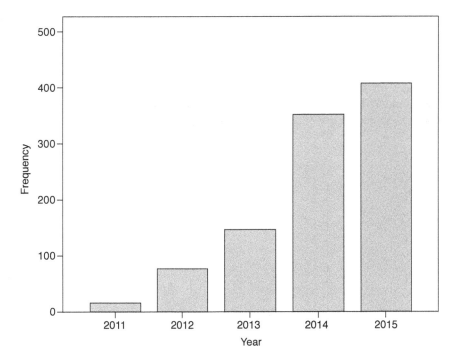

Figure 6.1 Caseload 2011–2015.
Source: author.

2015, there were 461 reported judgments of the NGT that year. There has been a dramatic growth in the caseload of the NGT during this period rising from 1.6 per cent of the 1130 total recorded judgments in 2011 to 40.8 per cent in 2015. The NGT appears to have found favour with 'persons aggrieved' seeking to access environmental justice.

Benches (principal and regional)

Figure 6.2 represents the number of decided cases in the regional benches as a percentage of the total cases. The Principal Bench, Delhi, was the first to be established. Out of the 1130 reported judgments, 475 cases (42 per cent) were decided in Delhi. Chennai, also with two benches, has decided 350 cases (31 per cent), followed by Pune with 191 cases (16.9 per cent) and Bhopal with 112 cases (9.9 per cent). The Kolkata Bench decided 2 cases (0.2 per cent), the probable explanation for this low figure rests with its late establishment in 2014 and initial infrastructure issues. The increased caseload in both Delhi and Chennai resulted in the creation of extra benches.

Nature of disputes

Figure 6.3 examines the categories of disputes throughout all benches. There were 328 EC cases accounting for 29 per cent of the data analysed. The main purpose of the EC is to assess impact of the planned project on the environment and people and to try to abate/minimise this impact.[5] For example, 172 EC cases related to mining issues including sand, coal, iron ore and stone. Construction and infrastructural development, followed by thermal power projects, accounted for 57 and 35 ECs cases respectively. Pollution disputes that include air, water, noise, waste and related environmental degradation constitute 232 cases (20.5

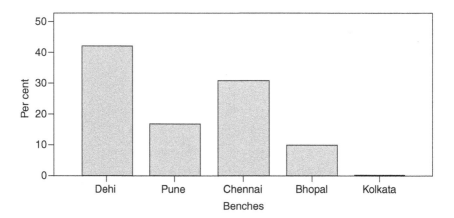

Figure 6.2 Benches (principal and regional).
Source: author.

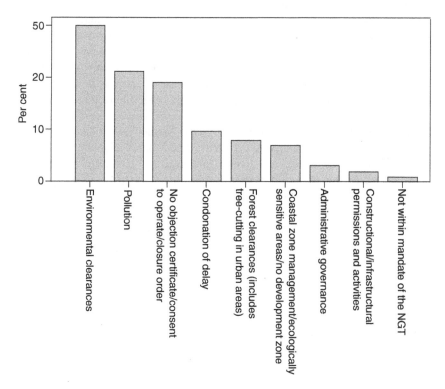

Figure 6.3 Nature of disputes.

Source: author.

per cent). The breakdown reflects air pollution (105 cases); water pollution (42 cases); waste pollution (27 cases); frequency of noise pollution (20 cases).

This is followed by 208 cases (18.4 per cent) dealing with no objection certificates/consent to operate/closure order to operate any industry, enterprise or activity. For example, 102 industrial units operated without proper certification.

There were 105 reported judgments (9.3 per cent) on condonation of delay. Sixty-five of these cases dealt with crushing units, mining activities and industrial enterprises. These are cases that were not filed before the NGT within the limitation period to invoke the jurisdiction of the Tribunal.[6] The policies underlying the law of limitation are ultimately based on justice and convenience – an individual should not live under the threat of a possible action for an indeterminate period because that would be unjust. Prescription of limitation takes in its ambit fairness and expeditious trial. Indefinite uncertainty in relation to bringing an action would be against public policy.[7]

Forest clearances, including tree-cutting in urban areas for developmental projects, account for 86 cases (7.6 per cent). The term 'forest land' refers to reserved forest, protected forest or any area recorded in the government record.[8]

Proposals for diversion of such areas for a non-forest purpose, even if the area is privately owned, require the prior approval of central government. The term 'tree' has the same meaning under any forest act[9] that may be in force in the forest area. The NGT has decided controversial cases for diversion of forest land for a non-forest purpose to include underground mining within mining and linear projects to include the laying of new roads, canals, railway lines, widening of highways and setting up of transmission lines, optical fibre lines and other activities.

Cases relating to development in ecologically fragile zones including coastal and NDZs constitute 75 cases (6.6 per cent). The MoEF declared eco-sensitive zones around protected areas to prevent ecological damage caused by developmental activities around national parks and wildlife sanctuaries. These areas act as 'shock absorbers' for the protected areas by regulating and managing activities. The basic aim is to regulate certain activities around national parks and wildlife sanctuaries in order to minimise the negative impacts of such activities on the fragile ecosystems encompassing the protected areas. Activities, including commercial mining, setting up of saw mills and industries causing pollution, commercial use of firewood, and major hydro-power projects, are prohibited in these areas. The MoEF also prohibits tourism activities, such as flying over protected areas in an aircraft or hot air balloon, and the discharge of effluents and solid waste into natural water bodies or terrestrial areas. Felling of trees, drastic change in agricultural systems and commercial use of natural water resources, including groundwater harvesting and the creation of hotels and resorts, are regulated activities.[10] The coastal zone, a transitional area between land and sea, needs protection and conservation against disproportionate growth in anthropogenic activities generating stress on natural ecosystems.[11] New industries and expansion of old industries are prohibited in CRZs. Discharge of untreated waste and effluents from industries, cities or towns and other human settlements is also prohibited, as is dumping of city or town waste, including construction debris and industrial solid waste.

Administrative governance cases (33 in number constituting 2.9 per cent) cover procedural error and impropriety including failing to observe the PNJ.[12] There were eight cases (7 per cent) that did not fall within the mandate of the NGT. For example, cases involving criminal law or those beyond the ambit of Schedule 1 NGT Act 2010. There is missing data for 35 cases constituting 3.1 per cent of the 1130 reported judgments.

Bench disputes distribution

Figure 6.4 is a cross-tabulation of bench-dispute variables. It shows the frequency, bench by bench, of key identified disputes which account for more than 10 per cent of the caseload of each bench.

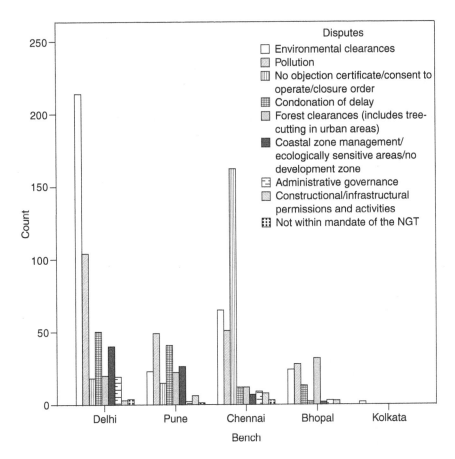

Figure 6.4 Bench disputes distribution.

Source: author.

Delhi Bench

ECs constitute the greatest number of disputes in the Delhi Bench. Out of a total of 472 reported cases, 214 dealt with ECs. This accounted for 45.3 per cent of the Delhi caseload and 65.2 per cent of the 328 ECs cases decided by the five benches. Pollution-related matters in the Delhi Bench numbered 104 cases being 22 per cent of the bench caseload and 44.8 per cent of the 232 pollution cases heard nationally. There were 50 cases dealing with condonation of delay, accounting for 10.6 per cent at this bench and 47.6 per cent at the all India level, out of 105 reported cases.

Pune Bench

The principal disputes in the Pune Bench are pollution and condonation of delay matters. Out of a total of 185 reported judgments, 49 dealt with pollution-related matters, being 26.5 per cent of the caseload. This bench accounted for 21.1 per cent of the 232 pollution cases heard in all benches. Condonation of delay cases amounted to 41 cases, being 22.2 per cent of the Pune caseload and 39 per cent out of 105 reported cases nationally. ECs were 23 cases, being 12.4 per cent of this bench and 7 per cent of the 328 cases heard nationally.

Chennai Bench

In Chennai, out of a total of 329 reported decisions, 162 cases related to no objection certificates/consent to operate/closure order to operate any industry, enterprise or activity being 49.2 per cent of the bench caseload. This was the largest disputes group decided by the southern bench. These cases accounted for 77.9 per cent out of 208 cases heard by all benches. ECs totalled 65 cases, being 19.8 per cent of all cases in Chennai and 19.8 per cent out of the 328 decided cases nationally. Fifty-one decided cases related to pollution. They amounted to 15.5 per cent of the Chennai Bench and 22 per cent of the 232 pollution cases heard by all benches.

Bhopal Bench

The Bhopal Bench witnessed a proportionate distribution of disputes in four major categories: forest clearances, pollution, ECs and no objection certificates/consent to operate/closure order. There were 32 cases, being 29.9 per cent concerning forest clearance matters (including tree-cutting in urban areas). Of 86 cases nationally, 37.2 per cent were decided in Bhopal. Pollution cases numbered 28, being 26.2 per cent of the 107 cases decided by the Bhopal Bench. They comprised 12.1 per cent of the national figure of 232 pollution cases. Thirteen cases related to no objection certificates/consent to operate/closure order to operate any industry, enterprise or activity, being 12.1 per cent of the bench caseload and 6.3 per cent of the 208 national figures.

Kolkata Bench

The Kolkata Bench heard two cases, both being on ECs.

Year disputes distribution

Figure 6.5 reflects a cross-tabulation examining major dispute categories on an annual basis from 2011 (7 July 2011) to 2015 (30 September 2015) in all benches thereby reflecting growth in particular categories. Selected categories constitute 10 per cent or more for the annual reported judgments.

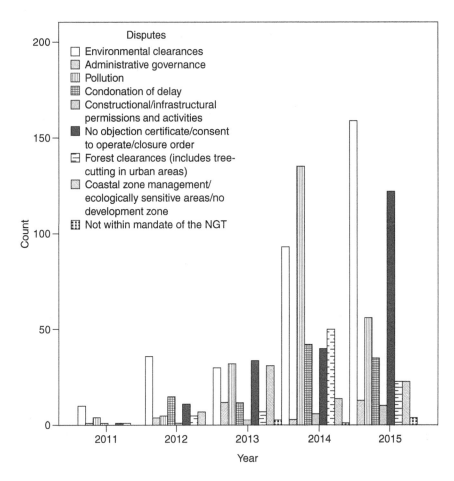

Figure 6.5 Year disputes distribution.
Source: author.

2011

The first judgment was delivered on 7 July 2011[13] and a total of 18 cases were reported. There were 10 EC cases; four pollution-related matters; and one in each of the administrative governance, condonation of delay, constructional/infrastructural activities, no objection certificate/consent to operate/closure order and forest clearances categories.

2012

There were 84 cases out of which 36 (42.9 per cent) related to ECs – 11 per cent of the total 328 ECs cases (2011–2015). Fifteen (17.9 per cent) cases were condonation of delay and constituted 14.3 per cent of the total 105 cases related to this category of disputes (2011–2015). No objection certificate/consent order/closure order amounted to 11 (13.1 per cent) cases and was 5.3 per cent of the total 208 cases in this category (2011–2015).

2013

Out of the 164 cases, 30 (18.3 per cent) related to ECs and constituted 9.1 per cent of the total 328 ECs cases (2011–2015). Pollution matters were 32 (19.5 per cent) cases and reflected 13.8 per cent of the total 232 cases in this category (2011–2015). No objection certificate/consent order/closure order amounted to 34 (20.7 per cent) cases and was 16.3 per cent of the total 208 cases in this category (2011–2015). Finally, coastal zone/ecologically sensitive area/NDZ had 31 (18.9 per cent) cases that amounted to 41.3 per cent of the total 75 cases related to this category (2011–2015).

2014

There were 384 cases out of which 93 (24.2 per cent) related to ECs, amounting to 28.4 per cent of the total 328 ECs cases (2011–2015). Pollution matters were 135 (35.2 per cent) cases and reflected 58.2 per cent of the total 232 cases related to this category (2011–2015). No objection certificate/consent order/closure order amounted to 40 (10.4 per cent) cases and was 19.2 per cent of the total 208 cases within this category (2011–2015). Fifty (13 per cent) cases related to forest clearances (including cutting of trees in urban areas) and represented 58.1 per cent of the total 86 cases of this category (2011–2015).

2015

159 (35.7 per cent) related to ECs out of a total of 445 cases and constituted 48.5 per cent of the total 328 EC cases (2011–2015). Pollution matters were 56 (12.6 per cent) cases and reflected 24.1 per cent of the total 232 cases within this category (2011–2015). No objection certificate/consent order/closure order amounted to 122 (27.4 per cent) cases and was 58.7 per cent of the total 208 cases in this category (2011–2015).

Plaintiffs

Figure 6.6 shows both the percentage of cases and category of plaintiffs (in these cases both original applicants and appellants) who approached the NGT as 'person aggrieved'.[14] The most frequent plaintiffs are NGOs/social activists/public-spirited citizens. They account for 533 plaintiffs (47.2 per cent) of 1130 cases. This significant number demonstrates both the opportunity to, and the ability for, public-spirited citizens and organisations to use the NGT as a route to seek remedies through collective proceedings instead of being driven into an

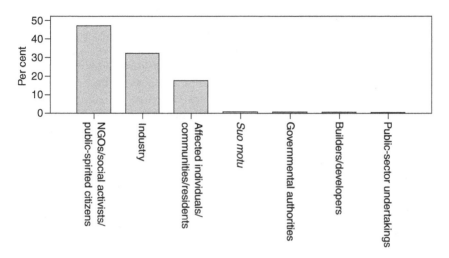

Figure 6.6 Plaintiffs.
Source: author.

expensive plurality of litigation, thereby, affirming participative justice. In *Jan Chetna v MoEF* (Judgment 9 February 2012) the NGT allowed an application by Jan Chetna, an NGO, concerning the grant of EC for the installation of a steel and power plant. The NGT ruled that the NGO was an aggrieved party and that its claim for a public hearing concerning the grant of an EC was sustainable.

The next largest category is industry, constituting 366 plaintiffs (32.4 per cent), both under original and appellate jurisdiction of the NGT. For example, in *P S Vajiravel v Chairman Tamil Nadu Pollution Control Board* (Judgment 28 February 2013), the appellants, M/S Shiva Shakthi Dyeing Ltd challenged the legal validity of the closure and disconnection of power supply order passed by the pollution control board. The NGT upheld the appeal on the grounds that the order passed by the pollution control board was a glaring example of non-application of mind, utter carelessness and also flagrant violation of the PNJ. Accordingly, the order was set aside as invalid.

Next, persons and communities directly affected constitute 200 plaintiffs (17.7 per cent). For example, in *R J Koli v State of Maharashtra* (Judgment 27 February 2015), the court allowed an application filed and argued in person by traditional fishermen seeking compensation for loss of livelihood due to infra-structural project activities.[15]

The NGT in nine cases (0.8 per cent) initiated *suo motu* proceedings.[16] For example, in *Tribunal on its Own Motion about Muttukadu Back Waters v Union of India* 2014 SCC OnLine NGT 2346, the NGT in the wake of reports in the *Indian Express* newspaper took up the matter *suo motu* relating to the Muttukadu estuary. Due to uncontrolled development and discharge of untreated sewage and effluents, the Muttukadu estuary faced the threat of harmful algal bloom of microcystis aeruginosa. In *Suo motu v Secretary, MoEF* (Judgment 30 January 2015), the NGT initiated *suo motu* proceedings based on a newspaper reporting in the interest of the environment against the proposed plan for an international cricket stadium at the foot of Tirumala hills, a rich catchment area with around 4 lakhs of mature trees, including the precious and endemic red sanders. The NGT directed that a mandatory EC must be obtained from the MoEF or State Level Environment Impact Assessment Authority (SEIAA) after finalisation of all the details of the proposed international cricket stadium project.

Governmental authorities constituted nine plaintiffs (0.8 per cent) of the data analysed. For example, in *Department of Environment, Kerala v K Savad* (Judgment 18 May 2015), the NGT allowed an application filed by the state of Kerala for extension of time to identify the forest cover in 142 villages as it required physical verification. The time was extended from two to six months. In *State Pollution Control Board v M/S Swastik Ispat Private Ltd* (Judgment 9 January 2014), the NGT upheld the decision of the pollution control board to direct the industrial unit to furnish a bank guarantee for compliance of conditions of consent order to operate the industry, installation of anti-pollution devices and ensuring that it is a pollution-free unit. In default of which and upon inspection, such bank guarantee would be liable to be invoked/encashed for environmental compensation and restoration purposes. Making such provision ensured, on the one hand, that the industry did not cause avoidable pollution and, on the other, the board performed its functions timely and effectively.

Builders and/or developers were seven plaintiffs (0.6 per cent) of the reported judgments analysed. In *M/S Aadi Properties v SEIAA* (Judgment 26 September 2015), the NGT refused to give relief to the appellant, M/S Aadi Properties, in relation to the construction of a district centre in Greater Mumbai without prior EC. The appeal was entertained by the NGT under section 16 NGT Act.

Public sector undertakings were person aggrieved in three cases (0.3 per cent). In *Rajasthan Rajya Vidyut Utpadan Nigam Ltd v Cess Appellate Committee* (Judgment 20 July 2015) the NGT allowed the appeal filed by the appellant against the payment of cess order passed by the Cess Appellate Committee. The assessing authority did not afford an opportunity of hearing to the affected party. Accordingly, the order was set aside with the direction to consider the matter afresh after affording the right to be heard to the appellant.

Defendants

Figure 6.7 identifies defendants and the percentage of their appearance in front of the NGT. Regulatory agencies (comprised of MoEF, state government, local authorities and pollution control boards) made up 942 defendants (83.4 per cent) of 1130 reported judgments. The MoEF was the defendant in 284 cases (25.1 per cent); state government appeared as defendant in 341 cases (30.2 per

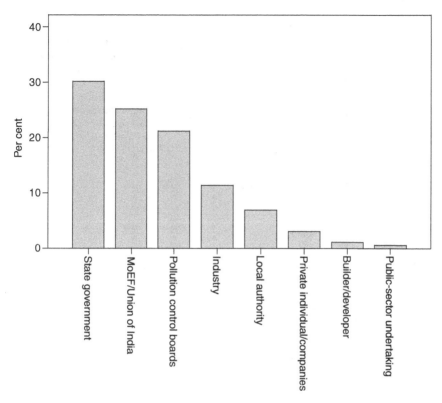

Figure 6.7 Defendants.
Source: author.

cent); a local authority was listed in 78 cases (6.9 per cent); and pollution control boards in 239 cases (21.2 per cent).

The remaining defendants included industry (129 cases, 11.9 per cent); builders/developers (14 cases, 1.2 per cent); public sector undertakings (seven cases, 0.6 per cent); and private individuals/companies (35 cases, 3.1 per cent).

Plaintiffs and defendants: common parties

Figure 6.8 is a cross-tabulation of the plaintiff–defendant variables showing the number of cases where the parties are constant. The figure reflects cases in the five benches. The selection of plaintiffs and defendants is based upon the frequency of appearance in the Tribunal. The plaintiffs include NGOs/social activists/public-spirited citizens, affected individuals and communities, and also industry. The defendants comprise MoEF, state government, local authority, pollution control boards and industry.

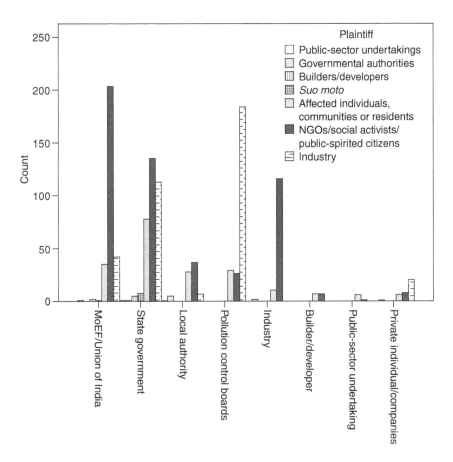

Figure 6.8 Plaintiffs and defendants: common parties.
Source: author.

Plaintiffs (NGOs/social activists/public-spirited citizens) v various defendants (MoEF, state government, local authority, pollution control boards and industry)

The MoEF was a defendant in 284 cases out of which 203 cases were brought by NGOs/social activists/public-spirited citizens as plaintiffs. The 203 cases accounted for 71.5 per cent of the 284 cases and also 38.1 per cent of the total 533 cases brought by NGOs/social activists/public-spirited citizens against various defendants. The state government was a defendant in 341 cases out of which 135 cases (39.6 per cent) were brought by NGOs/social activists/public-spirited citizens. This accounted for 25.3 per cent of the total 533 cases commenced by the NGOs/social activists/public-spirited citizens against a range of defendants. The local authority defended 78 cases out of which 37 (47.4 per cent) were brought by NGOs/social activists/public-spirited citizens. This amounted to 6.9 per cent of the total 533 cases against various defendants. Pollution control boards appeared in 239 cases. NGOs/social activists/public-spirited citizens brought 26 (10.9 per cent) cases. These 26 cases represent 4.9 per cent of the total 533 cases brought against numerous defendants. Industry was a defendant in 116 (89.9 per cent) cases brought by NGOs/social activists/public-spirited citizens out of a total of 129 cases. This accounted for 21.8 per cent of the total 533 cases commenced by NGOs/social activists/public-spirited citizens against a range of defendants.

Plaintiffs (affected individuals and communities) v various defendants (MoEF, state government, local authority, pollution control boards and industry)

The MoEF was a defendant in 284 cases. Thirty-five (12.3 per cent) cases were brought by affected individuals and communities. The affected individuals and communities brought a total of 200 cases against various defendants; 17.5 per cent against the MoEF. Out of the 341 cases defended by the state government, 78 (22.9 per cent) were brought by affected individuals and communities. These cases represented 39 per cent of the total 200 cases brought against various defendants. The local authority defended 28 (35.9 per cent) cases brought by affected individuals and communities out of a total of 200 cases. This accounted for 14 per cent of the total 200 cases brought against various defendants. Pollution control boards defended 29 (12.1 per cent) cases brought by the affected individuals and communities out of a total of 239 cases. The 29 cases represent 14.5 per cent of the total 200 cases brought by affected individuals and communities against various defendants. Industry defended 11 (8.5 per cent) cases brought by affected individuals and communities out of a total of 129 cases. This accounted for 5.5 per cent of the total 200 cases brought by the affected individuals and communities against multiple defendants.

Plaintiffs (industry) v various defendants (MoEF, state government, local authority, pollution control boards and industry)

The MoEF defended 284 cases of which 42 (14.8 per cent) cases were brought by industry. These cases represent 11.5 per cent of the total 366 cases brought by industry against various defendants. The state government defended 113 (33.1 per cent) cases brought by industry out of a total of 341 cases. These cases represented 30.9 per cent of the total 366 cases brought against various defendants. The local authority was the defendant in seven (9 per cent) cases brought by industry out of a total of 78 cases. This represents 1.9 per cent of the total 366 cases brought against a range of defendants. Pollution control boards defended 239 cases out of which 184 (77 per cent) cases were brought by industry. These cases represented 50.3 per cent of the total 366 cases brought against numerous defendants.

Disputes outcomes

Figure 6.9 is a cross-tabulation of disputes by categories and the Tribunal outcomes. The outcomes are classified as: allowed; not allowed/dismissed; partly allowed/dismissed; dissent; application/appeal withdrawn; and not to interfere or decide, including matters pending in the higher courts. The final category has an unusually high number of cases. This was because in January 2015,[17] the Tribunal disposed of 96 connected original applications with common questions of law based on similar facts and identical prayers without deciding, as the matter was pending in the Supreme Court of India.

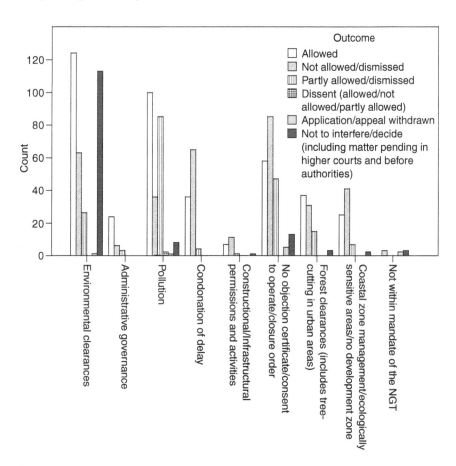

Figure 6.9 Disputes outcomes.
Source: author.

Environmental clearances

ECs produced 327 cases of which 124 (37.9 per cent) were allowed and constituted 30.2 per cent of the 411 allowed cases in all categories. There were 63 (19.3 per cent) not allowed cases that constituted 18.5 per cent of the 341 not allowed cases in all categories. There were 26 (8 per cent) partly allowed/dismissed cases that amounted to 13.8 per cent of the 188 partly allowed/dismissed cases in all categories. There were 113 (34.6 per cent) cases categorised as not to interfere/decide, including matters pending in the higher courts.[18] This amounted to 79 per cent of the total 143 cases. There was only one case relating to application/appeal withdrawn.

Administrative governance

Twenty-four (72.7 per cent) cases were allowed out of 33 cases relating to administrative governance. This amounted to 5.8 per cent of the 411 allowed cases in all categories. There were six (18.2 per cent) not allowed administrative governance disputes that constituted 1.8 per cent of the 341 cases in all categories. There were three (9.1 per cent) partly allowed/dismissed cases that amounted to 1.6 per cent of the 188 partly allowed/dismissed cases in all categories.

Pollution

Out of the 232 pollution cases, 100 (43.1 per cent) were allowed and constituted 24.3 per cent of the 411 allowed cases in all categories. Thirty-six (15.5 per cent) were not allowed and amounted to 10.6 per cent of the 341 cases in all categories. There were 85 (36.6 per cent) partly allowed/dismissed cases that amounted to 45.2 per cent of the 188 partly allowed/dismissed cases in all categories. Eight (3.4 per cent) cases were categorised as not to interfere/decide, including matters pending in the higher courts. This amounted to 5.6 per cent of the total 143 cases. There was only one dissent judgment.[19] However, it was reported twice as the two judges wrote separate judgments. There was only one case relating to application/appeal withdrawn.

Condonation of delay

Thirty-six (34.3 per cent) cases were allowed out of 105 cases relating to condonation of delay. This amounted to 8.8 per cent of the 411 allowed cases in all categories. Sixty-five (61.9 per cent) were not allowed and amounted to 19.1 per cent of the 341 cases in all categories. There were four (3.8 per cent) partly allowed/dismissed cases that amounted to 2.1 per cent of the 188 partly allowed/dismissed cases in all categories.

Constructional/infrastructural permission and activities

Out of the total 20 cases, seven (35 per cent) were allowed and constituted 1.7 per cent of the 411 allowed cases in all categories. Eleven (55 per cent) were not allowed and amounted to 3.2 per cent of the 341 cases in all categories. There was one case each relating to partly allowed/dismissed and not to interfere/decide, including matters pending in the higher courts cases.

No objection certificate/consent to operate/closure order

This category produced 208 cases of which 58 (27.9 per cent) were allowed and constituted 14.1 per cent of the 411 allowed cases in all categories. There were 85 (40.9 per cent) not allowed cases that constituted 24.9 per cent of the 341 not allowed cases in all categories. There were 47 (22.6 per cent) partly allowed/dismissed cases that amounted to 25 per cent of the 188 partly allowed/dismissed cases in all categories. Thirteen (6.3 per cent) cases were categorised as not to interfere/decide, including matters pending in the higher courts. This amounted to 9.1 per cent of the total 143 cases. Five applications/appeals were withdrawn.

Forest clearances (including tree-cutting in urban areas)

Thirty-seven (43 per cent) cases were allowed out of 86 cases in this category. This amounted to 9 per cent of the 411 allowed cases in all categories. Thirty-one (36 per cent) were not allowed and amounted to 9.1 per cent of the 341 cases in all categories. There were 15 (17.4 per cent) partly allowed/dismissed cases that amounted to 8 per cent of the 188 partly allowed/dismissed cases in all categories. Three cases were located in the category of not to interfere/decide including matters pending in the higher courts.

Coastal zone management/ecologically sensitive area/NDZ

Twenty-five (33.3 per cent) cases were allowed out of 75 cases in this category. This amounted to 6.1 per cent of the 411 allowed cases in all categories. Forty-one (54.7 per cent) were not allowed and amounted to 12 per cent of the 341 cases in all categories. There were seven (9.3 per cent) partly allowed/dismissed cases that amounted to 3.7 per cent of the 188 partly allowed/dismissed cases in all categories. Two cases were placed in the category of not to interfere/decide including matters pending in the higher courts.

Not within the mandate of the NGT

Out of eight cases, three were not allowed/dismissed, three related to not to interfere/decide, including matters pending in the higher courts, and two applications/appeals were withdrawn.

Plaintiffs' outcomes

Figure 6.10 is a cross-tabulation between plaintiffs by categories and Tribunal outcomes. The success or otherwise of different plaintiff groups is identified by reviewing outcomes from all benches as a whole. The plaintiffs include affected individuals/communities/residents; NGOs/social activists/public-spirited citizens; industry; builders/developers; government authorities; public sector undertakings; and *suo motu* cases.

Affected individuals/communities/residents

Affected individuals/communities/residents were plaintiffs in 199 cases of which 112 (56.3 per cent) were allowed and constituted 26.9 per cent of the 416 allowed cases in all categories. There were 66 (33.2 per cent) not allowed cases that constituted 18.5 per cent of the 357 not allowed cases in all categories. There were 16 (8 per cent) partly allowed/dismissed cases that amounted to 8.3

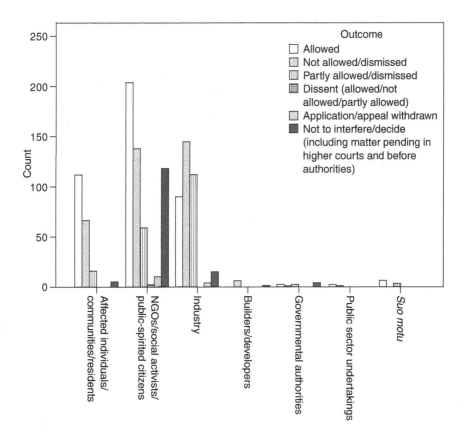

Figure 6.10 Plaintiffs' outcomes.
Source: author.

per cent of the 192 partly allowed/dismissed cases in all categories. Five cases were located in the category of not to interfere/decide including matters pending in the higher courts.

NGOs/social activists/public-spirited citizens

There were 204 (38.4 per cent) cases allowed out of 532 decided cases with this category of plaintiff. This amounted to 49 per cent of the 416 allowed cases in all categories. There were 138 (26 per cent) not allowed cases that constituted 38.7 per cent of the 357 cases in all categories. There were 59 (11.1 per cent) partly allowed/dismissed cases that amounted to 30.7 per cent of the 192 partly allowed/dismissed cases in all categories. There were 118 (22.2 per cent) cases categorised as not to interfere/decide, including matters pending in the higher courts.[20] This amounted to 82.5 per cent of the 144 of the total cases. There was only one dissent judgment.[21] There were 10 (1.9 per cent) cases relating to application/appeal withdrawn that constituted 71.4 per cent of the 14 cases in all categories.

Industry

Out of the 366 industry cases brought, 90 (24.6 per cent) were allowed and constituted 21.6 per cent of the 416 allowed cases in all categories. There were 145 (39.6 per cent) not allowed, amounting to 40.6 per cent of the 357 cases in all categories. There were 112 (30.6 per cent) partly allowed/dismissed cases that amounted to 58.3 per cent of the 192 partly allowed/dismissed cases in all categories. Fifteen (4.1 per cent) cases were categorised as not to interfere/decide including matters pending in the higher courts. This amounted to 10.5 per cent of the 144 of the total cases. Four applications/appeals were withdrawn.

Builders and developers

Out of seven cases, six were dismissed and one was a no interference result.

Governmental authorities

Out of nine cases, two were allowed; one was dismissed; two were partly allowed/dismissed; and four were subject to no interference.

Public sector undertakings

There were three cases: two allowed and one dismissed.

Suo motu cases

There were nine *suo motu* cases out of which six were allowed and three partly allowed.[22]

Conclusion

The 10 figures provide evidence that offers answers to the questions presented at the beginning of this chapter. The case growth in the five benches is significant. In particular, the Principal Bench in Delhi and the regional bench in Chennai demonstrate extraordinary growth. Between the two benches they have heard 73 per cent of the 1130 cases decided by the five benches. This high workload resulted in the creation of extra benches both in Delhi and Chennai. The rapid growth of the overall caseload suggests that this specialised forum has attracted the positive attention of people seeking environmental justice. The term 'standing' has been reformulated as 'person aggrieved' who has the right to approach the Tribunal under its jurisdiction. The growing public awareness and the confidence in the NGT is likely to produce a continuing growth in cases filed. However, on the other hand, there is no current suggestion of either the establishment of new benches or the appointment of additional judges as provided by the NGT Act. Without such expansion, including circuit benches the spectre of court-clogging, the bane of Indian courts, casts a potential shadow on the NGT's current speed, efficiency and access to justice.

The key disputes at the national level are ECs and pollution-related matters. ECs account for almost one-third (29 per cent) of the total cases heard over the five years traced. Pollution matters represent a fifth of all cases. Between them they make up half all judgments traced. There are different patterns emerging in the nature of the caseload from bench to bench. In Delhi, ECs make up 45.3 per cent of its total caseload. In Chennai the bench has been particularly concerned with issues relating to industry, especially the dyeing sector. Half of Chennai's cases have dealt with no objection certificate/consent order/closure order affecting industry. In Pune, pollution-related matters, particularly groundwater pollution, constituted a quarter (26.5 per cent) of the bench's workload. In Bhopal, forest clearances (including cutting of trees in urban areas) dominated, amounting to almost one-third (30 per cent). The jurisdictional responsibility of this bench has the largest forest cover in India.

The most active and successful plaintiffs are the NGOs/social activists/ public-spirited citizens who brought 47.2 per cent of all cases. The history of PIL and relaxed *locus standi* has developed this group as an experienced active body of plaintiffs,[23] hence their regular and successful appearance in all NGT benches. The group success rate in cases they brought stands at 38.3 per cent. Affected individuals/communities/residents brought 17.7 per cent of all cases with a success rate of 56 per cent. The relatively low costs of bringing the case coupled with positive encouragement by the NGT to litigants in person reflect a conscious effort on the part of the Tribunal to promote access to environmental justice. Indigent and illiterate litigants have been encouraged to speak in their vernacular language (especially at regional benches) to ventilate their grievances and personal and community experiences. Confidence-building in the NGT has and will result in motivating litigation from within these groups who traditionally had little or no access to justice. This reflects a broad-based, people-oriented approach by the NGT.

The principal defendant was the MoEF and it was involved in 25.1 per cent of all cases. State governments were involved in 30.2 per cent of all cases. Local authorities and pollution control boards were also frequent defendants. These regulatory authorities were the first named defendants but were also joined by industry in many of the cases.[24] For example, the POSCO case[25] has the first defendant as Union of India (MoEF) joined by a subsequent defendant M/S POSCO-India Ltd. The MoEF's frequent appearance before the Tribunal suggests a failure of appropriate regulatory administration, such as granting ECs and permissions that were arbitrary and illegal. The data suggest a repeated failure on the part of regulatory authorities to undertake their statutory environmental protection duties and social responsibilities in regard to environmental matters.

There are numerous cases where there is a repetition of parties. For example the MoEF was a defendant in 284 cases out of which 203 cases, 71.5 per cent, were brought by NGOs/social activists/public-spirited citizens. Additionally, state government was a defendant in 341 cases out of which 135 cases, 39.6 per cent, were brought by NGOs/social activists/public-spirited citizens. This finding shows a dominant pattern of a select group of plaintiffs bringing regular actions against powerful regulatory authorities for non-compliance of procedural safeguards and maladministration.

In essence, the data demonstrate that the NGT has grown from a small caseload to a significant size with every expectation of further growth. The benches are active, with the exception of Kolkata, and are dealing with a range of environmental issues that reflect the special regional circumstances. The *locus standi* and the liberal interpretation of 'person aggrieved' has opened up access to the Tribunal to promote diffused and meta-individual rights. This has resulted in the frequent appearance of known parties, both as plaintiffs and defendants, before the Tribunal.

Notes

1 www.greentribunal.gov.in/.
2 To access this database, contact the author personally.
3 Section 38(3) NGT Act.
4 See Chapters 2 and 7.
5 See Chapter 3.
6 See Chapter 3.
7 See *S K Samanta v West Bengal Pollution Control Board* (Judgment 24 July 2014); *V K Tripathi v MoEF* (Judgment 1 October 2014); *Nikunj Developers v State of Maharashtra* (Judgment 14 March 2013).
8 Forest (Conservation) Act 1980.
9 Indian Forest Act 1927.
10 MoEF, Guidelines for Declaration of Eco-Sensitive Zones around National Parks and Wildlife Sanctuaries, F No 1–9/2007 WL-1(pt).
11 Coastal Regulation Zone Notification 2011.
12 See Chapter 3.
13 See *Deepak Kumar Rai v M/S Prabhu Nath Rai Udyog Ltd* above.

14 See sections 14, 16 and 18 NGT Act 2010 and Chapter 3.
15 See Chapters 3 and 4.
16 For a detailed discussion, see Chapters 3, 6 and 7.
17 *Goa Paryavaran Savrakshan Sangharsh Samitee v M/S Sociedade Timblo Irmaos Ltd* (Judgment 13 January 2015).
18 See text to n 17 above for this unusually high figure.
19 *Jal Biradari v MoEF* (Judgment 22 January 2015); see also Chapter 6.
20 See text to n 17 above for this unusually high figure.
21 See above n 18.
22 See Chapter 3 and 6 for a discussion of *suo motu*.
23 See Chapter 2.
24 All cases were classified by the first named plaintiff and first named defendant due to the complexity and number of parties to the dispute. Some cases had as many as 96 defendants.
25 *Prafulla Samantray v Union of India* (Judgment 30 March 2012).

7   The National Green Tribunal's journey

Challenges and success

In 2015 Elizabeth Mrema, Director, Environmental Law and Convention, UNEP stated:

> ...the Rule of Law lies at the core of a just administration of justice and is a prerequisite of peaceful societies, in which environmental obligations, equality before the law and the adherence to the principles of fairness and accountability are respected by all. Law coupled with strong institutions is essential for societies to respond to environmental pressures and crucial for the international community to address the environmental challenges of our time.
>
> (Mrema 2015: 7)

Access is a primary step to the achievement of environmental justice. It involves articulation in the language of equity of the assurance of legal standing for all affected and interested parties; the right of appeal or review; specialised environmental courts and other practical dispute resolution mechanisms.

Several international declarations and institutions call for judicial specialisation, envisaging expert courts and judges and lawyers trained in environmental matters to promote the environmental rule of law and achieve sustainable development.[1] Chief Justice Brian Preston of the State of NSW, Australia, Land and Environment Court, stated:

> An environmental court is better able to address the pressing, pervasive and pernicious environmental problems that confront society (such as global warming and loss of biodiversity). New institutions and creative attitudes are required to address these problems. Specialization enables use of special knowledge and expertise in both the process and the substance of resolution of these problems. Rationalization enlarges the remedies available. An environmental court is better positioned to develop innovative remedies and holistic solutions to environmental problems.
>
> (Preston 2012: 427–428)

At present, there are 1200 ECTs functioning in 44 countries (Pring and Pring 2016).[2] According to Pring and Pring:

...there is no one best model for an Environment Court and Tribunal (ECT) – no 'one size fits all' design. This is understandable because what is 'best' for each country is an ECT that fits the country's unique historical, ecological, legal, judicial, religious, economic, cultural and political environment. It is the one that results in the most effective environmental dispute resolution process with access to justice for all affected interests. What will work best should be explored in an open, transparent planning process...

(Ibid.)

In this context, India's commitment to a 'green court' assumes significant practical importance. India's record as a progressive jurisdiction in environmental matters through its proactive judiciary is internationally recognised (Peiris 1991; see also Anderson 1998: 1–23). India's environmental justice discourse responded to a growing judicial realisation and appreciation of the connection between human rights and environmental protection. The deficiencies in environmental regulation, contradictions and gaps in institutional mechanisms, inefficiencies in administrative enforcement, multilayered corruption (including political corruption for personal gain) collectively prompted the Supreme Court of India to adopt the de facto role of caretaker of the environment through PIL. Thus, judicial activism promoted environmental justice through judge-fashioned processes and remedies.[3]

The active engagement of the Indian judiciary in imparting environmental justice nonetheless raised concerns about the effectiveness of PIL in relation to rapidly increasing numbers of petitions; complex technical and scientific issues; unrealistic court directions; individual judicial preferences, more often personality-driven rather than reflecting collective institutionalised adjudication; and the issue of creeping jurisdiction. The Law Commission of India (2003) strongly advocated the establishment of 'environment courts' bearing in mind decisions of the Indian Supreme Court. In its judgments in *AP Pollution Control Board v M V Nayudu* (1999) 2 SCC 718 and (2001) 2 SCC 62, *M C Mehta v Union of India* (1987) 1 SCC 395, and *Indian Council for Enviro-Legal Action v Union of India* 1996 (3) SCC 212, the Supreme Court advocated the establishment of environmental courts. These would benefit from the expert advice of environmental scientists and technically qualified persons as part of the judicial process. Accordingly, the Indian Parliament passed the National Green Tribunal (NGT) Act in June 2010. The NGT Act institutionalised the procedural element of environmental justice by establishing the NGT, thereby enhancing the principles of environmental democracy that include fairness, public participation, transparency and accountability.

The NGT – officially described as a 'specialised body equipped with necessary expertise to handle environmental disputes involving multi-disciplinary issues'[4] – is a forum offering greater plurality for environmental justice. Exercising wide powers, the NGT is staffed by judicial and technical expert members deciding cases in an open forum. It avails itself of adversarial, inquisitorial, investigative and collaborative procedures throughout the decision-making process.[5] In this chapter, these features are briefly re-examined in the context of their impact within judicial and ministerial circles, as well as their wider social and environmental acceptance and effectiveness. It provides an overview of the challenges and successes related to the activities of the NGT since its establishment in 2010.

The NGT: challenges

For an institution to be fully functional and effective, the necessary infrastructure, courtrooms and associated staffing must be in place. From its inception, the NGT faced major institutional challenges due to limited co-operation and hesitant operational commitment of both federal and state governments. The NGT Delhi Bench started operating from two premises, one being a temporary office and the other a make-shift court.[6] In essence, it did not get off to a good start.

The under-staffed bench and inadequate logistic and infrastructure facilities, coupled with inappropriate housing for bench appointees, led to the resignation of three judicial members: Justices C V Ramulu, Amit Talukdar and A S Naidu. The state inaction required intervention by the Supreme Court in order to remedy the situation. Senior counsel, Gopal Subramaniam, appeared on behalf of the NGT and informed the Supreme Court about 'a very sorry state of affairs' affecting the green Tribunal. He said:

> ...the members have been put up in the middle of quarters of Class III and IV employees in Van Vigyan Bhavan in Delhi. The initial budget of Rupees 32 crores was slashed to Rupees 10 crores to be further reduced to Rupees 6 crores. Each of the members is paying from his own pocket for travel. They don't even have a supply of food at work and they are compelled to get food from the canteen. Is this how the government proposes to treat the sitting and former judges of the High Courts and Supreme Court of India?[7]

The Supreme Court described the treatment experienced by the members of NGT as 'utterly disgusting'.[8] The two-member bench of the Supreme Court was comprised of Justices G S Singhvi and J Mukhopadhaya. They required the government to ensure the

> effective functioning of the tribunal by providing all the facilities and amenities to the judicial members, who are former judges of the High Court at par with the sitting judges and also to the expert members. They [members of NGT] must function with dignity.[9]

Accordingly, the Supreme Court stated that the NGT benches must become fully functional by 30 April 2013. The Principal Bench, established in Delhi, moved to permanent, spacious premises with modern infrastructural facilities in

October 2013. The Delhi Bench is currently supported by extra benches that share the increasing caseload.[10]

The Chennai Bench became operational in November 2012. At present it has two benches sharing the caseload but the infrastructural facilities could be improved, considering the increasing workload of this regional bench.[11] The Bhopal Bench started functioning in the basement of a building, despite affidavits being filed by the state government claiming suitable accommodation had been provided to the NGT. Justice Singhvi reacted sharply by observing 'we cannot appreciate that a misleading statement was made before the highest court. A false affidavit was filed before the apex court. Accommodation does not mean basement'.[12] Presently, the Bhopal Bench has appropriate infrastructural facilities.

The Pune Bench was treated in a similar derisory manner. It was inaugurated on 17 February 2012, but the lack of state support resulted in delays into March 2013. Kolkata fared even worse. Exasperated by the indifferent treatment by the three state governments, Madhya Pradesh (Bhopal Bench), Maharashtra (Pune Bench) and West Bengal (Kolkata Bench), the Supreme Court in March 2013 ordered the NGT benches to become operational and requested the Additional Solicitor General to contact the secretaries of the relevant departments and make them personally responsible for the operational functionality of the NGT benches, writing:

> ...we hope that the concerned functionaries of the State would realise the importance of having the NGT benches and avoid the situation in which the court may require their presence. We have to take up the matter because we don't want the people to suffer.[13]

The court's order resulted in state governments taking the necessary steps for the Bhopal and Pune Benches to become operational. This involved the provision of appropriate office space, chambers for the judges with sufficient staff, a registrar office, a staff room, library, administrative and accounts sections and a video-conferencing room to allow those litigants unable to attend the court in person to be heard.

The state of West Bengal failed to respond to the orders of the Supreme Court. The NGT chairperson inspected the Kolkata Bench and found the premises, particularly the accommodation offered to judges, to be 'shabby, uninhabitable and without a toilet'. The flouting of orders by the state government prompted the Supreme Court to advise the central government to consider moving the Kolkata Bench to Guwahati or Ranchi. The Supreme Court observed:

> there is no point fighting over these issues. It is a sheer wastage of the Court's time and energy. The Chairperson should not have visited the places at all. The NGT bench in Kolkata may have been set up because of purely political reasons. But because of total non-cooperation by the West

Bengal government, we would like the Centre to consider shifting it to Guwahati or Ranchi.[14]

There is a dual explanation for this dismal treatment which affected the establishment and the early operational effectiveness of the NGT. First, there existed an unresponsive and dysfunctional state administration that failed to appreciate the importance of green issues. For instance, the 2013 CAG report on granting forest clearances highlighted serious regulatory lapses on the part of MoEF in monitoring diversion of forest land for non-forest (industrial, commercial and other development projects) purposes. The MoEF failed to appropriately discharge its responsibility of monitoring of compliance with the conditions of the Forest (Conservation) Act 1980 relating to diversion of forest land. The CAG report observed non-compliance with regulatory conditions in specific cases. For instance, the states of Rajasthan and Odisha did not get prior approval from the central government when renewing mining leases thereby rendering them unauthorised. The report stated 'numerous instances of unauthorised renewal of leases, illegal mining, continuance of mining leases despite adverse comments in the monitoring reports, projects operating without environment clearances, unauthorised change of status of forest land and arbitrariness in decisions of forestry clearances were observed'. CAG found that in 219 cases the state government concerned had renewed mining leases without the approval of MoEF.[15]

Second, and more importantly, from the outset NGT decisions identified the MoEF and related administrative offices as demonstrating indifference, *ultra vires* or negligence in the exercise of their responsibilities.[16] Frequently, the MoEF has been subjected to severe criticism by the NGT for failing to observe its own procedural rules such as the improper granting of licences without prior EIAs being completed or appropriately conducted or appointing members without appropriate qualifications to the EACs.[17] The Tribunal has been prepared to call senior civil servants to the court to hear, often inappropriate or implausible, explanations for MoEF decisions.[18] Indeed, in *Sudeip Shrivastava v State of Chhattisgarh* (Judgment 24 March 2014), the Tribunal took the unusual step of criticising the Minister of State for Environment and Forest and MoEF for acting arbitrarily and ignoring relevant material issues that would have contributed to a holistic appraisal of the environmental problem.

In the Delhi air pollution case (*Vardhman Kaushik v Union of India* Judgment 7 April 2015), the NGT observed:

> ...the authorities, departments and the state governments have not even initiated the process for compliance of the (earlier) directions. With the increasing pollutants in the air, life of residents in the NCR, Delhi is becoming more and more vulnerable to various diseases and the greatest sufferer of these pollutants are young children of today and India's tomorrow. The slackness and casual attitude of the Authorities of the state Government is exhibited from the very fact that the air pollution is increasing

and has reached to an alarming level which would make it difficult for the people of Delhi even to breathe freely much less fresh air.

(Para 2)

In *Jai Singh v Union of India* (Judgment 18 February 2016), the NGT identified a failure of government and regulatory authorities in preventing and controlling pollution arising from illegal and unauthorised mining, transportation and running of screening plants/stone crushers. The Tribunal observed:

> ...the activity must be brought within the control of legal and regulatory regime. The concerned authorities of the Government and Boards should not only realise their responsibility and statutory obligation but should ensure that there is no unregulated exploitation of the natural resources and degradation to the environment. Respondents, including the State Government, the Boards, MoEF and other concerned authorities have permitted such activity despite orders of the Hon'ble Supreme Court of India, the High Courts and the Tribunal. There is definite evidence on record to show that illegal mining has continued ... Merely denying the authenticity of the photos, videos and other documentary evidences on the pretext that they were doctored would not amount to discharge of the onus placed upon the respondents...

(Para 93)

Early exposure by the NGT embarrassed both civil servants and politicians to such an extent that they were reluctant to provide appropriate support in the expectation that it would restrict the activities of the NGT. Neither the ministry, state governments nor the various environmental statutory bodies were accustomed to being questioned in a probing, informed and systematic manner nor having their decisions subjected to regular public 'merit review'.[19] Previously, these authorities enjoyed both an official and unofficial decision-making licence power directly associated with various expert committees, boards and officials, as well as the Minister. The result was arbitrary approval of projects without undertaking the proper environmental and social impact assessments and disturbingly often in violation of pertinent laws and rules. Indeed, as the case data in Chapter 6 indicates, the failure of central and state agencies to follow due process has been a regular and major cause of complaint from affected parties seeking redress from the NGT.

The vulnerability felt by the MoEF concerning the activity and willingness of the NGT to criticise the ministry whenever appropriate and justified took practical form with the establishment by the MoEF of the High Level Committee (HLC) to review forest and environment related laws. T S R Subramanium was appointed as the chairperson (HLC 2014). Its terms of reference were:

i   to assess the status of implementation of each of the six Acts[20] vis-à-vis the objectives;

ii to examine and take into account various court orders and judicial pro-
    nouncements relating to these Acts;
iii to recommend specific amendments needed in each of these Acts so as to
    bring them in line with current requirements to meet objectives; and
iv to draft proposed amendments to each of the aforesaid Acts to give effect to
    the proposed recommendations.

Perhaps surprisingly the HLC report was highly critical of regulatory agencies
dealing with environmental matters. It said:

> ...the Executive, as pointed out has not covered itself with glory – indeed
> it has invited the attention of the judicial branch through lack of basic
> care.... The institutional failures include lack of enforcement, flawed regu-
> latory regime, poor management of resources, inadequate use of technology;
> absence of a credible, effective enforcement machinery; governance con-
> straints in management; policy gaps; disincentives to environmental con-
> servation, and so on.
>
> (HLC 2014: 8 and 22)

Importantly, what was missing from the HLC's terms of reference was the
authority to review the NGT Act. Nevertheless, the HLC exceeded its mandate
and made recommendations which, if implemented, would have severely
restricted the operational effectiveness of the NGT by the creation of extra
institutional layers – district environmental courts and an Appellate Board.

The HLC recommended the establishment of special environmental courts
in every district to be headed by a judge of the rank of a sessions judge or an
additional session judge. Further, the HLC recommended a new 'umbrella' law
– Environmental Laws (Management) Act (ELMA). The ELMA provided for
the creation of two institutions, the NEMA, at central level, and the State
Environment Management Authority (SEMA), at state level, as full-time
processing and EC and monitoring agencies (HLC 2014: 62, 63 and 68–71).
ELMA was also to be provided with an Appellate Board against the decisions
of NEMA or SEMA or the MoEF and Climate Change (MoEFCC) in respect
of project clearance, prescribing a three-month time limit for disposal of
appeals. The Appellate Board would be constituted by the government and
presided over by a retired High Court judge and include two officers of the
rank of secretaries to the government of India retired or serving (ibid.: 64, 65,
74 and 75). The decisions of the government, NEMA or SEMA under this
proposed law would not be questionable before nor enquired into by any court
or tribunal either via *suo moto* or at anyone's behest on any ground (ibid.: 75).
The jurisdiction of the NGT was to be limited to entertaining applications by
parties aggrieved by the decisions in appeals under NEMA or SEMA for
review on grounds permissible and subject to limitations applicable to judicial
review of administrative actions by the High Courts and the Supreme Court
of India (ibid.).

Had the HLC recommendation been accepted and acted upon, the NGT would have been stripped of its first instance hearing powers and restricted to act as an appellate court employing judicial review, but unable to exercise *suo motu*. The proposed provisions were regressive as they would have significantly reduced the powers of the NGT, including the power of merit review. This is important as merit review in environmental matters is capable of highlighting environmental misdeeds and wrongful decisions by regulatory agencies. In the words of Chief Justice Preston:

> merit review has numerous benefits including providing a forum for full and open consideration of issues of importance; increasing accountability of decision makers; clarifying meaning of legislation; ensuring adherence to legislative principles and objects; focusing attention on the accuracy and quality of policy documents, guidelines and planning instruments; and highlighting problems that should be addressed by law reform.
>
> (Preston 2012: 404)

Such a change would inevitably have restricted the effectiveness of the NGT. The HLC report was completed within three months and submitted to the government on 18 November 2014. It was subsequently considered by the Parliamentary Standing Committee on Science and Technology, Environment and Forests. The committee submitted its findings on 3 July 2015. The committee did not accept the HLC report on the ground that the period of three months allotted to the HLC for reviewing the six environmental Acts was too short and that there was no cogent reason for rushing the report without comprehensive, meaningful and wider consultations with all stakeholders (Parliamentary Standing Committee 2015: 9). A careful reading of the text further suggests that the committee was supportive of the existing environmental judicial framework, particularly the NGT, and that it should not be disturbed. The Parliamentary Committee stated:

> Some of the essential recommendations of the HLC have been doubted and would result in an unacceptable dilution of the existing legal and policy architecture established to protect our environment. Further, an impression should not be created that a Committee whose constitution and jurisdiction are itself in doubt, has been used to tinker with the established law and policy. Should the government wish to consider specific areas of environmental policy afresh, it may consider appointing another Committee by following established procedures and comprising of acclaimed experts...
>
> (2015: 9)

Additionally, representatives of civil society, NGOs and experts expressed serious reservations concerning the recommendations contained in the HLC report. For instance, Ritwick Dutta of the Legal Initiative for Forest and Environment organisation stated that the

> HLC knew that … laws (NGT Act) which have worked and which are (is) the hope for environmental movement and have (has) given a new voice and a new right … and the National Green Tribunal is dealing with more than 5,000 cases.
>
> (Ibid.: para 7.10)

Chandra Bhushan of the Centre for Science and Environment stated:

> …a lot more thought needs to go into deciding what kind of an institution this country needs in the future. Already there are National Green Tribunal; District Courts; High Courts and the Supreme Court. The HLC is recommending to add two more institutions, an appellate authority as well as District Courts.
>
> (Ibid.: para 7.4)

Nevertheless, the NGT has overcome suspicion bordering on hostility with the support of the Supreme Court and its own commitment to ensure the terms of the NGT Act are given practical effect throughout India. Despite initial setbacks and continuing concerns from powerful agencies it is a story of endeavour and success, as the Tribunal grows both in strength and public approval.

The NGT: a success story

In this final section, the life history of the NGT is located within the theoretical framework offered by two management academics, Roy Suddaby and Thierry Viale.[21] The organisation theory they advanced in 2011 is placed alongside the material, fieldwork and case analysis data presented in this book. These scholars set out four principles concerning professionals, institutional change and external impact, namely field-level change arising as a consequence of the interaction between professionals and institutions:

1   professionals use their expertise and legitimacy to challenge the incumbent order and define a new, open, uncommitted space or occupy committed space;
2   professionals use their inherent social capital and skill to populate the field with new actors and new identities;
3   professionals introduce nascent new rules and standards that recreate field boundaries; and
4   professionals manage the use and reproduction of social capital within a field thereby conferring a new status hierarchy or social order within the field (Suddaby and Viale 2011: 424).

The four principles recognise NGT bench members as professionals (Jowitt 1977: 1442). The *first principle* is illustrated by the organisational theory empirically researched and applied by Dezalay and Garth (1996). They demonstrated how powerful judges, businessmen and lawyers defined new operational territories.[22] Their work traced the creation of new categories of economic and intellectual activity that embraced international commercial disputes. This new category fell outside established jurisdictional boundaries of existing judicial institutions. By redefining the intellectual and geographical space of localised dispute settlement an opportunity was created for marginal actors, including academics and retired judges, to become the new legal experts within a new framework.

Specifically, NGT internal procedural change also brought about field-level change as the external is affected and altered by the internal. The proactive NGT bench colonised intellectual space partly by the public promotion of its jurisdiction and through its effectiveness in protecting both the environment and the interests of affected parties, particularly tribals and adivasis. It created inviting, accessible opportunities for the dispossessed and representative NGOs, through the liberal interpretation of the term 'aggrieved person', to enter an informed judicial environment receptive and capable of appreciating, addressing and responding to the concerns of the applicant.[23] The institutionalisation of the larger welfare and interest of public and the environmental protection has championed parity of participation thereby alleviating inequality and promoting recognition, capabilities and functioning of individuals and communities in India's environmental justice discourse. For example, in May 2016, in *Paryawaran Sanrakshan Sangarsh Samiti Lippa v Union of India* (Judgment 4 May 2016) the NGT recognised the rights of villagers to be consulted concerning the construction of the Kashang Integrated Hydroelectric Project.[24] The Tribunal directed the MoEF and state government to ensure that, prior to the forest clearance for the project, the proposal is placed before a Gram Sabha[25] of villages in Kinnaur district of the state of Himachal Pradesh.[26] The recognition and participation of the local community in the decision-making process promotes social and economic equity thereby advancing environmental justice. Thus, field-level awareness was altered in sequence and as a consequence of the internal promotional activity of the NGT.

Nevertheless, colonialisation, as India well knows, is never without struggle and cost. Seldom is colonised territorial space 'empty' prior to the arrival of the coloniser. There are winners and losers. The process of seeking to take control of inhabited intellectual space was undertaken by the NGT through internal procedural expansion and change, but it has not occurred without struggle. Both the Supreme Court and High Courts in particular already heard environmental cases. They were occupying environmental jurisdictional space prior and subsequent to the establishment of the NGT. The Supreme Court had transferred environmental cases to the NGT and advised the High Courts to do likewise because of the unmanageable backlog of these cases.[27] However, there was concern within some High Courts about the way in which the NGT has unilaterally and questionably expanded its powers to include *suo moto* powers despite the fact that they had previously been exercised exclusively by the High Court.[28] Hence, when the Tribunal commenced to use *suo moto* powers, the earlier and ongoing conflict between MoEF and the NGT was joined by some High Courts concerned with the alleged self-assignment by the Tribunal of further jurisdictional power.

The exercise of *suo moto* powers by the NGT was initially raised and challenged by the MoEF. The ministry had refused to confer this power on the Tribunal, despite repeated requests to do so. In an affidavit filed before the Supreme Court of India in 2013, the MoEF stated: 'the government of India has not agreed to confer *suo motu* powers on the Tribunal. It is for the NGT, an adjudicatory body, to follow the provisions of the NGT Act 2010'.[29]

On the other hand, justifying the exercise of *suo motu* power, the Chairperson of the Tribunal stated: 'Our job is to protect environment. Anything under the sun is environment. We are liberal in procedure and we are reaching out to people.'[30]

The claim of alleged judicial over-reach was bolstered when the High Court of Madras restrained the NGT Chennai Bench from initiating *suo motu* proceedings. The High Court stated:

> NGT is not a substitute for the High Courts. The tribunal has to function within the parameters laid down by the NGT Act 2010. It should act within four corners of the statute. There is no indication in the NGT Act or the rules made thereunder with regard to the power of the NGT to initiate suo motu proceedings against anyone, including statutory authorities.[31]

Further an order passed by Madras High Court dated 7 July 2015[32] stated that the NGT should not further initiate *suo motu* proceedings.

Some lawyers that were interviewed expressed their reservations concerning the exercise of *suo motu* power. For instance, Lawyers 4 and 5, both of whom appear before the NGT, stated 'a tribunal is a statutory body whose jurisdiction and powers are stated within the statute. A tribunal cannot enlarge its jurisdiction'.[33] The legitimate use of *suo motu* powers by the NGT is moot for, while claimed lawful by the NGT, its usage has been challenged both by High Court judges and the MoEF.[34] Jurisdictional expansion in this regard remains unsettled, although its procedural value is significant. It allows the NGT to self-initiate proceedings and permits the Tribunal to roam far and wide searching for pressing environmental issues that it considers to be in the public interest.[35]

Additionally, the NGT conferred upon itself the power of judicial review, yet another important and controversial instance of strategic procedural growth.[36] The self-defined expansion of its powers reflects further territorial extension at the potential cost of alienation and challenge by those traditional actors who had previously and exclusively enjoyed the exercise of these powers. Nevertheless, in 2014, in the cases of *Wilfred v MoEF* and *Kalpavriksh v Union of India* (both Judgments 17 July 2014), the NGT ruled that:

> [The] tribunal has to exercise powers which are necessary to administer the justice in accordance with law … it certainly would have to expand its

powers and determine the various controversies in relation to fact and law arising before it. This Tribunal has the inherent powers not only by implied application of the above enunciated principles of law but the provisions of the NGT Act particularly Section 19 of the NGT Act which empowers the Tribunal to regulate its own procedure and to be guided by the principles of natural justice.

(Wilfred v MoEF: para 44)

Bolstering its power further, the NGT observed:

> ...it will be travesty of justice if it was to be held that the Tribunal does not have the power to examine the correctness or otherwise or constitutional validity of a notification issued under one of the scheduled acts to the NGT Act. In the absence of such power, there cannot be an effective and complete decision on the substantial environmental issues that may be raised before the Tribunal, in exercise of the jurisdiction vested in the Tribunal under the provisions of the Act.

(Wilfred v MoEF: para 58)

This second illustration of a controversial procedural growth through adopting the power of judicial review has been viewed by some constitutional experts as the NGT overstepping its statutory brief and the improper acquisition of powers restricted to the superior courts. It is settled law that judicial review in general – and the High Courts' power to exercise judicial superintendence over the courts and tribunals in their respective jurisdictions in particular – is a part of the basic structure of the Indian Constitution. In *L Chandra Kumar v Union of India* (1997) 3 SCC 261 the Supreme Court observed:

> ...the tribunals are not substitutes for the High Courts, and they can carry out only a supplemental, as opposed to substitutional role, since the power of the High Courts and Supreme Court to test the constitutional validity of legislations can never be ousted or excluded. The tribunals are therefore not vested with the power of judicial review to the exclusion of the High Courts and the Supreme Court.

(At 302)

Constitutional experts feel that it is the superior courts of record that decide the substantial questions of law. To quote Rajeev Dhawan: '...the NGT cannot strike down a statute. It can only examine the decisions that are taken and consider if they are in compliance with the three principles laid down in Section 20 of the Act'.[37] Justice Ruma Pal, former judge of the Supreme Court of India, questioned: 'Who do we include within the term "judiciary"? Is it limited to constitutional courts or does it also include those tribunals which decide rights and merely have the trappings of a court?'[38] Increasing tribunalisation is viewed by some, particularly those directly affected, as a serious encroachment on the senior judiciary's independence and powers, thereby causing institutional confusion, collusion and complexity.

The NGT has also adopted and practises investigative[39] and stakeholder consultative procedures.[40] As a result, the NGT improves active participation through dialogue, argument and norms for eliciting factual realities and expert knowledge in order to respond to environmental problems. The ongoing Yamuna river[41] and air pollution[42] cases are illustrations of participatory mechanisms. According to Chairperson Kumar:

> ...we call everybody. We call chief secretary Haryana, chief secretary Delhi, chief secretary, Uttar Pradesh, all the environmental pollution control Boards, all nigams, Delhi jal board [regulatory agencies] ... we try to understand from them what difficulties or impediments they are going to face if the judgment was to be implemented. We are dealing majorly with mass issues so therefore it is important to have all the stakeholders ... We have to adopt a system which will give results to us because we are dealing with cases which affect mass at large and there are very few cases where individuals are concerned. By and large we are trying to make an effort that we give judgments which are more practical, more sustainable and more effectively implementable. That is the way we deal with the issues before us.[43]

The NGT's willingness to employ different procedural enquiry strategies to resolve the environmental issues reflects its expansive self-created procedure[44] that consequently produces changes both in institutional and external landscapes. The NGT, because of its status, power and public approval, is expanding and redefining its jurisdictional boundaries through its procedural growth and knowledge expertise. It has both trespassed upon but simultaneously challenged established public authorities,[45] particularly the MoEF and High Courts, for the right to regulate or respond to environmental issues. As a consequence, the turf war remains unresolved, but the NGT consistently appears to be gaining enhanced public recognition and support.

The *second principle* reflects on how professionals restructure institutions by creating and supporting new categories of legitimate social actors. Suddaby and Viale point out that most studies of institutional change review how professionals engage in the institutional work necessary to generate new categories of organisation (2011: 430). However, they progress this point by identifying how organisations either promote or create new actors whose talents and attributes, previously possibly undervalued, are absorbed into the changing organisation and thereby receive formal recognition for their contribution to that institution. By examining the NGT, it is apparent that external actors are absorbed into the NGT's investigative activities in order to promote a judgment securely based on and underwritten by third-party technical input. Each bench has the power to appoint external actors in order to provide an independent and impartial scientific response to issues identified by the bench. Although each bench has a technical expert, his knowledge base is limited to a specific scientific area or areas. Consequently, an expert on water pollution and allied matters may not be able to respond appropriately to a case involving forest questions.[46] It is at this point that the bench may reach out to a qualified external expert, carefully selected as being independent of both parties to the case. The involvement of university departments and independent research bodies[47] illustrates how new, non-legal third parties are introduced to the NGT fact-finding and scientific evaluation processes. A bench judge described this process as follows:

> If a particular case requires scientific input unavailable within the bench as currently comprised, we ask a university such as an Agricultural College or an organisation like NEERI. The university or research organisations as they stand apart from state or federal control are better able to provide us with independent but qualified feedback. For instance if the matter deals with agricultural land our appointed external experts visit the site and make an assessment as Court Commissioners. The Court Commissioners provide assistance to us by making technical assessments regarding the loss of agricultural land and crops and appropriate compensation payable to the farmers. We are careful to insist upon independence of the external experts. Panels and consultants have a history elsewhere of having an interest in the project so that a conflict may arise. We are not confident that people have either the required expertise or independence.[48]

A technical bench member pointed out his specialised area of expertise and the value of third-party involvement in cases that require a specific scientific evaluation which he is not qualified to carry out:

> we are getting good support and reports from technical organisations and universities. We are willing to appoint third party technical experts when my expertise does not cover the case in point. For example we recently appointed M S University Baroda for their expert input.[49]

FFCs are another mechanism to populate the institution with new actors. In the Amrit Mahal Kaval case,[50] the NGT appointed a FFC of experts to assess and advise on case-related environmental issues. The NGT noted:

> ...the Tribunal made a thorough scrutiny of the FFC report and also comments made by the parties thereon. After doing so, the Tribunal is of the considered opinion that the report of FFC was thoroughly satisfactory, can be safely relied upon and is of good assistance to decide on the environmental issues that arise in this case.
>
> (Para 160)

The appointment of *amicus curiae* is a further illustration of how the NGT engages with external actors.[51]

There exists a symbiotic relationship between the construction and usage of third-party actors. The recognition of external, independent scientific, non-legal actors promotes their professional value while simultaneously expanding the status and reach of the institution that has recognised the value and import-ance of their contribution.[52] As stated above, growth and change within the institution produces field-level change, namely both public recognition and support for the NGT.

The *third principle* emphasises how professionals promulgate new rules and standards that redefine the boundaries of their field. Suddaby and Viale state: 'a key mechanism through which professionals use their expertise to change field logics and boundaries while simultaneously furthering their own professional projects is by promulgating rule systems designed in the broader social interest...' (2011: 432).

The interdisciplinary relationship and outcomes of legally qualified judges working alongside scientific environmental expert judges as joint decision-makers of equal standing has moved case adjudication beyond traditional func-tions and legal remedies. The essence of a court is to make a decision that is binding on the parties to the dispute. However, the NGT, on occasions, is capable of going much further, thereby reconfiguring its jurisdictional bound-aries. Its decisions, through expansive rationale and innovative judgments, go beyond the 'courtroom door' and have had far-reaching social and economic impact. A major innovation is the NGT's willingness to offer scientifically-based structural planning and policies that respond creatively to weak, ineffec-tive regulation or even the absence of regulation. Examples of its creativity include the preparation and promulgation of policies on waste management,[53] noise pollution,[54] tyre-burning[55] and cumulative EIA.[56] To quote Expert 4: 'Where there are gaps or limitations in the policy, the NGT interferes and gives directions to the government to incorporate the same...'[57] Another example for the need for creative policy-making was given by Expert 2 who stated:

> ...environmental issues are complex. We are dealing with natural systems and future events based upon impacts. While framing the rules or regula-tions no one had visualized the scenario that activities such as bio-medical waste treatment facility would come up in the near future. However, in today's world bio-medical waste and associated activities need serious con-sideration based upon the likely impacts and magnitude. So, if we feel that the activity is injurious to public health and environment, we pass appro-priate orders of expanding the scope of rules and regulations by adopting the principle of constructive intuition to give it a wider meaning to attain the primary object and purpose of the Act in question. Such an interpreta-tion would serve the public interest in contrast to the private or individual interest.[58]

These environmental social policies reflect the NGT's willingness to recognise the greater public interest, welfare and environmental protection and demonstrate its readiness to undertake internal growth resulting in the intentional promotion of external field-change. This increased level of its creativity becomes embedded within the institutional structure and further extends the NGT's growing status and its power to offer environmental solutions to the public.

Finally, the *fourth principle* deals with the reproduction of social capital that confers enhanced occupational status and prestige within the field. The social capital does not depend upon income or economic capital, but is essentially dependent upon a wealth of knowledge, gained through education and training, and its practical application within the institution (Suddaby and Viale: 433).[59] Within the NGT, the bench members, through their exercise of power based upon their expert knowledge and status, are capable and, indeed, able to apply their legal, technical or scientific knowledge to solve environmental questions.

The judicial members have many years of court experience as judges of the High Court or, in the case of the chairperson, as a former judge of the Supreme Court or chief justice of a High Court.[60] The present Chairperson, Justice Swatanter Kumar, is a former judge of the Supreme Court and former Chief Justice of Bombay High Court. The extensive judicial experience of these individuals, coupled with their sensitivity to environmental questions, provides them with the authority to turn an institutional framework laid down by statute into a dynamic flexible legal framework within which they can exercise and apply their expert knowledge.

The scientific expert members of the NGT constitute an epistemic community as described by Hass.[61] He characterises epistemic community as comprising experts with professional training enjoying social authority based upon their reputation for impartiality.[62] The engagement of the NGT's scientific experts in the decision-making process as 'constructive science scholars' has contributed to the development of environmental jurisprudence that not only encompasses legal doctrines but also science-based knowledge resulting in the solution of domain-specific problems.[63]

Institutional theorists refer to the ability 'to motivate others to cooperate ... the ability to engage others in collective action' (Suddaby and Viale 2011: 434). The co-operative bench activity identified by Harry T Edwards (2003) as 'collegiality' includes discourse between two disciplines: law and science. Collegial decision-making process that involves interdisciplinary discourse provides motivation to co-operate and engage in collective action. Strong, positive collegial relationships accept and promote judicial independence of mind and discussion, resulting in an interdependent and interdisciplinary decision-making process. Thus, collegiality helps to reproduce the professional capital, which sits and grows within the NGT, and thereafter affects its field credibility in the eyes of the general public. To quote a bench member:

> The matter is taken to a logical end and it is only possible with the blend of judicial and technical minds. We are two in number. We meet regularly – morning, afternoon and evening. Communication is not an issue. Formally as well as informally we discuss the issue before going to the hearing as well

as before settling any judgment or theme of a judgment. We discuss and all the time we are on the same track. The judicial and technical inputs are given by the respective members. This happens because there is a regular communication. The thought process is the same. A common blend amounts to qualitative judgment and delivers justice from such a combination.[64]

The four principles presented by Suddaby and Viale provide a framework that allows a clearer understanding of the life and activity of the NGT. From a stuttering start to its current established and successful profile its professional actors have created both internal and external change that has proved successful and continues to operate in the public interest and environmental protection.

The final word

The NGT's institutional form legitimises sustainable environmental governance by adopting reflexive practices (Voss and Kemp: 2006).[65] By offering ecological, technological and scientific resource knowledge, the NGT judicial and technical members either formulate policies or assist states with the implementation of these policies, thereby adopting both problem-solving and policy-creation approaches. The legitimacy not only includes the decision-making process (accountability and transparency), but also refers to the process through which the 'environment and public interest', as opposed to the 'economic development interest', has a determining influence. Nevertheless, the NGT's judicial and scientific experts and the use of their knowledge within a judicially controlled forum offers an internalised, accountability-focused approach whereby a diverse set of actors, such as governmental and local authorities, companies and multinational corporations, are restrained from compromising human welfare and the ecology.

The NGT has and is changing the environmental jurisprudential landscape in India. This is occurring not simply through greater public access created by its wide definition of 'aggrieved party'. Originally, it attracted litigants because of its decision-making speed. It is enhancing public expectation through its judgments and policy directions that clearly reflect a commitment to its statutory obligation to decide cases according to the principles of environmental sustainability. The composition of the bench and the involvement of technical experts has introduced a new dimension into the decision-making process. The legal lens has been expanded by the new and dramatically different composition of the bench. Science has a profound effect upon our understanding of and response to environmental issues. Science has a similar role and effect within the NGT. Independent, in-house, scientific knowledge has become part of the analysis that produces judicially binding decisions.

The very success of the NGT, by its provision of forthright decisions and far-reaching remedial actions affecting aggrieved persons throughout India, has resulted in expressions of anxiety focused on the powerful position achieved by the tribunal within a relatively short period. It is to be hoped that no Thucydides trap has been set.

This book has charted and analysed the growth of a powerful judicial body staffed by technical experts and lawyers that functions not only as an adjudicatory body but also moves its focus beyond traditional, individualised legal issues and associated common law remedies. The tribunal's ability to engage, produce and enforce scientifically supported policy has taken its remit beyond the courtroom and into the wider community. The NGT has impacted upon and expanded the country's environmental jurisprudence, developed wide-ranging environmental policies and exposed serious administrative weaknesses. Its stamp upon India's environmental jurisprudence is indelible. Its public credibility is widespread and the results of its decisions continue to reach ever further across India.

Notes

1 See Chapter 1 for details.
2 Ibid.
3 See Chapter 2 for a detailed discussion.
4 See the NGT website http://greentribunal.gov.in.
5 See *Vitthal Gopichand Bhungase v Gangakhed Sugar and Energy Ltd* (Judgment 20 December 2013).
6 'Green tribunal gets short shrift' DownToEarth 30 June 2012 www.downtoearth.org.in/news/green-tribunal-gets-short-shrift-38426; 'A new era for environmental litigation in India' India in Transition, 30 January 2012 https://casi.sas.upenn.edu/iit/ghosh.
7 'SC slams poor facilities for green tribunal' Legal India, 20 September 2012 www.legalindia.com/news/sc-slams-poor-facilities-for-green-tribunal.
8 Ibid.
9 Ibid.
10 See Chapter 6 for caseload growth in all benches.
11 See Chapter 6 for figures demonstrating the caseload growth of the Chennai Bench.
12 See above n 7.
13 'SC asks states to provide offices to green tribunal' TwoCircles.net, 15 March 2016 http://twocircles.net/2013mar15/sc_asks_states_provide_offices_green_tribunal.html#.VuqqvuaHjdM.
14 'Kolkata may lose green tribunal bench to Guwahati or Ranchi' *Times of India*, 10 July 2016 http://timesofindia.indiatimes.com/city/kolkata/Kolkata-may-lose-green-tribunal-bench-to-Guwahati-or-Ranchi/articleshow/20996616.cms.
15 'Environment ministry failed to monitor forest diversion: CAG' Down To Earth, 8 September 2013 www.downtoearth.org.in/news/environment-ministry-failed-to-monitor-forest-diversion-cag-42131.
16 *Sarpanch, Grampanchayat Tiroda v State of Maharashtra* (Judgment 12 September 2011); *Jan Chetna v MoEF* (Judgment 9 February 2012); *Prafulla Samantray v Union of India* (Judgment 30 March 2012); *Adivasi Mazdoor Kisan Ekta Sangathan v MoEF* (Judgment 20 April 2012); *Osie Fernandes v MoEF* (Judgment 30 May 2012); *Rohit Choudhary v Union of India* (Judgment 7 September 2012).
17 *Sreeranganathan K P, Aranmula v Union of India* (Judgment 28 May 2014); *Prafulla Samantray v Union of India* (n 16 above); *Rohit Choudhary v Union of India* (n 16 above); *Samata v Union of India* (NGT Judgment 13 December 2013); *Kalpavriksh v Union of India* (Judgment 17 July 2014).

18 'NGT issues warrant against MoEF secretary' *Hindustan Times*, 27 March 2015 www.hindustantimes.com/india-news/ngt-issues-warrant-agianst-moef-secretary/article1–1331135.aspx; NGT summons Environment Secretary over MoEF's absence from hearings' *Times of India*, 1 December 2013 http://articles.economictimes.indiatimes.com/2013–12–01/news/44619558_1_joint-secretary-the-ngt-moef.

19 'Law of the jungle' *The Hindu*, 18 October 2013 www.thehindu.com/opinion/op-ed/law-of-the-jungle/article5244600.ece.

20 Environment (Protection) Act 1986; Forest (Conservation) Act 1980; Wildlife (Protection) Act 1972; Water (Prevention and Control of Pollution) Act 1974; Air (Prevention and Control of Pollution) Act 1981; and Indian Forest Act 1927.

21 I am grateful to Professor Suddaby for bringing his work to my attention.

22 This change has been experienced in India with the growth of the mega-law, practices such as Amarchand & Mangaldas, Suresh A Shroff & Co, AZB & Partners, J Sagar Associates, Luthra & Luthra, Khaitan & Co and Trilegal that focus on international commercial work and cross-border dispute settlements. These large specialised practices present a dramatic contrast to the traditional, sole-practice Indian lawyer who focuses on litigation within the established Indian courts.

23 See Chapter 3 for a detailed discussion.

24 The construction of the 130 megawatt Kashang Integrated Hydro Electric Project involved the acquisition of forest land, thereby affecting the forest cover, valuable pine trees and jeopardising the livelihood of the community. See, generally, the Scheduled Tribes and Other Traditional Forest Dwellers (Recognition of Forest Rights) Act 2006 and condition 16 of the 'In Principle' forest clearance.

25 Gram Sabha is described as the foundation of the Panchayati Raj system. It consists of all the adult members of a village and keeps a check on the activities of Gram Panchayat and influences their decisions for the welfare of the village.

26 In a landmark judgment, *Orissa Mining Corporation v MoEF* on 18 April 2013, the Supreme Court directed that the smallest units of local governance use their powers and take a decision on whether the Vedanta Group's $1.7 billion bauxite mining project in Odisha's Niyamgiri Hills should go forward. The decision validated the Gram Sabha's power under the Scheduled Tribes and Other Traditional Forest Dwellers (Recognition of Forest Rights) Act 2006.

27 *Bhopal Gas Peedith Mahila Udyog Sangathan v Union of India* (2012) 8 SCC 326. The Supreme Court observed:

> keeping in view the provisions of the NGT Act 2010 … it can be safely concluded that the environmental issues and matters covered under the NGT Act, Schedule 1 should be instituted and litigated before the National Green Tribunal. Such approach may be necessary to avoid likelihood of conflict of orders between the High Court and NGT. Thus, in unambiguous terms, we direct that all the matters instituted after coming into force of the NGT Act and which are covered under the provisions of the NGT Act and/or in Schedule 1 of the NGT Act shall stand transferred and can be instituted only before the NGT. This will help in rendering expeditious and specialised justice in the field of environment to all concerned.
>
> (347)

In *Adarsh Cooperative Housing Society Ltd v Union of India* (Order 10 March 2014), the Supreme Court of India stayed its own order by which it had transferred all environmental cases from High Courts to the NGT. In *Vellore Citizen Welfare Forum v Union of India* 2016 SCC OnLine Mad 1881 the Madras High Court stated. '…however, it appears that the application was withdrawn on 11.8.2014' (para 78). Additionally, the Supreme Court transferred more than 300 cases to the NGT in 2015. The Green Bench, headed by the then Chief Justice H L Dattu, decided to let go of several cases for swift decisions, thereby also shedding its pendency. See Chapter 3 for further details.

28 In *suo motu* proceedings a court acts on its own volition in the absence of parties. Interestingly, the NGT Act 2010 does not expressly provide the authority to initiate *suo motu* proceedings. In *Baijnath Prajapati v MoEF* (Judgment 20 January 2012), the NGT commented that 'at the same time it is mentionable that we are not conferred with suo motu powers' (para 9). However, recently a further controversy has arisen in *Manoj Misra v DDA* (Order 25 May 2016) concerning the legitimate usage of contempt powers by the NGT. The matter is pending awaiting hearing.

29 'No suo moto powers provided for you, MoEF tells green tribunal' *Indian Express*, 26 August 2013 http://archive.indianexpress.com/news/no-suo-motu-powers-provided-for-you-moef-tells-green-tribunal/1160046/.

30 www.oneindia.com/india/government-should-focus-on-cleanliness-of-environment-national-green-tribunal-1681721.html. Additionally, the chairperson had previously informed me in an interview, dated 16 July 2014, regarding his position on *suo motu* power. Judges 2, 4 and 6 agreed with the chairperson in their interviews, dated 6 and 8 April 2015, on exercising *suo motu*.

31 'Green tribunal's wings clipped, Madras High Court halts suo motu proceedings', *Times of India*, 3 January 2014 http://timesofindia.indiatimes.com/city/chennai/Green-tribunals-wings-clipped-Madras-high-court-halts-suo-motu-proceedings/articleshow/28346066.cms.

32 *P Sundarajan v Deputy Registrar NGT* (2015) 4 LW 23 at 27; *Vellore Citizen Welfare Forum* (n 27 above).

33 Interviews 10 and 16 April 2015.

34 See above n 31 and n 32. In an affidavit filed before the Supreme Court, the MoEF stated that: '… the government of India has not agreed to confer suo motu powers on the Tribunal. It is for the NGT, an adjudicatory body, to follow the provisions of the NGT Act 2010'. 'No suo motu powers provided for you, MoEF tells green tribunal', *Indian Express* (Archive), 26 August 2013http://archive.indianexpress.com/news/no-suo-motupowers-provided-for-you-moef-tells-green-tribunal/1160046.

35 *Tribunal on its Own Motion v District Collector, Sivaganga District* 2014 SCC OnLine 1450 to prevent pollution of the Sambai; *Tribunal on its Own Motion v Union of India* 2014 SCC OnLine 1433 on a news item published in *The Hindu* dated 21 November 2013 under the caption 'Plan for stadium at Tirupathi raises eyebrows'; *Tribunal on its Own Motion v Union of India* 2014 SCC OnLine 2352 about 'Setting up of petrol bunk in Sathyamangalam Reserve forest' published in *The Hindu*, dated 1 August 2013; *Tribunal on its Own Motion v The Secretary, MoEF* 2013 SCC OnLine 1086 regarding unauthorised constructions in Muttukadu coastal zone, report in *New Indian Express* dated 7 July 2013; *Tribunal on its Own Motion v State of Tamil Nadu, Municipal Administration and Water Supply Department* 2013 SCC Online 1105 regarding quality water to be delivered by public tap, based on letter dated 24 July 2013 from Shri Ramchandra Srivatsav.

36 See Chapter 3.

37 'Tribunal on trial' Down To Earth, 30 November 2014 www.downtoearth.org.in/coverage/tribunal-on-trial-47400.

38 'When tribunals undermine the judiciary' Rediff News, 25 October 2013 www.rediff.com/news/column/when-tribunals-undermine-the-judiciary/20131025.htm.

39 See Chapter 5.

40 Ibid.

41 *Manoj Misra v Union of India* Judgment 13 January 2015, now referred to as the Maily se Nirmal Yamuna Revitalization Plan 2017.

42 *Vardhaman Kaushik v Union of India* and *Sanjay Kulshrestha v Union of India* (Order 7 April 2015).

43 Speech of Justice Swatanter Kumar, Orientation Programme on Environment and Law, Delhi Judicial Academy http://judicialacademy.nic.in/index.php?option=speech &view=content&id=1.

44 Section 19 NGT Act.
45 For example, the Chief Minister of Meghalaya, Mukul Sangma, urged Prime Minister Modi to allow the state government the right to regulate the previously largely unregulated mining activities in view of the peculiar ground conditions in the Hill state. This intervention was the result of a wave of protests against the NGT's ban on unscientific rat-hole mining in Meghalaya. Coal-mining is a major source of livelihood for people and of revenue for the government. However, the NGT decided that the unscientific, unlicensed and illegal coal-mining affected water sources and the landscape, and overall it degraded the ecology: *Impulse NGO Network v State of Meghalaya* (Order 9 June 2014).
46 This illustration was given to me by a judge, interview 30 March 2015.
47 *Ashok Gabaji Kajale v M/S Godhavari Bio-Refineries Ltd* (Judgment 19 May 2015); *Subhas Datta v State of West Bengal* (Order 28 July 2015); *Paramjeet S Kalsi v MoEF* (Judgment 15 May 2015).
48 See n 46 above.
49 Interview 31 March 2015.
50 *Environment Support Group v Union of India* (Judgment 27 August 2014).
51 See *Mahalaxmi Bekar v SEIAA, Mumbai* Order 27 February 2015.
52 See above n 43. Chairperson Kumar in his speech stated:

> we call experts, we appoint technical teams, consisting of members from Indian Institute of Technology to give their opinion. The recommendations of these Committees are further vetted by the expert members we have at NGT. So we have double check method that means we collect something from outside which is filtered through expert members and then converted into a judgment.

53 *Pathankot Welfare Association v State of Punjab* (Judgment 25 November 2014).
54 *D B Nevatia v State of Maharashtra* (Judgment 9 January 2013); *Indian Spinal Injuries Hospital v Union of India* NGT (Judgment 27 January 2016).
55 *Asim Sarode v Maharashtra Pollution Control Board* (Judgment 6 September 2014).
56 *T Muruganandam v MoEF* (Judgment 11 November 2014); *Samata v Union of India* (n 17 above).
57 Interview 25 July 2014.
58 Interview 15 July 2014.
59 Suddaby and Viale quoted Friedson (1994: 104) as:

> I suspect that the prestige attached to professions stems less from the social origin of their members than from the fact of their attending institutions of higher education … Aristocratic origins have not been characteristic of those drawn into the professions.

60 See Chapter 3.
61 See Chapter 5.
62 Ibid. Haas 2007: 19–43; and 2014: 19–43.
63 Ibid. and for a detailed discussion see Chapter 5. See also Schrefler 2010; and 2014.
64 Interview dated 30 July 2014.
65 Reflexive governance implies 'one calls into question the foundation of governance itself, that is, the concepts, practices and institutions by which societal development is governed, and that one envisions alternatives and reinvents and shapes those foundations' (Voss and Kemp 2006: 4).

References

Ambrus, M, Arts, K, Hey, E and Raulus, H (eds) (2014) *The Role of 'Experts' in International and European Decision-Making Processes* (CUP).

Anderson, M R (1998) 'Individual rights to environmental protection in India' in A E Boyle and M R Anderson (eds), *Human Rights Approaches to Environmental Protection* (OUP).

Dezalay, Y and Garth, B (1996) 'Merchants of law as moral entrepreneurs: constructing international justice from the competition for transnational business disputes' 29(1) *Law and Society Review* 27.

Edwards, H T (2003) 'The effects of collegiality on judicial decision-making' 151(5) *University of Pennsylvania LR* 1639–1690.

Friedson, E (1994) *Professionalism Reborn* (University of Chicago Press).

Haas, P M (2007) 'Epistemic communities' in D Bodansky, J Brunee and E Hey (eds), *Oxford Handbook of International Environmental Law* (OUP).

Haas, P M (2014) 'Ideas, experts and governance' in M Ambrus, K Arts, E Hey and H Raulus (eds), *The Role of 'Experts' in International and European Decision-Making Processes* (CUP) 19–43.

High Level Committee on Forest and Environment Related Laws (2014) *Report* (MoEF&CC) http://envfor.nic.in/sites/default/files/press-releases/Final_Report_of_HLC.pdf.

Jowitt, E (1977) *Dictionary of English Law* (Sweet & Maxwell).

Law Commission of India (2003) *Proposal to Constitute Environment Courts* 186th Report http://lawcommissionofindia.nic.in/reports/186th%20report.pdf.

Mrema, E (2015) *Environmental Rule of Law: Trends from the Americas* (Organization of American States) www.oas.org/en/sedi/dsd/EnvironmentalRuleOfLaw_SelectedEssay_English.PDF.

Parliamentary Standing Committee on Science and Technology, Environment and Forests (2015) *263rd Report on High Level Committee Report to Review Various Acts Administered by MoEF&CC* (Parliament of India).

Peiris, G L (1991) 'Public interest litigation in the Indian subcontinent: current dimensions' 40(1) *International and Comparative Law Quarterly* 66–90.

Preston, B J (2012) 'Benefits of judicial specialisation in environmental law: the Land and Environment Court of New South Wales as a case study' 29(2) *Pace Environmental LR* 396.

Pring, G and Pring, C (2016) *The ABCs of the ECTs* (UNEP).

Schrefler, L (2010) 'The usage of scientific knowledge by independent regulatory agencies' 23(2) *Governance* 309–330.

Schrefler, L (2014) 'Reflections on the different roles of expertise in regulatory policy making' in M Ambrus, K Arts, E Hey and H Raulus (eds), *The Role of 'Experts' in International and European Decision-Making Processes* (CUP) 63–81.

Suddaby, R and Viale, T (2011) 'Professionals and field-level change: institutional work and the professional project' 59(4) *Current Sociology* 423–442.

Voss, J and Kemp, R (2006) 'Sustainability and reflexive governance: introduction' in J Voss, D Bauknecht and R Kemp (eds), *Reflexive Governance for Sustainable Development* (Edward Elgar).

Index